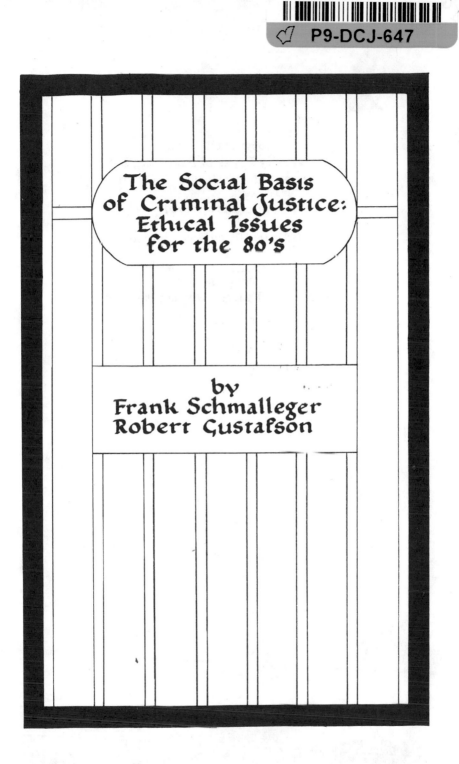

The Social Basis of Criminal Justice: Ethical Issues for the 80's

by
Frank Schmalleger
Robert Gustafson

Copyright © 1981 by
University Press of America, Inc.
P.O.Box 19101, Washington,D.C. 20036

All rights reserved .

Printed in the United States of America

ISBN:0-8191-1686-6(Perfect)
0-8191-1685-8(Case)
Library of Congress Number:80-6175

PREFACE

This book is being published at a time
when the future of American criminal justice is
in serious doubt. The 1960's and 1970's created
a crisis of legitimacy for police and other
criminal justice practitioners nationwide. The
1980's are witness to the economic consequences of
this situation. The Law Enforcement Assistance
Administration, along with the numerous splinter
groups it sponsored, are being eliminated. The
ideal of police community relations, born of
the last two decades, has rarely progressed
beyond crime prevention programs. Police can
now depend more fully on the services of
volunteers, but their acceptance by the citizenry
is still questionable.

We believe that all components of the
American system of justice need to develop an
ethical awareness which can guide them through
these trying times. Without such awareness
the entire system stands apart from the rest of
society-an automation without heart. American
justice must reflect the ideals of American
society, for such ideals are inherent in the
notion of justice we all hold.

We have tried in the pages that follow to
build an understanding of the need for ethical
awareness among criminal justice practitioners.
We have not suggested particular ethical systems,
believing that social values rise and fall with
the temporal flow. Some of the articles we have
included are empirically oriented and explicate
existing ethically-informed behavior. Others are
intended simply to be thought-provoking, and ask
the student or practitioner what actions on his
or her part are necessary to insure a successful
future for the justice system. Each contribution
is from a well-informed practitioner who comes
into daily contact with the problems we've

mentioned. Two contributions include an international perspective, and have the potential to highlight current ethnocentristic practices and attitudes we here in America so often fall victim to.

The authors wish to thank all the contributors, many of whom have no doubt wondered when this project would come to fruition. We also thank our typist and proof-reader, and the Pembroke State University Faculty Development Fund for helping with the financial aspects of manuscript preparation. Emily Whittle, an excellent artist, by any standard, was kind enough to provide our cover and title page. Our families gave of their time, assuming tasks which might otherwise have been ours so that we might complete this work. Finally, and most importantly, we wish to thank University Press of America for seeing value in this manuscript, which, although it provides a long-overdue analysis, may not have wide market appeal – the criteria used so unabashedly by far too many other publishers in manuscript selection.

Robert K. Gustafson
Laurinburg, N.C.
April, 1981

Frank Schmalleger
Pembroke, N.C.
April, 1981

iv

CONTENTS

INTRODUCTION

Frank Schmalleger, Ph.D.

The principles which gave birth to American democracy were undergirded by a strong faith in ethical justice. Our founding fathers understood that "justice for all" begins on the individual level. To insure that this ideal was not bent to momentary whims or future petty needs, they created a systematized process for the determination of criminal cases. Justice and ethics are tied closely together in this system. Justice refers primarily to a fair resolution of disputes. Ethics, on the other hand, is concerned with moment-to-moment fairness during the process through which the dispute settlement occurs.

The adversary system of due process places hurdles along every step of the road from arrest to conviction. These hurdles exist to insure that the accused is not railroaded into a loss of liberties.

This is not to say that the American founding fathers (who established procedural safeguards in the Constitution) were not interested in the control of crime. Indeed they were, but they believed the interests of society could be best served by insuring that the agents of justice were also subject to the law. They were willing, in short, to sacrifice efficiency for fairness.

Recent history has been quite different, however, and its consequences provide clear evidence of the wisdom of those early American patriots. By the late 1800's, technology began to make a tremendous impact upon society. The agents of justice found themselves surrounded by new ideas and gadgets, each holding previously undreamed of possibilities for efficient enforcement of the law. Meanwhile, mobility, communications, firepower, and organization were increasing among society's criminal element. As justice practitioners fought to enforce the laws the technological spiral continued its growth until, at some

1

point, the ideal of individualized justice lost ground to visions of efficiency and mechanical sophistication.

Today, well-managed bureaucracies and efficient judicial processing survive as measures of justice in our modern world. The literature of the justice professions reflects these concerns, consisting primarily of topics in criminalistics, investigation and organizational management. We have arrived at the point where we believe that the justice practitioner who clears the most cases, whether from the police blotter or the court docket, somehow dispenses the best justice. Quantity has replaced quality as the hallmark of daily justice in America.

Conceptions of justice which go beyond systematized processing are thought by professionals themselves to have little place in the "real world"; surviving appropriately, if at all, only in the heads of academicians who need not face life "on the streets." But efficiency as the measure of justice bodes ill for the future of American justice institutions, for while the technological sophistication of criminal justice agencies has increased dramatically in the past few decades, the acceptance of those agencies by the public they serve has suffered greatly. During the protest years of the 1960's justice agencies bore the brunt of social unrest not because any large portion of our population had suddenly adopted criminal lifestyles, but because many people felt that traditional concepts of justice, both at home and abroad, were being violated. Perhaps, in this sense, the protestors of the 1960's were more conservative than the established institutions with which they clashed.

The 1960's brought justice practitioners under fire and left behind a paranoia which continues to separate them from the society they serve. Today's law enforcement officer, hearing himself referred to as a "pig," may, at the very least, feel unappreciated by his verbal assailant, and yet fail to realize that his declining legit-

2

imacy is a legacy of the "justice as efficiency" model of his forebearers. The disrespect he faces can only be heightened by clinging to the old model and resorting to more and faster processing. American justice must be impartial, but not blind to human needs.

Societal acceptance is necessary for the smooth functioning of our system of justice. Low acceptance means little public cooperation and frustrates the gathering of criminal intelligence. As declining public acceptance weakens the framework of social legitimacy upon which our system of justice depends, efficient processing becomes more difficult. Tasks assigned to practitioners demand more effort and more time. Job satisfaction, professionalism, and even life satisfaction decline for police officers, prosecutors, judges, and treatment personnel as public mistrust and criticism question even the nature of the goal to be pursued. "What am I doing in this job?" "Why am I here?" "What am I trying to accomplish?" "How am I seen?" All these are commonly asked questions among today's practitioners.

While, in general, the situation in America is still tolerable, criminal justice practitioners fully realize that they are viewed with hostility and suspicion by elements of the citizenry. As American criminal justice enters the 1980's, it faces a crisis the likes of which it has not seen before -- a crisis of identity in which the very purpose of our system is called into question, along with the meaning of justice in our culture.

This crisis has not, however, arrived without warning, nor have the warnings been entirely ignored. Efforts to insure the legitimacy of the American justice system have been with us since the 1800's and especially flourished in the late 1960's and 1970's. Those two decades saw the development of numerous "standards and goals" of relevance to (and often created by) criminal justice agencies.

But standards, although they may increase professionalism by insuring uniform and predictable
practices, can be based as easily upon criteria of
efficiency as upon ethical considerations. Ethics
means, simply, a respect for the rights of others.
Those rights flow less from court precedent or constitutional guarantees than they do from a recognition of the basic humanness of those with whom
we are dealing. The cop who goes strictly "by the
book" may efficiently enforce the law according to
every technical standard ever published, and yet
daily violate his public's sense of fairness.
Discretionary decision making can never be entirely
subsumed under laws or standards because each situation has its unique aspects. Hence, discretion
within the system becomes an important realm for
ethical action.

Public relations and community programs have
also been tried as ways to increase the acceptance of justice practitioners by the public.
These efforts have returned some dividends, but
run the danger of being viewed suspiciously,
especially where they turn public cooperation to
the advantage of enforcement agencies.

To achieve social legitimacy, all programs,
standards, and daily actions of justice practitioners must meet the criteria of fairness to
which the public adheres, and it is these criteria
which form the basis for ethical behavior. Public
standards of fair play are not hidden from us. Indeed, they are known to almost everyone raised in
this society. Standards of fairness relative to
the justice system arise in the public mind from
one simple fact: most citizens fear contact with
representatives of the system, at least to some
extent. Such fears arise not from criminal purpose nor a guilty mind, but from the knowledge
that we all face tension-creating daily contacts
with enforcement agents. These contacts vary from
the sight of a patrol car in our rear-view mirror,
to false arrest for a serious offense. Whatever
the nature of the contact we all want to believe

4

that "If I'm innocent, I'll be all right." Or, if wrongfully apprehended, "I'll be set free soon, and in the meantime I'll be treated fairly." Such simple desires lay the ground rules for ethical action in criminal justice. Ethics require the practitioner to put himself in the place of those he deals with, and to ask, "If that were me, how would I want to be treated?"

Finally, ethical behavior is an indispensible aspect of professionalism. Self-regulation is the hallmark of any occupational group which has achieved the maturity necessary to consider the needs of others. Criminal justice ethics must be informed by societal standards, because the profession they undergird draws its legitimacy from public service.

The articles which follow examine justice institutions in contemporary America from an ethical perspective. They are all original contributions written expressly for this volume by practitioners who believe in the importance of ethical awareness. We have made no attempt to create an all-encompassing ethical code, for codes convey more the letter than the spirit of the concepts they deal with. We have tried, rather, to sensitize our readers to the existence of ethical dilemmas in the day-to-day actions of justice professionals. Such awareness, we feel, is the first step in increasing professionalism and creating social legitimacy and life satisfaction for all those who work in the system.

The articles begin with John Matthews and Ralph Marshall's demonstration of how organizational concerns with efficiency influence the ethics of criminal justice practitioners. They focus on the personal risks involved in ethical behavior, and find that the ethically-minded professional may be regarded as a "trouble-maker" by his peers.

Next, André Bossard, Secretary General of INTERPOL, describes ethical problems in law

5

enforcement which arise from the multiple roles of the officer. Familiar with the complexities of societal demands upon police behavior, Secretary Bossard points out that a police force cannot be adequately understood without reference to the cultural context in which it must function. He suggests criteria for international police cooperation that should be acceptable to diverse societies, and suggests the groundwork for an international code of police ethics.

Charles Johnson and Gary Copus narrow the focus to law enforcement ethics. Johnson and Copus analyze the ethical code of the International Association of Chiefs of Police for its relevance to day-to-day law enforcement problems. Merton's framework of "modes of individual adaptation" and Festinger's theory of cognitive dissonance are applied to police ethical behavior, and the realities of effective law enforcement are compared to the requirements of the official code.

A continuing analysis of police ethics is provided by Paul Murphy and T. Kenneth Moran who examine the potential for cyclical police corruption in New York City. Their article deals with city-wide police deviance and suggests that large-scale corruption, based upon police cynicism, secrecy, and anomie, will again surface in New York before the end of the century.

In the following article, John Jay Douglass, Dean of the National College of District Attorneys, describes the ethical issues facing prosecutors. Wide prosecutorial discretion is shown to form the crux of an ethical dilemma he calls the "white hat syndrome." Prosecutors who fall prey to the syndrome believe they represent an idealized good battling against evil, and are tempted to overstep the bounds of legitimacy in the interest of winning. Dean Douglass also examines the standards of professional organizations as they relate to all stages of the

criminal trial. Of special interest to the
reader will be his analysis of the ethics of
plea bargaining.

Carolynne Stevens' contribution focuses on
correctional ethics. She shows that agreement on
ethical standards is difficult in corrections because practitioners have diverse roles and
divergent self-conceptions. In fact, she says,
society has been unable to agree upon the fundamental purpose of corrections: to punish or
rehabilitate. Stevens argues that the ethics of
combat, upon which our adversary system of justice is based, may be applicable to the courtroom,
but not to corrections. A conflict perspective
may lead correctional personnel to perceive
inmates as enemies rather than clients.

Miller, Noury, and Tobia also deal with the
ethics of incarceration. They discuss the well-
known treatment versus punishment dilemma in
light of historical ethical developments in
American society. The treatment ideal is shown
to conflict with the inherent organizational
makeup of contemporary prisons. Values learned
in prisons are seen as directly opposed to
successful reformation.

In the next article, Ralph O. Marshall, former Executive Secretary of the Idaho Commission
for Pardons and Parole, explores the ethical
dilemmas of parole decision-makers. He points
out how his personal values and those of social
interest groups combined to influence parole
policy. The article contains an especially
interesting analysis of the conflict of ethical
perspectives which arises from the clash between
conformist and criminal values. Marshall's
concept of the "good man," for which parole
decision-makers search, underscores the values
board members bring to bear on the parole process,
and reveals how knowledgable inmates try to
imitate the ideal.

The final article, by Lawrence Bennett, Director of LEAA's Office on Program Evaluation, concerns ethics in criminal justice research. Bennett shows how ethical considerations enter any research project at the onset and remain a part of all evaluations. He outlines the crucial steps in evaluation research which are sensitive to ethical influences and suggests strategies for increasing ethical objectivity.

The book concludes with Robert Gustafson's philosophical look at criminal justice ethics. Gustafson, a philosopher and Chairman of Pembroke State University's Philosophy and Religion Department, explores the "state of the art" relevant to contemporary ethical thought in criminal justice. His concluding section examines the previous articles and suggests the likely course of future ethical developments in criminal justice.

Some Constraints on Ethical Behavior in Criminal Justice Organizations

John P. Matthews, Ph.D.
Ralph O. Marshall, Ph.D.

Introduction

Most commentaries concerning ethics and ethical behavior tend to focus on the individual and the alternatives he faces in the decisions made throughout life. Often this focus is drawn within the broad social milieu in which the individual operates. Seldom, however, do such treatises examine the organizational context in which much of our lives are spent, and the organizational consequences which stem from individual decisions and the resultant behaviors of those decisions. It is the purpose of the authors of this paper to examine one aspect of ethics in criminal justice--constraints placed on individuals by their employing organizations as these individuals carry out their duties.

The issues involved in criminal justice ethics cannot be adequately examined without also examining the organizational context in which these issues are manifest. To attempt to do so would obviate the investigation of these issues and would reduce all consideration of ethics to a generic exploration of a universal nature, thus losing the richness to be gained from viewing ethics from the perspective of criminal justice.

Etzioni (1964), in an often quoted passage, has pointed out that:

> Our society is an organizational society. We are born in organizations, educated by organizations, and most of us spend much of our lives working for organizations. We spend much of our

leisure time paying, playing, and praying in organizations. Most of us will die in an organization, and when the time comes for burial, the largest organization of all--the state--must grant official permission.(P.1)

Organizations are, then, one of the most pervasive elements, if not the most pervasive element in modern social life. To fail to recognize this while studying ethics, in the view of the present authors, makes such study of ethics fatally incomplete.

This paper does not attempt to analyze organizations, nor does it attempt to identify an inclusive set of organizational variables which affect ethical behavior. The intent here is to examine the relationship between ethical behavior and organizational reward structures, both formal and informal. If criminal justice organizations reward ethical behavior there will be an increased likelihood of the continuation of such behavior. If such behavior is not rewarded it is unlikely that it will be continued. If such behavior results in the application of negative sanctions the likelihood is increased that such behavior will be extinguished.

Service Ideal Versus Organizational Ideal

Many people naively believe that because criminal justice organizations are public service organizations there will be a perfect match between a service ideal and an organizational ideal, that is, that the organizational ideal is a service ideal. Such a belief is evidence of an unfortunate lack of sophistication concerning organizations. Criminal justice organizations, as is the case with all organizations, have a multitude of needs to which they must respond. One of these needs is service to their clients, but most of these needs have to do with survival, growth, maintenance, internal conflict, and threats from the environment. As a result, most of the expenditure of scarce resources will be directed to these internal needs and what is left over can then be directed toward client needs. Viewing this as a continuum, it becomes apparent that no organization can survive at either extreme. A total organizational orientation would mean that all resource allocation would be directed toward organizational needs and no client services would be granted. A total service orientation would mean that all resource allocation would be directed toward client needs, with no attention to maintenance of the organization. Obviously an appropriate location along the continuum must be found. It is our position that criminal justice organizations tend to operate much closer to the total organizational end than the total service end. There are several variables which affect an organization's position on this continuum. Among them are organizational size, whether the organization is public or private, and whether or not the organization is monopolistic. Large, public, and monopolistic organizations tend to have a strong organizational orientation and small, private organizations which are in competition with others for clients tend to have a strong service orientation. Criminal justice organizations are public, that is, they are not privately owned and operated. They are monopolistic; they are, so to speak, the only game in town. If a citizen is dissatisfied with the quality of police services, as an example, the option of selecting another police agency to provide service is not available. And, they tend to be large, although this is not necessarily the case.

All this is a rather lengthy, and possibly circuitous, way of setting a stage for understanding that ethical behavior is not simply a matter of individual choice. It is our conception that conventional ethical thought has focused on the individual actor and his choices. It has asked whether he is a good person, whether his conduct conforms to good principles and is directed toward the achievement of a good end-state and the like. Although we are unable to

11

comment on the directions which professional
ethicists are taking, it is our impression that
"street-level" ethical discussion has not been informed by the sociological insight that an organization is, itself, an actor--that it is more than
the combined desires of its members, and that it
has goals which transcend the goals of those
individual members. Therefore, we conceptualize
ethics in the criminal justice system not in terms
of the individual actor and the choices he makes
with reference to his society. Rather, we perceive that those choices are heavily influenced
by his organization, and the point at which they
become ethical choices is where he envisions his
organization as contributing to the good society.
It is at that point that the participant resolves
to make ethical decisions. Here this situation
assumes tragic proportions because, and we perceive this as an organizational axiom, criminal
justice organizations tend to reward participants
whose behavior focuses on organizational rather
than client needs.

     We are unable to locate our position on the
formal ethical map, although one of the coordi-
nates would undoubtedly be utilitarianism. We do
assume some sort of service ideal as an ethical
sine qua non. Further, the ethical principle
which we hold and which we believe is relevant for
this particular analysis is that ethical action
requires risk.

Ethical Behavior and Risk

     The organizational maxim central in this pre-
sentation is that "no good deed will ever go un-
punished." This whimsical Murphy-like law highlights our assumption that ethical behavior in
criminal justice organizations involves risk to
the individual and to his organization. The degree of risk is not at issue here, but the fact of
risk is. It should be clear to the student of human behavior that risk taking in organizational
role performance tends to be rare, especially in

12

cases where the individual has a "no-risk" alternative available.

Among the dilemmas encountered by those who evaluate organizations is the dilemma of effectiveness versus efficiency. Although it need not always be so, it appears that many organizations tend to choose between being effective and being efficient. In order to be effective the organization must examine and appraise its goals and the means selected to pursue those goals on a continuous basis. When a social service organization, especially, asks about its effectiveness, it opens itself up to the world beyond its boundaries and begins to consider what happens to other people as a result of what it does, or doesn't do. In contrast, the assessment of efficiency is an internal matter. The questions which are asked pertain to the smoothness with which the organization functions. The question of efficiency is much easier to answer and is far less threatening to ask. As a result criminal justice organizations tend to focus on efficiency (on organizational needs) rather than of effectiveness (service to clients). Behavior which enhances organizational efficiency is greatly valued by the organization, and is concomitantly rewarded. Behavior directed toward organizational effectiveness forces the organization to acknowledge difficult and threatening issues and, as a result, tends not to be rewarded.

One fairly straightforward way of conceptualizing this issue is to look at the behavior of criminal justice practitioners in terms of the potential problems for the organization resulting from their performance.

For purposes of this analysis, "problems" are defined in terms of the "effectiveness" of the organization. To attend to effectiveness means to place under scrutiny the goals of the organization and the allocation of resources. Since we are considering criminal justice organizations, the primary ethical dimension which modifies all consider-

13

ations of effectiveness is <u>justice</u>.

From this perspective a typology of three types of employees can be developed. This typology is to be evaluated from the vantage point of the organization.

    I.   Those who create problems
   II.   Those who neither create nor solve problems
  III. Those who solve problems

The Type I employee represents the individual whose behavior creates a need for the organization to expend resources to make up for the behavior. The organization, generally, removes these people from their positions in order to preclude further problems. There are two ways of doing this. The first is to terminate the employee. This would appear to be reasonable, but in the face of civil service, union contracts, and public opinion this option is not always available. In cases where termination is not a viable solution the organization generally opts for the alternative that Peter and Hull (1969) might call the "lateral arabesque" but which we prefer to call assignment to the organizational ceremonial burial ground. Most organizations of any size have positions where the person filling that position can do little damage. These are reserved for the "screw-ups" that the organization cannot terminate.

The second type represents the individual who does as little as possible, hoping to avoid situations in which he may be at risk. This is often the individual who "passes the buck," who "doesn't make waves" and who creates no controversy for the organization. He is often called a steady, dependable employee and he is highly valued by the organization because he places no demands on the organization to expend resources to deal with the issues he raises or in which he becomes involved. Niederhoffer (1967) in his well-known study of police cynicism pointed out that approximately one half of his sample reported that

14

they felt the average police officer simply
wanted to get through each eight hour shift without getting in trouble. The question arises of
how one "does nothing" and still stays out of
trouble. The answer lies in the concept of risk
behavior. These individuals have discovered means
by which they can look busy and productive without becoming involved in activities in which they
must make decisions for which they will be held
accountable. There are two primary ways in which
they can avoid the ethical issues inherent in the
situation. This simply requires that they focus
on "black and white" situations, and force as many
as possible of the other situations, in which they
become involved, into a "black and white" mode.
This is a subtle practice, but easy enough to
carry out, especially in criminal justice organizations where the law can be used to accomplish
this end, as most experienced criminal justice
practitioners are aware. The second way has to
do with the remainder of the situations in which
the individual becomes involved, those in which
a subjective decision must be made. In this case
the employee who falls into our Type II category
makes an evaluation concerning the risk involved
and the decision is made in favor of that choice
which represents the smallest amount of risk to
him. Specific examples of such behavior in criminal justice might include the prosecutor who
selects only clear-cut cases to prosecute and who
enters into plea bargaining in more difficult
cases; the judge whose sentencing practices are so
lenient as to discourage appeals; the police
officer who simply uses the law as the basis for
his decisions and who avoids consideration of the
circumstances surrounding the situation; and the
probation officer whose pre-sentence investi-
gations consistently recommend incarceration.
This category constitutes the majority of criminal justice practitioners today, as well as the
majority of employees in any endeavor.

The third category of employee in our typology
is that individual who solves problems. At first
glance this would appear to be the ideal employee
from the perspective of the organization as well

15

as that of the client. A more thorough consideration, however, points up problems for the organization as a result of this kind of behavior. The
solving of problems requires the mobilization of
organization resources, application of those resources, and evaluation of the effect of their
application. The net result is that these resources cannot then be expended on organizational
needs of the moment, and that they must be re-
focused away from organizational maintenance to
the problem at hand and then back to maintenance.
Organizations tend not to reward people whose
behaviors require the expenditure or the transfer
of resources. Thus, such behaviors are seen as
"making waves."

Let us present a scenario in which each of
the three types of individuals might be placed.
Assume a poor mother of two young children calls
the police department requesting that an officer
be dispatched to her apartment because of "an
emergency." The officer arrives on the scene,
knocks on the door, is admitted to the apartment
and is greeted with the following statement.
"Thank God you're here. My youngest child has
just been bitten by a rat right here in this
apartment. I've complained to the owner numerous
times about rats and he just says that if I don't
like it here I can move. Please help me. My
husband is in prison and I just don't know what
to do."

The Type I officer might respond by saying
"Lady, what in the hell do you want me to do? Do
you want me to hunt the rats and shoot them? Get
your kid to a doctor and move out of this crummy
place." At this point he might well turn on his
heel and walk out.

The Type II officer would be likely to respond
by saying "I would recommend that you do three
things. First, see to it that your child gets
medical attention. Second, call the health department first thing tomorrow morning and request
an inspection. Third, begin to look for another

16

place to live. There is really nothing that I can do, but if the health inspector finds this building to be in violation of the health code his department can require that the owner take care of the problem." At this point he might tip his hat and leave.

The Type III officer might respond by saying "Let me examine the child. If the bite has broken the skin, I will take you to the emergency room of the county hospital immediately in my patrol car. I personally will see to it that the health department sends an inspector out to examine this building, and before I leave you I'll give you the names of several organizations that may be able to assist you in finding more suitable housing."

This final response requires time away from routine organizational activities and the officer may attempt to use police resources to stimulate the initiation of a health inspection as well as to identify appropriate social service agencies to recommend. While such effort is, in our perspective, highly ethical, it is also very likely to result in the officer's being labeled "do-gooder" or "social worker" by his peers as well as to generate some negative commentary from his supervisors, including the possibility of a lowered employee evaluation rating. As a result, the officer is unlikely to expose himself to the risk, especially when the Type II response is likely to result in peer, as well as supervisory approval as a "professional" response. We will not quarrel that the Type II response is unethical; it is not. It is simply an avoidance of the ethical issues involved, and therefore, cannot be measured by standards of ethics.

Organizational Control of Employee Behavior: Internalization versus Externalization

Another important determinate of organization behavior centers on the modes of influence that

17

the organization uses to channel the activities of individual organizational members. This is most easily conceptualized in an internalization/externalization paradigm. Emphasis on internalization of the organizational goal, objectives and means of pursuing these ends results in techniques of influence designed to convince the employee that these ends are desirable in and of themselves and are, therefore, worthy of being accepted by the individual as his own, i.e., worthy of being internalized. Emphasis on externalization of the goal and objectives of the organization results in techniques of influence designed to impress upon the employee the means by which the goal and objectives are to be pursued, with no attempt being made to convince the employee to accept these ends as his own. Here the focus is on the idea that "this is the way we want things done. If you want to obtain the rewards and avoid the punishments we can levy, you will do these things as we say." The latter approach relies on authority; the former on normative control.

It is our perspective that ethical behavior can best be evaluated in the normative mode, at least in situations of little close supervision as is the case in most criminal justice organizations. This should not be construed as our endorsement of close supervision. Close supervision is necessary only when the ends sought by superiors and subordinates are divergent or when subordinates have not given adequate evidence of technical expertise. Most criminal justice practitioners do accept the goal and objectives of their employing organizations as being worthwhile, and most are competent to perform their duties. In spite of this, criminal justice organizations have attempted to bring about ethical behavior through external influences. It is almost as though they are saying "you will be ethical--or else!" Some of the external techniques used by criminal justice organizations include threats of criminal or civil sanction, employee

evaluation, internal affairs, pay structures, pro-
motional systems and means of job assignments. We
are not suggesting that these influences are
inappropriate. We are suggesting that they should
not be the primary approach to influence. Most
people are too sophisticated to appreciate threat
as the first, or only, attempt to bring about
compliance. To do so is diametrically opposed to
the idea of developing on organizational atmosphere in which ethical behavior will flourish.
The point to be emphasized here is that it is
difficult, at best, to evaluate behavior on
ethical grounds when that behavior occurs in the
presence of the sanctioning force. Thus the key,
or at least a key, to the idea of examining behavior from an ethical perspective is a determination of whether the behavior is internally or
externally motivated.

Absolute and Situational Ethics

The study of ethics is often organized in a
dichotomy--Absolute versus Situational ethics.
An absolute ethicist would hold that in order for
behavior to be ethical the actor must do the
"right," or ethical, thing, regardless of the
consequences for himself or for anyone else. The
situational ethicist would hold that ethical
behavior must take into account the greatest
good for the greatest number. Criminal justice,
or at least the law enforcement component, has
approached this dilemma through the development of
conceptual models guiding organizational activity.
The absolute ethical view is made manifest in the
"professional" model of policing--a view which
encourages strict invocation of the criminal
justice process in the face of criminal violation,
and the equal treatment of all individuals, who
have displayed like behaviors, regardless of the
situation surrounding the behavior or the consequences. The situational ethical view can be
seen in the "discretionary model" of criminal
justice--a view which includes the situation and
consequences in the decision of whether or not to

invoke the criminal justice process. (For a more complete examination of these models see: Herman Goldstein, _Policing a Free Society_, Ballinger Publishing Company, 1977.)

There is however, an area of ethical concern which has been largely neglected in criminal justice. We would call this area "expedient ethics." By this we refer to the invocation of an ethical principle to camouflage the more relevant, but more risky, ethical choice to be made. A judge justifies giving a mother probation while giving a maximum sentence to her male co-defendant with the principle: "Because there is nothing which matches a mother's love, we must not separate her from her children." A parole board avoids the heat by pronouncing: "Although we believe he would be a law-abiding parolee, the public will not tolerate our placing someone who committed a crime like that in its midst. Decisions like that will lead to the ending of the indeterminate sentence." A policeman says: "We depend on each other for back-up in life and death situations; therefore, you have to overlook your fellow officers' indiscretions."

Earlier in this paper we commented on the truism that ethical decisions involve risk. Our examples here show that decisions in organizations will be based on the least risk to the decision-maker. If ethical decision-making is to be encouraged in criminal justice organizations, the organizational environment must be conducive to such behavior, for if it is not, ethical be-havior will only occur in spite of, rather than because of, the organizational climate. Without change in the organizational climate, no signi-ficant change in the amount of ethical behavior can be reasonably be expected.

20

BIBLIOGRAPHY

Etzioni, Amitai. Modern Organizations. Englewood
    Cliffs, N.J.: Prentice-Hall, Inc. 1964.

Goldstein, Herman. Policing a Free Society. Cam-
    bridge, MA: Ballinger Publishing Company,
    1977.

Peter, Laurence, and Hull, Raymond. The Peter
    Principle. New York: William Morrow and
    Company, Inc., 1969.

Niederhoffer, Arthur. Behind the Shield. Garden
    City, N.Y.: Doubleday and Company, Inc.,
    1967.

John P. Matthews, Ph.D., is an Associate
Professor of Criminal Justice and Coordinator
of the Law Enforcement and Police Science Program at Sam Houston State University. A former
police officer, Dr. Matthews received the B.S.
degree from California State University at Long
Beach, the M.S. degree from Michigan State
University, and the Ph.D. degree from Texas
A & M University.

Ralph O. Marshall, Ph.D., is an Assistant
Professor of Criminal Justice at Sam Houston
State University. Formerly the Executive Secretary of the Idaho Commission for Pardons and
Parole, Dr. Marshall received the B.A. degree
from Monmouth College, the M.A. degree from
the University of Iowa, and the Ph.D. degree
from Washington State University.

Police Ethics
And International Police Cooperation

André Bossard

Police ethics is a problem which is broached more and more frequently nowadays; although it may often give rise to controversy, it never fails to arouse interest.

The United Nations has drafted a Code of Conduct for Law Enforcement Officials which has recently been adopted by the 3rd Committee.[1] On 8th May 1979, the Council of Europe adopted a resolution on the same subject.[2]

The police themselves are very much concerned with the problem in many countries. During a symposium for the heads of police colleges held at Interpol Headquarters in Saint-Cloud, France, in October 1979, twenty-one of the countries represented reported that lectures on professional ethics were included in the curricula of their police colleges. Indeed, the participants asked that the subject of methods of dispensing this type of instruction be included on the agenda for the next symposium.

However, the topic raises many problems. Before even broaching the subject of police ethics as such, I feel it is important to first define what we mean by "police" and then pinpoint the

[1]U.N. 3rd Committee, Code of Conduct, item 88C, 34th Session, 1979, A/C.3/34/L/65.

[2]Parliamentary Assembly of the Council of Europe: Resolution 690 (1979) on the Declaration on the Police, 31st Session, 2nd Sitting, 1979.

23

particular moral, political and legal system within which the concept of ethics is to be considered.

The very idea of "police" covers a multitude of realities. The etymology of the word implies the "administration of the city." Today, the duties of the police vary considerably from country to country, according to the different national political or legal structures. But, in general, it seems safe to say that police work falls into three main categories: the maintenance of public order and security, intelligence work and crime investigation.

Just as these three tasks differ, so do the duties of the officers involved; the role of a member of a force responsible for maintaining order in the street and public security has something in common with that of a soldier. Indeed, these forces are often organised on semi-military lines, and their training places special emphasis on discipline, teamwork and respect for a strict hierarchy which leaves the lower ranks little room for personal initiative and responsibility.

Intelligence work, on the other hand, calls for skills akin to those of the journalist: the ability to seek out and cross-check items of information (but with no obligation to respect the strict rules governing the gathering of evidence to be produced in court), objectivity, accuracy and various other intellectual qualities such as a good, analytical mind.

Finally, the criminal investigation officer responsible for providing the courts with proof that a given person has committed a given offence, must display qualities similar to those of the magistrate to whom, under certain legal systems, he is answerable. He has to find evidence which can be produced in court, in accordance with penal law and strict rules of procedure. He is in direct contact with people, takes down statements with a view to subsequent prosecution, searches premises, makes seizures or arrests -- and all these actions will be scrutinized later during court proceedings. Such officers are often held personally responsible for their action.

It is therefore quite impossible to expect police officers performing these different tasks to have the same attitude to their work. A criminal investigation officer will not be very successful if he approaches his work in the same way as an intelligence agent, who does not have to constantly bear in mind the need for "evidence which will stand up in court." And a police officer responsible for maintaining public order could seriously jeopardize the outcome of some carefully planned joint action if he suddenly decided to do something on his own initiative.

Clearly, then, no rules of conduct could apply in every particular to all police officers, since they have very different tasks to perform. Any such rules of conduct would have to be tailored to the main types of work they do, but the problem is to find tasks which are common to all three of the categories outlined above. Could a single code of conduct be drawn up to apply to a soldier, a journalist and a magistrate?

The problem is further complicated by the fact that in many countries the same police officer may be required -- in the normal course of his work -- to perform duties from all three categories, for example, when he is a member of a non-specialised local police force. A similar situation arises with regard to cooperation on crime prevention.

Consequently, any attempt to draw up a code of conduct must focus on general rules capable of being used as guidelines for all police officers - in other words, general professional ethics, combined with specific rules of conduct for each of the three main categories mentioned.

However, we must not lose sight of yet

another important characteristic of police work. Generally speaking, it is basically a matter of carrying out orders. Police officers have no part to play in the drafting of laws, nor are they empowered to take legal decisions concerning law enforcement or to govern. In other words, they have no legislative, judicial or executive power.

Most of the duties that the police have to carry out -- no matter which of the three main categories of police work is involved -- are imposed upon them. In other words, the basic decision is normally taken by some outside authority -- a central or local government authority, or a judicial authority. The decisions are taken within the framework of specific laws or regulations, which means that these duties must be performed according to certain rules which themselves can vary in time and space and according to the type of work involved.

But the rules governing police action are themselves affected by various considerations: procedural (laws and regulations, the principle of legality, "everything that is not specifically forbidden is permitted," etc.) political (governmental instructions) and social (the acceptability of police action).

And so the police have only a rather limited field of action within the bounds of which they are free to choose the way in which they carry out their duties: they can choose what action to take, they can list priorities, and they can decide which method of intervention is to be used, but such options are often made automatically, as part of professional practice.

It therefore seems almost impossible to envisage a code of conduct for the police as a separate entity, independent of political and judicial ethics or indeed, of a given moral and legal system existing within a given social context at a given time and in a given place.

It is evident that the general concept of "the police" cloaks a complex reality, varying as it does according to the actual work involved and with scope for action depending on the law and on authorities external to the police. Consequently, attempting to determine a code of ethics is an extremely difficult undertaking.

Can anything helpful be learned from international police cooperation?

For many years now, the International Criminal Police Organization, Interpol, has devoted its energies to promoting cooperation between member countries in an attempt to prevent and combat offences against ordinary criminal law.

The Organization operates in a twofold context which may well affect any light we can bring to bear on this problem:

First, its work is carried on by a large number of countries - 127 at the time of writing - with very different political and social structures. This allows us to draw quite far-reaching conclusions.

Secondly, its activities are confined to crime investigation, which means it can collect only very limited information about the technical aspects of the maintenance of public order and about non-judicial intelligence work.

However, within these limits we can see whether any principles likely to help in devising a code of ethics for international police cooperation emerge from our practical experience; we can also sketch a broad general outline of the conditions with which a police officer must comply if he wishes to cooperate with his counterparts in other countries.

We should first emphasize that international police cooperation through Interpol channels is carried on in strict compliance with the conditions and limits laid down by the Organization's Constitution. This provides a certain number of basic principles which could be said to constitute a "Charter of Cooperation."

The first of these is respect for national sovereignty. Article 2 of the Constitution stipulates that the aim of the Organization is to ensure and promote the widest possible mutual assistance between all police authorities within the limits of the laws existing in different countries.

Such cooperation therefore excludes all possibility of supranational powers, or of one country's laws taking precedence over another's. Nor can there be any question of any type of coercive power, or sanctions, being brought to bear on member countries.

Article 2 of the Constitution also specifies that cooperation shall be carried on within the context of "the spirit of the Universal Declaration of Human Rights." The main principles laid down in that Declaration must therefore be used as guidelines for common action, and when a country becomes a member of the Organization -- and so accepts the terms of its Constitution -- it also implicitly accepts these general principles.

Finally, Article 3 of the Constitution forbids the Organization to undertake any intervention or engage in any activities of a political, military, religious or racial character.

Over the years, these principles have become enshrined in various texts or practices which can to some extent be taken as a rough outline for a "Code of ethics for international police cooperation."

At its General Assembly session in October 1949, the International Criminal Police Commission (which became the ICPO-INTERPOL in 1956) adopted

28

a resolution reminding the police -- and more
particularly the criminal investigation departments -- that they must make use of all the
advances provided by technology, forensic science
and criminology in their work, and that all acts
of violence or inhuman treatment committed by the
police in the exercise of their duties must be
reported to the judicial authorities. The
resolution also recommended that in all police
training colleges special importance be attached
to the recognition of the right of all persons,
including those suspected of having committed a
criminal offence, to receive fair and humane
treatment.

On many occasions the Organization has
drawn member countries' attention to the fact
that whenever action is required in connection
with a wanted offender, full details of the
criminal offence involved must figure prominently
in the appropriate request. Only then can we
decide whether or not the request is compatible
with the terms of the Organization's Constitution.

The non-political nature of the Organization's
activities is one of the fundamental principles
of cooperation. The refusal to allow cooperation on political cases has a two-fold objective:
to base all combined action on general agreement
as to the purpose of that action, and to guarantee
the Organization's impartiality, thus allowing
the police forces in countries with widely
differing political regimes to work together on
cases which will not give rise to controversy.

In practice, the question of whether a case
is predominantly political, military, religious or
racial in character is not decided on the basis
of abstract criteria; the General Secretariat
studies each case on its own merits, in collabora-
tion with the country or countries concerned, and,
where appropriate, can refuse to assist in the
investigation. In some circumstances, the countries
concerned may themselves decide that their national
laws will not allow them to cooperate on a case

which does not seem to them to have sufficient
justification or to be compatible with their laws.

In fact, this is what happens when countries
receive requests for arrest with a view to extra-
dition. As countries have cooperated over the
years, a basic pre-extradition procedure has
emerged, theoretically resulting in any wanted
person being handed over to the judicial authorities. Any such request with no adequate justification, or involving someone implicated in a
political, and not a criminal offence, could
result in a refusal to cooperate, in the light of
the terms of the Organization's Constitution and
of the principle of national sovereignty. To
some extent, therefore, a refusal to cooperate
can be construed as an indirect sanction against
those who do not comply fully with generally
accepted international policy.

Finally, Interpol cooperates with other
international organizations also working in the
spirit of the Universal Declaration of Human
Rights. In particular, a special agreement
has been drawn up between our Organization and
the United Nations Economic and Social Council,
and we were consulted when the previously-mentioned
"Code of Conduct for Law Enforcement Officials"
was being drafted.

And so it can be seen that practical, day-
to-day experience of cooperation has given rise
to a certain number of rules which can be considered as a potential code of international
police ethics: respect for national laws;
compliance with the terms of the Universal Declaration of Human Rights; non-intervention in
cases of a political, military, religious or
racial nature; justification of requests for cooperation by reference to a violation of ordinary
criminal law; and, finally, indirect sanctions
in the form of a refusal to cooperate.

These principles apply more to national
police forces than to individual police officers.

And yet, we have been able to gain some idea of
the potential rights and duties of the typical
law enforcement official as a result of the regular
and frequent contacts we have had with law enforcement officials from all over the world, the
meetings and exchanges of ideas which take place
at the various conferences and symposia we organize, the reports we prepare showing differences
in working methods in member countries, and the
study of the draft code of conduct recently
submitted to the United Nations.

The police officer investigating a crime is
involved in the whole judicial process. Very
often, his enquiries are the first link in the
judicial chain which logically ends in conviction
or acquittal. His activities are not confined
to handling documents -- he has to establish and
report facts. He also has the first contacts
with the people directly involved and who might
subsequently be the subject of proceedings. Any
error of judgment made by the investigator handling the initial enquiries can drastically
affect the freedom, reputation, livelihood and
even the life of the people concerned, since he
can set subsequent enquiries off in a direction
that can be very difficult to change later.

And so, in the light of this enormous
responsibility, what rules should govern the
police officer's conduct?

The first - and most obvious - rule is that
he must respect the law. Since the police
officer is the servant of the law, responsible
for its enforcement, he should naturally be the
first to obey it in every respect. This means
that he must never go beyond what the law orders
or allows -- in other words, he must never exceed
his powers. And of course he must never take the
law into his own hands, even if he feels that it
does not correspond to his own ideas of what
justice and the protection of society should be.
He is a servant of the law and of justice, not an
avenger.

The second rule is a natural consequence of the first. The police officer must serve the law and nothing but the law. He must never use his position as a police officer to further his own personal interests or those of other people. Apart from excluding any form of direct or indirect corruption, this also means that his private life, like that of Caesar's wife, must always be irreproachable and untainted by any breath of suspicion.

Thirdly, he must always be objective and impartial. This is extremely difficult, since it is practically impossible to prevent our personal ideas and opinions from influencing our judgment or the way we report things, even if the process is not conscious.

We believe that this means that the police officer must be absolutely non-political in the performance of his duties. This in no way implies that he cannot have his own personal opinions or beliefs, just that he must perform his duties in a completely unbiased way. In many countries, criticism of the police most often arises in connection with trials involving political offences and it is here that police action can frequently give rise to controversy.

The need for the police to be non-political raises the question of their relationship with the government. This is a vast, complex and controversial question, and I do not intend to broach it here. My feelings on the matter are that any attempt to draw up a code of police ethics involves striking a balance between the need for the police to serve some authority (either central or local government) and obey orders from that authority, and the obligation they have to serve the community and not some political movement, the implication being that they must resist certain pressures and behave in an unbiased fashion.

It is here that the point I made earlier is

particularly valid: police ethics cannot be dissociated from the ethics of government.

The fourth rule is that the police officer's duties must be socially acceptable. Since he is there to serve the public, he must never forget that he is dealing with human beings and must behave accordingly. This rules out the use of any practice contrary to the respect for human dignity and also implies the need for discretion as far as the mass media are concerned. Although we must not underestimate the importance of keeping the public informed, we must remember that very often people can be seriously harmed if details of their private lives are made public before the whole truth has been definitely established.

There is another point here, in connection with the amount of freedom allowed the police officer to decide how to carry out his duties. When exercising that personal initiative, he must be aware that certain types of routine work and certain reactions can become almost automatic; consequently, he must not lose sight of the possible consequences of this--indeed, he must do everything in his power to break himself of such habits if they begin to take precedence over the strict rules laid down in laws and regulations. The same applies to the exercise of any discretionary powers he may have; he must never come to consider such powers as proof of his own personal superiority, but rather as an instrument entrusted to him to use for the public good.

Obviously, if it is important to try to establish a code of ethics for the lower ranks, it is equally--if not more--important to do so for those in command. There can be no code of conduct for the police in general without a code of conduct for the command level. Apart from the requirements outlined above, the latter must lay even greater emphasis on service and a sense of responsibility, since a commanding officer is responsible not only for his own actions, but also for those of his men. This is mainly evident with regard to the personal initiative allowed lower ranks; where their performance of their duties becomes routine and automatic, this is often due to a lack of effective leadership.

There is considerable truth in the saying that a team is only as good as its leader.

The whole notion of command raises the problem of orders that are illegal or contrary to professional ethics. This is a very complex problem since it involves preserving "the balance between the need for internal discipline of the agency on which the public safety is largely dependent on the one hand, and the need for dealing with violations of basic human rights, on the other." Conscious of the difficulty there is in preserving this balance, the Draft Code of Conduct for Law Enforcement Officials adopted by the 3rd Committee of the U.N. General Assembly recommends that when violations of the Code occur, law enforcement officials "shall report the matter to their superior authorities and where necessary, to other appropriate authorities or organs vested with reviewing or remedial power."

The rules we have tried to define are essential for effective law enforcement. They may seem to represent a somewhat idealistic goal, but Interpol's experience in many countries over many years would tend to indicate that this is an attainable goal -- in fact, in the vast majority of cases these rules of professional ethics are usually applied. There are of course certain regrettable lapses -- and we must in no way underestimate the gravity of such occurrences. But they are really so few in number that they are obviously exceptions to the rule. On the average professional crime investigators are as competent-- if not more so -- than the members of other professions. Indeed, in our opinion, their professional and moral standards are usually excellent. It takes a very special kind of person to do a job where he is exposed to so much danger on a constant, day-to-day basis. First of all, there is the actual physical danger -- and this does not just mean having to arrest dangerous criminals, the "big names" in the underworld; it also means the daily risks faced by the police officer who has to rush into the thick of things to break up a fight, to stop someone who is in the middle of committing a crime, or to overpower a dangerous maniac, an alcoholic or a drug addict. There is also considerable moral danger. Very few professions are so exposed to the risks of social contagion. The police officer is in permanent contact with crime, vice, corruption and the tremendous power of money that has been acquired quickly and dishonestly. It is any wonder, then, that he is particularly vulnerable to a wide variety of temptations? Not the least of these is discouragement in the face of the many duties he has to perform, with sometimes only very limited resources, in a permissive society which seems to encourage those who break the law and yet shows a total lack of interest in the victims of crime. Yes, it does take a very special kind of person to do this job.

What can be done to ensure continued respect for professional ethics and, indeed, even greater adherence to these rules?

There are international texts, and if they are to be enforced effectively, their provisions should be incorporated in national laws. There are various rules and regulations, prohibitions and penalties.

And yet we must not make it look as though, by advocating a code of ethics for the police, we have no confidence in a profession which, on the whole, performs its duties to the satisfaction of the majority of the general public. Rather, a code of police ethics should be regarded as a set of guidelines to facilitate the exercise of this dangerous profession. However, in my opinion, respect for the basic rules appears to be influenced much more by material factors than by the actual texts themselves. These factors include:

- Staff recruitment: When recruiting staff, as much weight must be given to the applicants' physical and educational qualifications as to their moral standards, their personality and their motivation for joining the police.

- Training: Young police officers must be given sound training -- in technical and legal subjects naturally (knowledge of the laws they will have to enforce, rules governing the use of force in law enforcement, etc.), but also in such things as civics, a sense of social responsibility and human relations. They must also be given refresher courses throughout their careers, not only to brush up their skills, but also to give them a change from the daily work routine.

- Discipline and training for commanding officers: As I said earlier, a team is only as good as its leader, and so particular attention must be paid to the selection procedure for commanding officers. Posts of command should not be given automatically as a reward for long service or merit -- such criteria as personality, natural authority, personal initiative, a sense of responsibility and an even temperament are equally important.

- Career prospects: Police officers must have a professional status involving job security and salaries high enough to protect them from outside influence. The police function must be structured.

- Technical resources: Criminal investigation officers must be able to call on all the technical resources made available by forensic science, thus facilitating the investigation of crime and the gathering of evidence.

36

- The non-political nature of police work:
I have already underlined the importance of this
and shall not enlarge on the subject.

   - Staff management policy: It is very important that specialized police officers should
not be frequently taken from their normal work
for temporary assignment to other, completely
different duties - for example, a detective
should not be assigned to street patrols, crowd
control duties or purely administrative work.
This means that the authorities concerned have to
adopt a staff management policy, which may well
present problems but is, in fact, essential.

   - Police/public relations: Efforts must be
made to promote a feeling of mutual confidence
between the police and the public. Obviously,
the problem is not the same everywhere, but
distrust of the representatives of the law does
seem to be almost second nature in some countries.
However, it must be realised that prevention is
one of the most effective ways of combating crime,
and prevention depends on mutual trust between the
police and the public and consequently on the
knowledge each has of the other.

   I said at the beginning of this article that
police ethics cannot be considered in isolation
from the ethics of justice or of government; in
fact, the problem is that of the ethics of society
as a whole. The police in general, and crime
investigation departments in particular, merely
reflect the society in which they work and the
moral standards they have to defend. The police
did not spring fully armed from the legislator's
brain, they were born of necessity and experience
and have to adapt to the conditions of life
within society and to the civilization of which
they are but one component part.

   It is almost ironic to think that, although
many claim that the age in which we are living is
marked by a decline in moral standards and rampant

permissiveness, great concern is nevertheless being expressed about the ethical standards required of those responsible for law enforcement, even while the very substance of the law is sometimes in dispute.

And so I believe that the search for a code of ethics for the police is in fact a search for a balance between the law and man, between society and the individual, between order and freedom.

Mr. André Bossard, Secretary General of Interpol, has a Doctorate in Law from Paris University and has been a Commissaire in the French National Police since 1950, working in various operational services of the Police Judiciaire. He was seconded to the International Criminal Police Organization-- Interpol in 1971 as Head of Division; he was elected Secretary General of the Organization in 1978.

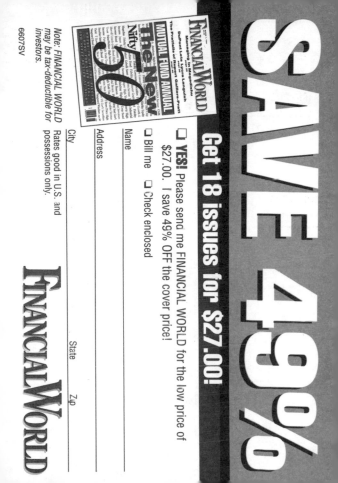

BUSINESS REPLY MAIL

FIRST-CLASS MAIL PERMIT NO. 22 FLAGLER BEACH, FL

POSTAGE WILL BE PAID BY ADDRESSEE

FINANCIALWORLD

P.O. Box 420144
Palm Coast, FL 32142-9558

Law Enforcement Ethics:
A Theoretical Analysis

Charles L. Johnson, Ph.D.
Gary B. Copus, Ph.D.

There exists in criminal justice several
professional and "emerging professional" relationships which are either formally (attorney-client)
or informally (police-citizen) governed by a
stated or implied code of ethics. The purpose
of this paper is to examine theoretically the
areas of law enforcement ethics, more specifically the often quoted and "the accepted" Law
Enforcement code of ethics. The examination of
this topic is especially important in that for
police, the actual mechanics available for
insuring adherence to a code of ethics are less
formal and obvious than in other professions
conventionally and historically recognized as
such. Specifically, where less public awareness
and public review is involved, where greater
latitude in the use of discretion is involved,
where the ultimate impact upon the client has
more potential for life changing results, the
more important it is to understand the effect a
code of ethics might have on police behavior. As
an integral part of the quest for professionalism,
the police as an occupational group have addressed
formally the need for a code of ethics. During
the 1957 conference of the International
Association of Chiefs of Police (IACP) a law
enforcement Code of Ethics was adopted. The
Code was first developed by the California
Police Officers Association and the Peace
Officers Research Association of California,
later being adopted by the National Conference
of Police Associations (German, et al, 1973). It
is the order of attention given to ethics which
may shed some light on the actual importance of
this area in the police organization. Generally
speaking, it is fair to say that ethical considerations for conventional professions grew out
of a moral obligation felt by those professions

for their constituency. It would appear today however, that oftentimes the initial and primary impetus for formal written ethical guidelines is not a concern for constituency but rather to meet one of those accepted criteria for being recognized as a profession (you must have a code of ethics),then this code must be generated. If this is the case you might expect to find such a code of ethics reflecting more of an emphasis on form and style rather than on practical substance. What may be reflected is not so much an ideological commitment but rather a committment to appearances. One way to "get at" this issue is to identify if in fact there are issues and constituency relationships within the occupational environment of police that should be governed by a formally stated code of ethics. If there are, does the stated code of ethics address in an utilitarian manner these issues and relationships? While there are many avenues from which to approach a discussion of these issues and relationships and their emphasis on form or substance [1] perhaps two of the most fertile and yet relatively untouched (in this area) theoretical approaches are found in the works of sociologist Robert K. Merton and social psychologist Leon Festinger. Ethics in any social/professional sphere is a complex phenomena to analyze. To illustrate this complexity, realize that there is no unique way to view the phenomena as exemplified by the varied possibilities from a structural perspective alone. For instance, one can discuss ethics and ethical behavior in any part of the criminal justice system from the unit of analysis of individual, organization, or system. Further, the subject may be approached from other perspectives such as the psychological, social interaction, political, or economical. The approach chosen

[1] If the emphasis is on substance, is this emphasis consistent with police attitudes? If the emphasis is on form, does its nebulous form render it useless as an ethical guideline?

40

here is to utilize two well-known theoretical
perspectives from the social/psychological disciplines, namely, Merton's Anomie and Festinger's
Cognitive Dissonance. These perspectives were
chosen for several reasons. First, they have
established themselves as useful perspectives
through which to view a variety of complex
phenomena ranging from explanations of deviant
behavior as in the case of anomie to the analysis
of psychological disturbances at the individual
level as in the case of cognitive dissonance.
Further, the application of these two perspectives
to the study of ethics in criminal justice
proves capable of looking at future implications
for all levels of structural components--under the
assumption that criminal justice practitioners
will in the future internally adopt the ethics
into their individual modes of behavior. As will
be seen, the adoption process may result in
unanticipated consequences for the individual
actor as well as the organization in which the
actions occur.

The Perspective of Anomie

        The concepts of anomie, as used in this
chapter, are those developed by Robert K. Merton
(1968). Although Merton was concerned with the
explanation of deviant behavior, it is emphasized
that Merton was open on the definition of what
a deviant act is. Indeed, if taken in a narrow
sense, that is deviant behavior being equated
with a criminal act, anomie as a perspective to
examine ethics would be seriously questionable,
since an act of non-ethical behavior is not
necessarily an act of illegality. Merton contended   that deviant behavior refers to

        conduct that departs significantly from
        the norms set for people in their social
        statuses ... and, that deviant behavior
        had to be related to the norms that are
        socially defined as appropriate and

41

morally binding for people occupying
various statuses (Merton and Nisbet,
1966, p. 805).

Merton was strongly stated on this point, stres-
sing that anomie is a theory that distinguishes
general forms of deviant behavior which can be
removed from those which represent formal legal
violations. By viewing ethical statements of
conduct as setting the ethical norms of any
professional organization, it is assumed that
anomie is applicable to examining ethical versus
non-ethical conduct and further that the implications of ethical violations for the various
component levels of any organization. Based on
this initial assumption, attention is now turned
to developing a case for applying the anomie
perspective to an examination of ethical issues
in law enforcement. In other words, on what
rational basis can it be argued that anomie
theory is indeed a perspective through which to
examine ethics?

The Code and Reality: An Anomic Situation

Anomie is in essence based on the conceptual
dichotomy between cultural goals and institutional
means to achieve these goals. Merton placed
cultural goals in a cultural structure defined as
"that organized set of normative values governing
behavior which is common to members of a
designated society or group" (1968, p. 216).
Institutional means are the product of the social
structure consisting of the institutional norms
which define and regulate the means by which
cultural goals can be achieved, presumably
legitimately. Anomie, a conceptual condition,
arises when the equilibrium between cultural
goals and societal means of achieving these goals
is upset. For example, a cultural goal in the
American society is the maintenance of a minimal
level of living through the associate acquisition
of economic and material wealth. Given further

that this minimal level is to a great extent
defined by the advertising industry, anomie
theory would have it to mean that individuals
are coerced to believe they are entitled to a
comfortable home, one or more automobiles, and
the financial means to pursue selected types of
recreational and entertainment activities.
Merton recognizes this accent on success is not
peculiar to the American type of society nor
strictly economic, but states

> nevertheless, there is something pecul-
> iar about the emphasis on success in our
> open class society. Aspirations for
> place, recognition, wealth, and socially
> prized accomplishments are culturally
> held to be appropriate for all, what-
> ever their origins or present condition
> (Clinard, 1964, p. 217).

Yet, it is obvious that for a large sector of
our society these goals are virtually unobtain-
able thus giving rise to the conflict between
the promise of the culture and the realities of
the societal structure. It also follows that
there exist different rates of anomie by such
characteristics as social class, ethnic or
racial status, and other characteristics. The
latter is of particular interest given the
expansion of these characteristic examples to
include police organizational role differences
and the various police organization ranks. This
line of reasoning implies that differential
anomie rates may exist between various ranks and
divisions within the law enforcement organization.
To establish the legitimacy of anomie as a valid
perspective to view ethics, the conceptual
relationships between the key components of
anomie and those of ethics have to be identified
and substantiated, via discovering the
theoretical relationship between these components.
The objective is to find for each major component in anomie the corresponding component in
ethics (or more precisely their stated codes

43

and/or functions). Once these correspondences are identified, one could read anomie theory substituting terminologies to make the theory address specifically the area of ethics. Given that the conceptual components in anomie are cultural goals and societal means, what are the counterparts in ethics? Ethical standards, as expressed in Law Enforcement Code of Ethics, are equated to anomie's culturally defined legitimate goals. These standards delineated what the professional member can adopt as a level of expectation to aspire to. This point needs to be emphasized. Just as the previously cited example of a cultural goal (i.e. recognition and socially prized accomplishments) does not describe how one should live, neither do codes of ethics necessarily do so. Indeed, codes of ethics can be viewed in both ways, namely as simply a set of statements by which one can judge one's own behavior or the behavior of others and as a legitimate level of aspiration. The second perspective corresponds precisely to the culturally defined goal concepts of anomie. That is to say, ethical codes go far beyond specifying behavioral standards, and in actuality are a set of promises by which higher order individual needs (in the sense of Maslow's Hierarchy) can be met. Those codes describe qualities which it is assumed most persons would choose given the opportunity. The assumption, of course, is itself based on the belief that man is basically ethical and moral and thus inherently strives toward those states of being so well portrayed in the eloquent language used in the codes of professional organizations. For example, quoting from the Law Enforcement Code of Ethics adopted by the IACP:

> As a law enforcement officer my funda
> mental duty is to serve mankind; to
> safeguard lives and property; to pro
> tect the innocent against deception,
> the weak against oppression and intimi
> dation, and the peaceful against vio
> lence and disorder; ...maintain courages calm

44

in the face of danger, scorn, or
ridicule; ... I will never act
officiously or permit personal
feelings, prejudices, animosities
or friendship to influence my
decisions.

The intention of providing an abstract set of
values to which one can aspire is as apparent as
the intention to specify a set of identifiable
characteristics which a person is merely expected
to adopt. But are not culturally defined goals
such as a quality life style, striving to become president, and having the opportunity for a
college education, simply sets of promises to
which most persons can be assumed to aspire?
Given further these are examples of culturally
defined goals, and in essense their being no
different than the promises provided by codes of
ethics, it therefore follows in the terminology
of anomie, that a code of ethics can be viewed
as those culturally defined characteristics
which are legitimate goals to which members
of a profession can aspire. Having offered
reasons for the cultural/ethics relationship,
what about societal means? The counterpart to
Merton's societal means of goal accomplishment
is argued to be that social/organizational
milieu in which the levels of law enforcement
personnel are involved. Take for example,
the street patrolman confronted with a situation.
As is well-documented, this situation can be
viewed as a social scene involving the officer
and the apparent offender in a void of all but
legal considerations. It also can be viewed as
a social setting involving characteristics of
the officer, the offender, and on-lookers, in
conjunction with departmental regulations and
procedures. The social scene, as a combination
of all the above characteristics, defines the
means to accomplish the goals of the Code of
Ethics. In addition, the goals of the Code may
or may not be harmonious with the functional
goals immediately to be dealt with, that being
the performance of duty, much less the possibility

45

of being harmonious with the specific circumstances dictated by the immediate social setting. The literature well establishes the idea of the social/organizational scene in terms which are basic to the anomie perspective-- namely those conditions analogous to the social structure preventing, or at least being an obstacle to an individual officer in attaining the personal status described in the Code of Ethics. For example, Niederhoffer (1967) describes the difficulty faced by new officers when first handling cases. He says,

> On these cases the new patrolman must resolve the dilemma he has learned at the academy and the pragmatic precinct approach. In the academy, where professionalism is accented, the orientation is toward that of the social sciences and opposed to the 'lock-them-up' philosophy (Niederhoffer, 1967, p. 56).

Given that this latter philosophy is not reflected in the Code of Ethics, immediately the social scene begins to create obstacles to achieving the status of the ethically ideal professional. Sullivan (1971) cites a case in point of an officer in a West Coast city who spotted the local judge's car illegally parked. Given than the Code of Ethics clearly prohibits discrimination because of race, color, creed, or station in life ("I will never act officiously or permit personal feelings, prejudices, animosities or friendships to influence my decision."), the officer was faced with an obvious problem. The immediate choice boiled down to avoiding embarrassment and possible trouble that could result if the officer ticketed the judge's car. (To finish the story, the officer ticketed the car and later received public praise by the judge for his fortitude in doing the right thing.) Becker, citing from a study of a state police system, described the pressures placed on the new recruits to conform to accepted behavioral

46

patterns as defined by the experienced officers.
"Many past pundits suggested that probationary
policemen should forget everything they learned
in recent school, the implication that the rejection of school material was merely convenient, but
often necessary, if one were to gain approval of
field officers" (Becker, 1970, p.30). Wilson
(1968) points out that if an officer abides by the
phrase "You can't go by what the book says" (p.31),
it becomes feasible that higher order aspirations
defined by the Code of Ethics may be as inappli-
cable to handling a situation as may be strict
adherence to departmental rules and regulations.
In each of the above cases, and there are many
such citations supportive of the social scene
idea, there are pressures to conform in a manner
such that ethical codes become, if not irrelevant,
at least placed in a perspective not related to
the real world. And yet, the Code is still describing that most elevated state of aspirations
to which it is assumed most men and women would
aspire and who perceive the legitimacy of their
desire to do so. The conclusion is therefore that
the social/organizational milieu is equatable to
anomie's social structure.

The responses to anomic situations, like
human responses to any social situation requiring
resolution, is complex. The possible responses,
referred to as adaptive patterns, are diagrammat-
ically presented by Merton (1968, p.194).

FIGURE 1
A TYPOLOGY OF MODES OF INDIVIDUAL ADAPTATION

Modes of Institutionalized Adaptation Means	Cultural Goals	
I. Conformity	+	+
II. Innovation	+	-
III. Ritualism	-	+
IV. Retreatism	-	-
V. Rebellion	+/-	+/-

(+ = Acceptance; - = Rejection; +/- = Rejection
of prevailing values and substitution of new
values.)

47

As discussed by Clinard, Merton points out that "none of these adaptations is deliberately selected by the individual or is utilitarian, but rather, since all arise from strains in the social system, they can be assumed to have a degree of spontaneity behind them" (Clinard, 1964, p. 16). These adaptive patterns are assumed to exist in all social systems, particularly, that social system of law enforcement.

Conformity

As to the implications, attention is redirected toward Figure 1. The first mode, called Conformity, requires an individual to accept both the cultural goals and the institutionalized means of achieving those goals. In the current perspective this mode describes the law enforcement officer who accepts as legitimate the standards set forth in the Codes of Ethics and even more takes these standards as characteristics toward which to aspire. He also would accept that the social milieu in which they work is a component of the procedures that define their activity which are legitimate and workable ways to attain the desired end. Broderick (1977) describes a personality type he calls the Idealist, an officer who clearly accepts the ethical standards contained in the code. However, it is not clear from Broderick's description of the Idealist whether they also accept the institutionalized means as offering them the opportunity to achieve these goals. The conformity mode of adaptation is what most would probably refer to as a "good cop" according to middle-class American Standards.

The second mode of adaptation, Innovation, defines that officer who accepts the ethical standards as personal aspirations and yet rejects the means by which they can be achieved which is tantamount to the rejection of not the setting of their profession (this is unchangeable) but the rules, regulations, and procedures of

the department. A total rejection in the sense
of disobedience and/or insubordination is one
way rejection can be accomplished. More probable,
however, is a rejection through the "bending" of
the departmental rules and not always in a
socially undesirable manner. Consider the officer
who chooses, against department policy, to engage
in family counseling through offering advice and
simply acting the role of a professional counselor.
The reason the officer may choose this avenue
is related to anomie experienced. In order to
become that idealized person described in the
Codes of Ethics, the officer determined the
avenues open were inadequate, and thus chose to
innovate and open new paths for achievement.

Ritualism

Ritualism is a mode of adaptation by which
an individual officer scales down his aspirations.
If the officer cannot have an "unsullied" reputation and be "indiscriminating" in his behavior
to all, then a lower level of aspiration is
substituted. This was not necessarily dysfunctional in the original scheme of Merton,
especially when ritualism is approved by fellow
associates. The existence of this mode, reminis-
cent of the psychoanalytic protection process of
rationalization, could prevent a person from
choosing an adaptive pattern truly deviant and
dysfunctional to the society at large. For
example, if one were to be committed to
pecuniary success of a reduced level and to live
in a slum offering little or no opportunity to
achieve more than a basic level of living by
legitimate means, then from a societal order
point of view ritualism may be considered
desirable over retreatism to drugs and alcohol.
In law enforcement, however, the Code of Ethics
is unlike economic levels of possible achievement.
In the latter there are levels of choice--one may
choose one car instead of two, a black-and-white
television instead of a color one, or to live in

49

a less expensive neighborhood instead of the more expensive one. Ethical statements, however, unlike economic status, cannot be scaled up and down by individual choice. Whereas economic status, within certain parameters, may be determined by the individual, ethical statements are a result of group consensus. Therefore, partial acceptance of the ethical standards is not a viable option. Given this, ritualism, which implies a quantative choice, is not a possible mode of adaptation.

Retreatism

Through the mode of adaptation called retreatism ethical statements can also be rejected. Not only does the retreatist reject the ethical statements--"be an example to all"-- but also rejects the means, departmental policies, regulations, as well. As Merton states, "The retreatist pattern consists of substantial abandoning both of the once-esteemed goals, and of institutionalized practices directed toward these goals (Merton, 1957, p. 187). Retreatism, according to Merton, constitutes adaptive modes of behavior like psychotics, outcasts, chronic drunkards, and drug addicts (Merton, 1957). Although it would be far fetched to suggest that problems such as alcoholism can be completely traced back to the existence of anomie whose causal determinants in turn are in Codes of Ethics, it is clear that alcoholism in particular is a reaction to stress contained in the profession, or in anomie terms, in the social structure of law enforcement. That this stress is related to ethical aspirations is to be considered a theoretical possibility deserving a closer look.

Rebellion

The fifth and last mode of adaptation is

what Merton refers to as rebellion. Here, not only
are both the ethical standards and legitimate
institutionalized means rejected, but, there are
substitutions made to replace both. These substitutions can only be detrimental to the current
social structure. For example, an officer who
professes belief to generalities paraphrased
as "you have to get the job done no matter what,"
"hippies don't deserve the benefits of the law,"
"show me a minority and I'll show you a crook,"
"the only way to set the attention of law breakers
is to break their heads," are substitutions to
those lofty humanitarian, professional, ethical
statements with those reflecting their own views
of society and the attendant ways to deal with
law breakers held in those views. In a way,
this mode of adaptation offers little in the
way of positive change initiation that the
innovator does and is not mildly detrimental to
the social order as the retreatist.

The Perspective of Cognitive Dissonance

A second approach to the analysis of Law
Enforcement Ethics is that of Leon Festinger's
theory of cognitive dissonance. Festinger's
theory was first nationally proposed in the 1957
edition of his book, A Theory of Cognitive
Dissonance. Cognitive dissonance is a "moti-
vational state which exists when an individual's
cognitive elements (attitudes, perceived
behaviors) are inconsistent with each other"
(Wolman 1973, p. 66). When cognitive dissonance
does occur, this is an uncomfortable state for
the individual and cognitive equilibrium is
sought in order to reduce this dissonance. The
primary point here is that as soon as dissonance
occurs there will be pressures to reduce that
dissonance. A logical part of this process is
that the individual will also avoid inputs which
may have the affect of increasing dissonance.
When viewing the issues and relationships associated with ethics through the theoretical prism

51

of cognitive dissonance,a framework is necessary
in order to properly structure and address basic
problematic areas. The framework chosen for
this purpose is that of conventional police
attitudinal sets as portrayed by such authors as
Skolnick (1966), Wilson (1968), and Manning
(1971). Conventional police attitudes were
chosen when, upon review, it was determined
that these attitudes stem from and reflect many
of those issues and constituency relationships
which provide entry to the study of ethics in
relationship to law enforcement. In addition,
these conventional attitudes and the issues and
relationships they reflect, are for the most
part addressed by the widely adopted Law Enforcement Code of Ethics. This framework will
systematically bring to light those areas where
dissonance is present between the conventionally-
thought-of police attitudes and their code of
ethics, and the attitudes of the public which
are reflected in the current issues and constituency relationships associated with law
enforcement. When viewed through the theoretical
prism of cognitive dissonance the implications
of agreement or disagreement between the tri-
partite of police attitudes/assumptions, issues/
relationships, and the police code of ethics can
be discussed with increased structure and clarity.

Police Attitudes

The police personality and related attitudes
and assumptions have been a topic of both
emotional and empirical discussion for some time.
Police have been portrayed as being cynical
(Niederhoffer, 1969), isolated and alienated
(Skolnick, 1966), having a poor self-image
(Lawrence, 1978), defensive and distrustful of
outsiders (Wilson, 1968), dogmatic and authoritarian (Balch, 1972), no more dogmatic and
authoritarian than non-police (Culler, 1972;
Smith, Locke, Walker, 1968), and so on. The list
continues with respect to intelligence, sexual

identity, ability to relate to non-police, and many other traits. In addition, there is the question of whether the police occupation attracts certain personality types or whether the police occupational role molds individuals after becoming employed. While consensus as to a police "personality" may not have yet been reached, a great deal of discussion has been generated as to the presence or absence of a particular set of traits associated with police. While the jury is still out on the personality issue, there does seem to be some consensus as to the occupational culture of police and, the attitudes and means of dealing with the pressures associated with that occupation. This is of course not confined to the police occupation but rather is found in all occupations. The police, however, due for the most part to their unique position in society, seem to require special means of dealing with their occupational culture. As stated by Van Maanen:

> Workers in all occupations develop ways and means by which they manage certain structural strains, contradictions and anomalies of their prescribed role and task. In police work, with danger, drudgery, and dogma as prime occupational characteristics, these tensions are extreme. Correspondingly the pressure on new members to bow to group standards is intense. Few, if any, pass through the socialization cycle without being persuaded--through their own experiences and the sage-like wisdom passed from generation to generation of policemen-- to accept the occupational accepted frame-of-reference. This frame-of-reference includes, of course, both broad axioms related to police work in general (role) and the more specific corollaries which provide the ground rules of the workaday world (operations), (1970, p.116).

The occupational culture of police has generated attitudes based upon assumptions about their fellow officers, the citizens they protect and police, their own administration, the various branches of the government, and their role and relationships within these segments that make up society as a whole. The occupational culture contains the attitudes, values, and assumptions regarding the nature of man, in general those basic premises from which each of us make everyday decisions. Perhaps one of the best compilations of these assumptions/attitudes, is that by Peter K. Manning. Manning identified the postulates drawn from the works of Banton, Bordua, Reiss, McNamara, Niederhoffer, Skolnick, Westley, Rose, and Wilson; and qualifies then them by indicating that they (the postulates) are general reflections of the attitudes, norms, and values of primarily American, non-college educated patrolmen (Manning, 1971) [2] .

1. People cannot be trusted; they are dangerous.
2. Experience is better than abstract rules.
3. You must make people respect you.
4. Everyone hates a cop.

2
According to the National Manpower Survey (NMS) of the Criminal Justice System, 8.8 percent of sworn law enforcement personnel have completed 16 years of education and 46.4 percent have one year or more of college. The NMS projections for 1980 are 14.1 percent completing 16 years of education and 63.3 percent with one year or more college. The percentage of non-college educated patrolmen then (who do not make up all sworn personnel) would be quite high, and would represent the largest single group of police officers (NMS, vol. 2, p. 20, 1978).

5. The legal system is untrustworthy;
   policemen make the best decisions
   about guilt or innocence.
6. People who are not controlled will
   break laws.
7. Policemen must appear respectable
   and be efficient.
8. Policemen can most accurately identify
   crime and criminals.
9. The major jobs of the policeman are
   to prevent crime and to enforce the
   law.
10. Stronger punishment will deter crim-
    inals from repeating their errors.

Issues and Relationships

Given that the above assumptions reflect
attitudes held by police, what then are
associated issues/relationships that begin to
bring into focus the general concern of this
chapter, that of police ethics? The primary
and fundamental issues fall into five overlapping
areas:

1. police role/mandate
2. discretion
3. police/community relations
4. public perception of police
5. police perception of public

Police Role/Mandate

The police role has received considerable
attention over the years, however, as with the
"police personality," little consensus has been
reached. Dependent upon whether the police role
is perceived as peace keeping or law enforcement,
different conclusions are reached regarding the
role of police. The complexity of this problem
becomes better focused when the occupational
reality of the police role is considered. That
reality manifests itself in public expectations

55

of the police, the resultant political expectations of the police, and the acceptance by the police of those expectations. When the crime rate increases, the public singles out for accountability the most visible group, ie, the police. Yet when considered in an objective light, the police have little control over those factors that have become associated with increasing crime rates (ie, high unemployment, poor housing, ethnic ratios, deterioration of the inner city, crowding, age and sex ratios, and low educational attainment [Nettler, 1974]). What occurs then, as aptly stated by Manning and others, is that the police begin to manage their appearance, that is appearing to be able to manage their unreasonable mandate of controlling crime (Manning, 1971).

Discretion

Perhaps one of the most fundamental issues associated with law enforcement is the use and control of discretion on the part of the police. While the ultimate form of discretion is often viewed as the decision to place under arrest or not place under arrest, this by no means represents the total range of discretionary decisions on the part of police. The basic issue related to discretion is the logic associated with the decision to impose or not impose the full force of the law on an individual. Those situations in which the use of discretion is the most manageable are those dealing strictly with law enforcement. Those which are least manageable deal more closely with order maintenance. Since most current research indicated that the large majority of a police officer's time is spent in order maintenance situations, it becomes even more critical to appreciate the role of discretion in police work. While rules may be applied to lessen the magnitude of discretion, often these rules are necessarily ambiguous due to the variety of circumstances in which they may have applicability (Wilson, 1968). There remains then, as the compelling factor in decision making, the individual logic of the police officer.

In its truest form, police community relations is an attempt on the part of police to bring together the community and those persons charged with policing the community, for the purpose of dealing with problems and issues which have import for both parties (Cohn and Viano, 1976). While there have been charges that Police Community Relations is no more than an attempt on the part of the police at impression management, the ideal aim is to involve the citizens in decision making and policy setting for the police sector. The issue which arises out of these two extremes is whether the police are paying lip service to a useful mechanism or are intent on involving the community as a full partner in the control of crime. If the emphasis on the part of the police is "looking good, not necessarily on being good" (Radelet, 1977, p. 20), this then has certain implications for the police perception of the public. Even if the emphasis is on being good, the public response as a whole may not reflect acceptance of this effort on the part of the police community. The importance of this point lies in the fact that while the police group in any given community, via policy and rule, mandate a standard of behavior and put into action a program of community relations, the response from the community will vary dependent upon what part of the community you are addressing. In this sense, the community cannot be viewed as a wholistic concept, but rather must be viewed as several loosely knit groupings which reflect different and sometime opposing philosophies about what "being good" on the part of police actually is. This too makes even more difficult the task of formulating police-community relations policy which meets the needs of the community as a whole, and may result in the police falling back on the management of appearances rather than on building substantive participatory relationships with the community.

Public Perception of the Police

It would be safe to say that for most
citizens, contact with the police is for the
purpose of a negative sanction. Very few persons
have been stopped by their local police officer
and given praise and thanks for not speeding
or not assaulting another citizen. However,
there are two basic ways for the public to view
the police function. One is in the abstract
sense, when the individual is asked how the police
generally perform their function the response
is positive, that is, the belief that police do
not engage in serious misconduct, brutality,
take bribes, etc. (Radelet, 1977). This response
is not, of course, a static response, but varies
according to ethnicity, sex, age, and other
factors. While the majority of persons feel that
the police do perform appropriately, there are
two additional points worth noting. The first
is that the police do not deal with the majority
of the public, but rather a select few. For
example, the younger a person is, the more likely
he is to have a negative evaluation of police.
The second and related point has to do with
previous police contact. Specific contact with
law enforcement personnel removes one's perception
from the abstract to the situational. It is
worth repeating that almost without exception
public contact with police occurs because something has gone wrong or a wrong has been committed.
Given that this is the case, these situational
occurrences tend to personalize the individual's
view of the police with the result being a
generalization from this contact to the police
community as a whole.

Police Perception of the Public

Most of us, when making initial contact
with another individual, make some attempt to
place that individual in a category. The
category may be as encompassing as young or old,
or professional or non-professional, but never-

theless the attempt at categorization is made.
There have been general explanations offered for
this behavior, one of the most accepted being
that categorization "helps" us to understand
and thereby predict an individual's behavior. If
there is one occupational group which would
benefit from the ability to predict future
behavior, it would be the police. How do the
police view the public? Van Maanen indicated
that the police place citizens into one of three
categories, 1) "suspicious persons," 2) "ass-
holes," and 3) "know nothings" (Manning and
Van Maanen, 1978, p. 223). Campbell and Shuman
(1976) indicate that a high percentage of police
perceive ghetto residents as non-cooperative who
regard police as enemies or are indifferent
toward police; Westley indicates that the public
is hostile toward police resulting in the police
feeling isolated and "he (the policeman) regards
the public as his enemy, feels his occupation to
be in conflict with the community and regards
himself to be a pariah" (Manning, 1971, p. 177).
It would appear that police have a general
feeling about the public which could be described
as an adversary relationship, an "us against
 them" relationship. While this perception is
counter-productive, it is nevertheless understandable. It is understandable in that most
police contact with the public is the result of
a law violation or citizen disturbance. The
results of this contact more often than not ends
in the citizen being either indignant toward
the officers involved, becoming verbally abusive,
calling in a complaint, or in some cases
physically assaulting the officer. Given this
set of circumstances objectivity on the part of
the police toward the public is at a premium.

Law Enforcement Code of Ethics

In 1957, at the annual conference of the
International Association of Chiefs of Police
(IACP), a Law Enforcement Code of Ethics was
adopted. This code was not original to the IACP,

but rather had been developed the year preceeding
the 1957 IACP conference by the California Peace
Officers Association and the Peace Officers
Research Association of California (German, Day,
Gallati, 1973). The Code has since been adopted
by various other Law Enforcement Groups and
appears in many texts on law enforcement as the
accepted code of ethics for law enforcement
personnel. The Code consists of a four paragraph
code of ethics statement and is followed by
eleven articles which make up the Canons of
Police Ethics. The Code of Ethics and Canons
read as follows:

LAW ENFORCEMENT CODE OF ETHICS

AS A LAW ENFORCEMENT OFFICER, my
fundamental duty is to serve mankind;
to safeguard lives and property; to
protect the innocent against deception,
the weak against oppression or intim-
idation; and the peaceful against violence or disorder, and to respect the
Constitutional rights of all men to
liberty, equality, and justice.

I WILL keep my private life unsullied
as an example of all; to maintain cou-
rageous calm in the face of danger,
scorn, or ridicule; develop self-re-
straint; and be constantly mindful of
the welfare of others. Honest in
thought and deed in both my personal
and official life, I will be exemplary
in obeying the laws of the land and
the regulations of my department.
Whatever I see or hear of a confi-
dential nature or that is confided in
me in my official capacity will be
kept ever secret unless revelation in
the performance of my duty.

I WILL never act officiously or
permit personal feelings, prejudices,
animosities or friendship to influence

my decision. With no compromise for
crime and with relentless prosecution
of criminals, I will enforce the law
courteously and appropriately without
fear or favor, malice or ill will,
never employing unnecessary force or
violence and never accepting gratuities.

I RECOGNIZE the badge of my office
as a symbol of public faith, and I
accept it as a public trust to be held
so long as I am true to the ethics of
the police service. I will constantly
strive to achieve these objectives and
ideals, dedicating myself before God to
my chosen profession . . . law enforcement.

CANONS OF POLICE ETHICS

ARTICLE 1. PRIMARY RESPONSIBILITY OF JOB
The primary responsibility of the
police service, and of the individual
officer, is the protection of the people
of the United States through the upholding of their laws; chief among
these is the Constitution of the United
States and its amendments. The law
enforcement officer always respects
the whole of the community and its
legally expressed will and is never
the arm of any political party and
clique.

ARTICLE 2. LIMITATIONS OF AUTHORITY
The first duty of a law enforcement officer, as upholder of the law,
is to know its bounds upon him in enforcing it. Because he represents
the legal will of the community, be it
local, state, or federal, he must be
aware of the limitations and pro-
scriptions which the people, through
law, have placed upon him. He must

61

recognize the genius of the American system of government which gives no man, groups of men or institution absolute power, and he must insure that he, as a prime defender of the system, does not pervert its character.

ARTICLE 3.   DUTY TO BE FAMILIAR WITH
             THE LAW AND WITH RESPONSIBIL-
             ITIES OF SELF AND OTHER
             PUBLIC OFFICIALS

The law enforcement officer shall assiduously apply himself to the study of the principles of the laws which he is sworn to uphold. He will make certain of his responsibilities in the particulars of their enforcement, seeking aid from his superiors in matters of technicality or principles when these are not clear to him; he will make special effort to fully understand his relationship to other public officials, including other law enforcement agencies, particularly on matters of jurisdiction, both geographically and substantively.

ARTICLE 4.   UTILIZATION OF PROPER MEANS
             TO GAIN PROPER ENDS

The law enforcement officer shall be mindful of his responsibility to pay strict heed to the selection of means in discharging the duties of his office. Violations of laws or disregard for public safety and property on the part of the officer are intrinsically wrong; they are self-defeating in that they instill in the public mind a like disposition. The employment of illegal means, no matter how worthy the end, is certain to encourage disrespect for the law and its officer. If the law is to be honored, it must first be honored by those who enforce it.

ARTICLE 5. COOPERATION WITH PUBLIC
OFFICIALS IN THE DISCHARGE
OF THEIR AUTHORIZED DUTIES

The law enforcement officer shall cooperate fully with other public officials in the discharge of authorized duties, regardless of party affiliation or personal prejudice. He shall be meticulous, in assuring himself of the propriety, under the law, of such actions and shall guard against the use of his office or person, whether knowingly, or unknowingly, in any improper or illegal action. In any situation open to question, he shall seek authority from his superior officer, giving him a full report of the proposed service or action.

ARTICLE 6. PRIVATE CONDUCT

The law enforcement officer shall be mindful of his special identification by the public as an upholder of the law. Laxity of conduct or manner in private life, expressing either disrespect for the law or seeking to gain special privilege, cannot but reflect upon the police officer and the police service. The community and the service require that the law enforcement officer lead the life of a decent and honorable man. Following the career of a policeman gives no man special perquisites. It does give the satisfaction of safeguarding the American republic. The officer who reflects upon this tradition will not degrade it. Rather, he will so conduct his private life that the public will regard him as an example of stability, fidelity, and morality.

ARTICLE 7. CONDUCT TOWARD THE PUBLIC

The law enforcement officer, mindful of his responsibility to the whole community, shall deal with individuals of the community in a manner

63

such as will inspire confidence and
trust. Thus, he will be neither over-
bearing nor subservient, as the individual
citizen has neither an obligation to
stand in awe of him nor a right to
command him. The officer will give
service where he can, and require compliance with the law. He will do neither
from personal preference or prejudice
but only as a duly appointed officer
of the law discharging his sworn obligation.

ARTICLE 8.   CONDUCT IN ARRESTING AND
             DEALING WITH VIOLATORS
     The law enforcement officer shall
use his powers of arrest in accordance
with the law and with due regard to
the right of the citizen concerned.
His office gives him no right to prosecute the violator nor to mete out
punishment for the offense. He
shall, at all times, have a clear
appreciation of his responsibilities
and limitations regarding detention
of the violator; he shall conduct himself in such a manner as will minimize
the possibility of having to use force.
To this end he shall cultivate a dedication to the service of the people
and the equitable upholding of their
laws whether in the handling of laws
violators or in dealing with the law
abiding.

ARTICLE 9.   GIFTS AND FAVORS
     The law enforcement officer, repre-
senting government, bears the heavy
responsibility of maintaining, in his
own conduct, the honor and integrity
of all governmental institutions. He
shall, therefore, guard against placing
himself in a position which any person
can reasonably assume that special
consideration is being given. Thus, he

should be firm in refusing gifts,
favors, or gratuities, large or small,
which can, in the public mind, be interpreted as capable of influencing his
judgment in the discharge of his duties.

ARTICLE 10. PRESENTATION OF EVIDENCE
The law enforcement officer shall
be concerned equally in the prosecution
of the wrong doer and the defense of
the innocent. He shall ascertain what
constritutes evidence and shall present
such evidence impartially and without
malice. In so doing, he will ignore
social, political, and other distinc-
tions among the persons involved,
strengthening the tradition of the
reliability and integrity of an officer's word.

ARTICLE 11. ATTITUDE TOWARD PROFESSION
The law enforcement officer shall
regard the discharge of his duties as
a public trust and recognize his responsibility as a public servant. By diligent study and sincere attention to
self-improvement he shall strive to make
the best possible application of science
to the solution of crime and, in the
field of human relationships, strive
for effective leadership and public
influence in matters affecting public
safety. He shall appreciate the importance and responsibility of his
office, hold police work to be an
honorable profession rendering valuable
service to his community and the country.

There are several points which should be made
regarding the above code of ethics. The code has
been accepted and endorsed for the last twenty-
two years by the major police organizations in
the United States; the code specifically outlines
conduct which shall and shall not be engaged
in by law enforcement personnel; the code

specifies behavior which is honest, objective,
apolitical, competent, and subserviant to the
will of the populace as expressed in the constitution of the populace; while the implication
is that the code has been accepted by the police
community, there is little evidence that the
code has been understood and applied; and, the
tenor of the code is antithetical to the attitudes/
assumptions previously discussed in this chapter.

The above review of police assumptions/
attitudes, issues/relationships, and the police
code of ethics/canons of ethics all relate to
the singular question of how a code of ethics
contributes or detracts from ethical practices
on the part of police in relation to their constituency, the public. The following discussion
will attempt to systematically explore each of
the police attitudes/assumptions from the standpoint of the primary issue/relationships. Also,
the attempt will be made to discover if portions
of the code of ethics are supportive of, or
dissonant to parallel attitude/assumptions.
The first attitude/assumption presented is
"people cannot be trusted; they are dangerous."
The associated canon is Article Seven "Conduct
Toward the Public." First, it is obvious that
the attitudinal statement reflects a negative
portrait of the public by the police. At the
very least, the perception is not likely to result
in objective treatment of the public. While the
article in question states that the officer
should conduct himself in a manner which will
inspire confidence and trust, the preconceived out-
look that people cannot be trusted is likely
to result in the opposite effect. The question
which arises however is, can the police afford
to be totally trustful in their conduct toward
the public? In those situations which have the
potential of escalating into life-threatening
incidences, total objectivity may prove to be
counter-productive in protecting life and property. The second point to be made is that one
might feel an officer can mask this feeling of
distrust and dangerousness and give the appearance

66

of objectivity. However, this may beg the
question. Even if the behavioral manifestation
can be covered up initially, do years of such
practice result in the officer perceiving the
public as gullible and manipulable? The third
point concerns the question, how does such an
attitude influence the public perception of the
police? The often heard phrase, "I am an honest
tax paying citizen and he treated me as if I were
a criminal," may indicate that the police officer
is not successful in giving the impression of
being trustful. The resulting implication, in
the worst case example, is lack of public support
or at the very least a feeling of apathy towards
police in general.

The second attitude/assumption is "Experience is better than abstract rules." The
associated canons are Article Three, "Duty to
be Familiar with the Law and with Responsibilities
of Self and Other Public Officials" and Article
Eleven, "Attitude Toward Profession." Specifically, the working relationship of the police
officer results in a philosophy which portrays
experience, both in variety and length, as the
most efficient and expeditious source of information. While it should be stressed that a
great deal of the experience one gains on the
job is consistent with guidance provided in
rules, regulations, and procedure manuals, it
must also be noted that the attitudinal emphasis
here would seem to create an adversary relationship. Article Eleven exemplifies the high standard proposed by the canon of ethics stating that
"by diligent study and sincere attention to self
improvement he shall strive to make the best
possible application of science to the solution
of crime." The implication also found in
Article Three is that the officer should study
the "Principles" of the laws he is sworn to
uphold. Not mentioned are the informal station
house briefings of rookies by seasoned officers
or the coupling of experienced officers with
probationary officers. This by no means should

67

be construed as down-playing the importance of experience, but rather points out the emphasis placed by the occupational culture on deferring to experience in the streetwise sense rather than in the rulebook sense.

The third attitude/assumption is "You must make people respect you." The related issue/relationship is "Police/Community Relations" and the associated canon is Article Seven, "Conduct Toward the Public." The article in question indicates that the police must deal with the community in such a way that respect for the laws and police service is instilled in the community. In order to do this there should be some agreement between the public and the police as to who is serving whom and what police service actually entails. In reality, the police view the public as being those persons who generate their occupational problems while the public view the police as those persons who respond to a multitude of problem areas, including catching criminals. While there is agreement as to what tasks are being performed, there is disagreement as to whether these tasks should actually be performed and if they should in what priority. With regards to generating respect, the article would seem to indicate that respect by the public for the police should result from the adequate performance of service while the police feel that the office itself should generate respect, that is, citizens should respect the office because of what it is, and the power it represents, and this respect should carry over to the office holder. The difference would appear to be one of respect for merit as opposed to respect for power.

The fourth assumption/attitude is "Everyone hates a cop." The related issue/relationship is the "Public Perception of Police," and the associated canon is Article Eleven,

"Attitude Toward Profession." On the one hand,
the code of ethics is asking the officer to
appreciate the importance of his profession
and hold police work to be an honorable profession while rendering a valuable service to his
community. On the other hand, his day-to-day
contacts are with citizens who tell him he is
corrupt, racist, incompetent, and not aware
of who is paying his salary. What he is not
able to appreciate is the non-situational
citizen perception of the police which, in
the abstract sense, is that he is performing a
difficult task in an acceptable fashion. His
attitude then that everyone hates a cop is,
in part, the result of a biased sampling of the
citizen population.

The fifth assumption/attitude is "The
legal system is untrustworthy; police make the
best decisions about guilt and innocence."
The related issue/relationship is "The Use of
Discretion" and the associated canon, Article
Two,is that the police officer is the upholder
of the law and due to this responsibility, he
must be aware of the limitations placed upon
him to insure that his actions do not pervert
the character of the law. Since the police
officer is in a position to use discretionary
judgment, a philosophy which is premised upon
the untrustworthiness of the legal system and
portrays the individual officer as a Solomon-
like figure is completely antithetical to the
charge of Article Two.

The sixth attitude/assumption is "People
who are not controlled will break laws." The
related issue/relationship is again "Use of
Discretion" and the associated canon is
Article Eight, "Conduct in Arresting and Dealing
with Law Violators." The essence of Article
Eight is the charge to the officer to use his
powers in accordance with the law, indicating

69

that he has no right to prosecute, punish or use unnecessary force on the violator. The implication in the above attitude, however, when looked at in conjunction with all of the attitudes/assumption, is that police have the responsibility to control the public in order to insure that laws will not be broken. The control element is based upon the presumption that the individuals' behavior should be controlled so they will not break the law instead of the more limited notion of upholding the laws where and when a law is violated.

The seventh attitude/assumption is "Police must appear respectable and be effective." The related issue/relationship is "The Police Role/Mandate" and the associated canons are Article Six, "Private Conduct," Article Four, "Utilization of Proper Means to Gain Proper Ends," and Article Ten, "Presentation of Evidence." The appearance of respectability is addressed by Article Six, relating to Private Conduct. While the article in question mandates that the officer conduct his private life so that the public will regard him as an example of stability, fidelity, and morality, the police assumption is that the officer should "appear" respectable. Here again, the emphasis is on form as opposed to substance. The efficiency mentioned in the above assumption implies a Machiavellian-like approach exemplified by the officer who testifies in court that he recognizes the person to whom he gave a speeding ticket several weeks ago, when in fact, he cannot identify the person since during the interim he has given many similar citations. Parallel to this point is Article Ten, which charges that the officer should be mindful of the need for impartiality in his testimony to the facts of a case. Impartiality implies that the

70

the officer either has no personal investment
in clearing the case by conviction or if he
does, is able to remain totally objective. Given
that the police mandate (Manning, 1971), as
defined by the public, has been to catch criminals
and insure their conviction, it is hardly surprising that the police are concerned with
appearance of being efficient.

The eighth attitude/assumption is "Police
can most accurately identify crime and criminals."
The associated issue is the "Use of Police Discretion" and the related canon is Article Two,
"Limitation of Authority." It is fairly common
knowledge that a high percentage of crimes known
to the police are a direct result of citizens
informing the police that a crime has occurred,
or is occurring. While many of the citizen
call-ins may not actually reflect a criminal
incident, many do. Also, while many police are
able to state without question, in testimony,
that a citizen committed a crime, the accused
citizen does not actually bear the label until
he has been convicted with all the due process
safeguards being imposed. Again the philosophical set implied in this attitude/assumption
is that police can and should serve both the
law enforcement and judicial function with
regard to criminal identification and conviction.
Given the wide range of discretionary powers
vested in the police function, this attitude/
assumption will most likely manifest itself
in behavior which is dissonant to Article Two,
"Limitation of Authority." While this article
states that he (the police) must recognize the
genius of the American System of Government
which gives no one absolute power, the above
cited attitude/assumption is that the police
have special capabilities which equip him to
carry out the responsibilities of several
branches of the American System of Government.

The ninth attitude/assumption is "The major job of the policeman is to prevent crime and to enforce laws." The related issue is the "Police Role/Mandate" and the associated canon is Article One, "The Primary Responsibility of Job." Dependent upon which study is cited, from 50% to 80% of the police officers' time is spent in non-law-enforcement-related activities. The general perception, however, of both the public, and the image projected by the police is that police spend the large majority of the time in catching criminals, and arresting law-breakers. This also reflects the essence of Article One of the Police Code of Ethics. There is no difference in what the public perceives in an abstract sense as the law enforcement function, what the police feel the law enforcement function should be, and what the Code of Ethics addresses as the primary function of the police. The dissonance arises when these perceived functions are compared with reality.

The tenth attitude/assumption is "Stronger punishment will deter criminals from repeating their errors." The related issue/relationship is "Police Role/Mandate" and the associated canons are Article Two, "Limitation of Authority," Article Four, "Utilization of Proper Means to Gain Proper Ends," and Article Eight, "Conduct in Arresting and Dealing With Offenders." Of all the attitudes/assumptions, the tenth one is perhaps most consistent with public perception on the same issue. The Code of Ethics, however, warns the police that they should understand and not be bound by the limitations of their authority. Not included in their authority is the right to mete out punishment by using such measures as "street justice," falsifying testimony in order to insure what they consider

72

as an appropriate level of punishment or to
insure conviction at a more serious felony
level. It becomes fairly obvious that with
few exceptions there is considerable disagreement between how the code of ethics addresses
the above issues. The question which must be
dealt with is whose attitudes does the code
of ethics reflect? The most obvious answer
might be that it reflects the attitudes of
those persons who were a part of the group
which drew up the original code of ethics. In
addition, we might say that it must reflect
the attitudes of those persons who adopted
the code of ethics. Who then, are these
people? One would suppose that line patrol
officers, those attitudes and assumptions are
previously discussed, would have had a voice
in whether or not the IACP or similar organizations adopted the code of ethics. More likely,
however, the persons whose voices were most
prevalent at those adoption meetings were
high level administrative staff. If this is
the case, then it might be said that those
persons whose behavior should be most guided by
the code of ethics had little voice in its word-
ing or adoption. And yet, it serves as their
ethical guideline.

In his theory on Cognitive Dissonance,
Festinger describes a situation similar to
the one above, which he terms forced compliance.
This situation, as described by Festinger,
is one in which a "powerful communicator forces
a member of his audience to change his overt
behavior, while privately the member still holds
his original beliefs" (Festinger, 1959, p.85).
The force in question is one of either punishment
for noncompliance, or reward for compliance.
The critical point is that the compliance occurs

73

only on an overt or public level, and does not necessarily reflect a change in the individual's actual belief. An interesting question, based upon the above, is what punishment or reward could be given for noncompliance or compliance? The most obvious punishment would be when the behavior of an individual officer was inconsistent with both the code of ethics and statutory law. In this case there is the option of enforcing the law. It might also be possible that personnel rules and regulations may encompass parallel areas of concern, thereby giving methods of punishment through normal personnel policy. Another type of punishment might be a duty assignment which is conventionally considered as punishment. With respect to reward, there may be citations, good assignments, etc., which would enhance the officer's departmental image and make possible promotions or salary increases. All of this, of course, is based upon the premise that the departmental executives have an investment in the officer abiding by the code of ethics. Another possibility, however, is that the departmental executives have no such investment or if they do it is only ancilliary to an overriding concern of their public image being both ethical and professional. If this were the case then what you would expect to find is little emphasis on forced compliance via rewards or punishments and more emphasis on maintaining an appearance of concern for ethical behavior. While the above addresses the issue of forced compliance, it does not address the behavioral implications of forced compliance. Dissonance theory states that a subject will experience dissonance whenever he is presented with a communication discrepant with his own attitude. Given that dissonance is a motivating force, that is it causes something to happen, the person

74

will make attempts to reduce it. He may reduce
dissonance by finding support from others who
share his way of thinking, or he may find fault
to negate the reality and usefulness of what
the communicator is saying. He may decide to
change his mind and agree with the communicator,
or he may attempt to change the dissonant element
to be consistent with his way of thinking. In
other words, the person experiencing dissonance
can find support for his position or find fault
with the dissonant position, or bring dissonant
persons to his way of thinking, all of which
reduce or eliminate dissonance (Festinger, 1957).

Adding New Cognitive Elements

The first way of reducing dissonance, finding
support for his position, is what Festinger
calls adding new cognitive elements. As we shall
see, this option is readily available   to the
police officer.   Each of us often have
pre-determined beliefs about which we have strong
feelings. In the case of the police officer we
can use the example of the assumption that
experience is better than abstract rules. This
position is at best at odds with the code of
ethics which calls for the study of the principle
of the laws. If the officer becomes uncomfortable
due to this dissonance, he may attempt to reduce
the dissonance by adding new information to his
awareness which supports his contention that
experience is better than abstract rules. In
his search for new information, the officer can
go to no better place than his fellow employees.
This is because the attitudes/assumptions previously discussed are presumptions about certain
things. They are not to be identified with the
idividual alone, but rather are part of a shared
belief system which is passed from the experienced
officer to the new officer. This occupational
folklore is lent power through the consistency
and quantity of reiteration. It is from this
pool of like-thinking persons that new and
supportive cognitive elements can be obtained.

This information in turn provides material for aggressive debate of those arguments or positions which are the initial source of the dissonance.

Changing Behavioral and Environmental Cognitive Elements

The second method of reducing dissonance between attitudes/assumptions and the code of ethics is what Festinger terms changing a behavioral cognitive element. This process most closely parallels the changing of how one feels about something, resulting in the change of one's behavior. This, however, may have considerable consequences for the officer. If it is true that there is a strong and cohesive occupational culture, having developed its own mores, and these mores are antithetical to the portions of the Code of Ethics the officer has decided to agree with (thereby changing his behavior), he then has to face disagreement with the majority of his fellow officers. If this occurs, he then has a third option. Festinger refers to this option as changing an environmental cognitive element. In essence, as related to the above example, this involves bringing his fellow officers over to his way of thinking. For his fellow officers, this option would for them mean changing the environment which may have produced the code of ethics in the first place, that is changing the administrative concern for an image of ethical concern as opposed to a true concern for ethics.

Resistance to Change

While the above options for reducing dissonance are available to the police officer experiencing dissonance between his attitudes/assumptions and the code of ethics, this is not meant to imply that he is likely to choose one of these options. If dissonance is to be reduced using one of these options, then the resistance of

these cognitive elements to change must be considered. With respect to the change of behavioral
cognitive elements the first source of resistance
to change is the responsiveness of the element to
reality (Festinger, 1959). For example, if on a
day-to-day basis the behavior the officer sees
from most citizens he comes in contact with is
hostile or at best indifferent, he may have a
difficult time convincing himself that in fact
everyone does not hate cops and that he should
feel proud of his profession and have a positive
image of his profession. The reality of his
situation may reinforce the attitudes/assumptions
which he would like to change thereby providing
a source of resistance to change. With respect
to resistance to change of environmental cognitive elements, and adding new cognitive
elements, again the source of resistance to
change depends upon their relationship to reality.
For example, the officer who is experiencing
dissonance may attempt to change the attitudes/
assumptions of his fellow officers. He has as
his major tool to do so the power of persuasion.
As an example, consider the police officer who
says "the legal system is trustworthy, the courts
make the best decisions about guilt and innocence."
The resistance he encounters from his fellow
officers will be considerably stronger than his
singular argument. His fellow officers will most
probably experience some dissonance from his
argument and would have the option of adding new
cognitive elements to support their contention.
Given the strength of the occupational folklore
of the police, those persons supporting the
contention that the legal system is untrustworthy, would have a greater pool of information
from which new cognitive elements might be drawn.

Summary

The central question of this review is
whether or not the police code of ethics contributes to or detracts from ethical practices on
the part of police in relation to their con-

stituency, the public. It would appear when
viewing this problem through Festinger's Theory
of Dissonance, the current code of ethics does
little to contribute to ethical behavior. It
would also appear that it does in fact detract
from ethical behavior in that it is not closely
aligned with police reality. The police culture,
when faced with the code of ethics, is more
likely to add new cognitive elements to their
informational arsenal which are supportive of
their position, thereby reducing the dissonance
they may feel when their attitudes and assumptions
are compared with portions of the code of ethics.
Rookie officers, who may be more receptive to
the behavior implied in the code of ethics, are
more likely to change their behavior to be consistent with the behavioral mores of the police
occupational culture due to the insupportable
nature of the code of ethics as viewed within
the context of police reality. In addition, as
it is currently worded, the police code of ethics
adds to cynicism resulting from the attempt to
manage appearances via an unrealistic code of
ethics. As long as the focal point in this
area of police activity is to reduce dissonance
by the negation of the code of ethics as a useful
tool, very little support will be found among
their ranks to modify the code into a useful,
policy setting document. Finally, it becomes
obvious that ethical practices as reflected in
the police code of ethics, will have very little
impact on the individual logic involved in
discretionary decision making unless there is
some attitudinal change on the part of the
police. While the results of this review have
indicated the negative impact of the current
code of ethics, it may also provide some
theoretical direction for attempts to change the
current status of the code of ethics. The
first, and most obvious step, would be to modify
the code with input from line officers, so that
it reflects reality to a more reasonable degree.
This in time would reduce the resistance to change
by the occupational culture of the police. As
a further result, the more accurate reflection of

78

reality would allow the adding of new cognitive elements which are supportive of the modified code of ethics and yet not completely anti-thetical to the concerns reflected in the atti-tudes/assumptions of the police officer. This in no way should be taken to imply that the attitudes/assumptions previously identified should be conceded to by a modified code of ethics. Rather, what is implied is that given the strength of the current occupational culture and the related attitudes/assumptions held by that culture, the concerns implied in those attitudes and assumptions should be given careful consideration in any modification of the code of ethics. To not do so is to invite the continued exclusion of a workable code of ethics from police practices.

Conclusion

From the examination of ethics in law enforcement through the perspectives of anomie and cognitive dissonance, several common under-lying observations have emerged in both approaches. Both are concerned with the disjunction of reality and idealism. Given that there does exist a schism between the behaviors of officers in the real environment and those behaviors and attitudes which are expressed in the Code of Ethics, caution must be taken before it is con-cluded that the behavioral implications of dissonance and anomie will in fact manifest themselves. Even in situations where there exist wide differences between what is really happening and what the Code would have happen, there are situations where no dissonance would occur or any level of anomie be found. This could conceivably happen if at all stages of a law enforcement officer's career the disjuncture was recognized and the ethical end (idealism) was relegated to a role of lip service. No one would then take the Code of Ethics for anything but a set of elegant words not intending to affect the individ-ual officer's behavior and by no means taken as a set of legitimate aspirations. On the other hand, as law enforcement continues to emerge as a profession it is likely that at least in the academy stages of an officer's career more than lip service could be given to ethics to the extent that--in the extreme case--zealous instructors could emphasize the Code of Ethics to the extent of offering young officers not only the possibility, but also the necessity, of aspiring to these elevated states of individual attainment. Given that these same instructors cannot change reality, the implications of cognitive dissonance and anomie may become more accentuated in the future and demand more concern and scrutiny by those responsible for such issues. It could easily be deduced that the authors of this chapter have found little of a positive nature to say about the Law Enforcement Code of Ethics. One would be foolish to reject the general idea of a code of ethics. Professions for years have developed such codes, however, unlike some professions, law enforcement does not have a great degree of control over their occupational environment. Perhaps then, as earlier suggested, the occupational environment should be taken into account in any modification of the Codes of Ethics. The suggestion of modification of the Code of Ethics deserves clarification lest it be taken that the authors' stance is one of rejecting the present Code as it is now written. This chapter has not been an attempt to show cause for abandoning the adopted Code, but, rather an attempt to examine consequences. Aspirations to achieve the higher levels of human characteristics can be a most beneficial "holy grail" for members of any profession to seek, beneficial for both members and society at large. However, the theme of this chapter has been in general an admonition to the profession that ostentatious words are not enough, they must be examined in light of what we know from broader perspectives and their usage be so amended. Perhaps, by constant evaluation of what could be legitimately aspired to under ideal circumstances and what is possible will result in a movement toward the ideal state as reflected in the Law Enforcement Code of Ethics.

BIBLIOGRAPHY

Balch, Robert W. "The Police Personality: Fact or Fiction." Journal of Criminal Law, Criminology and Police Science. Vol. 63, No. 1, 1972.

Beckeiz, Haizold K. Issues in Police Administration. Metucher, N.J.: Scarecrow Press, Inc. 1970.

Broderick, John J. Police in a Time of Change. Morristown, N.J.: General Learning Press. 1977.

Campbell, Angus and Howard Schuman. Police in the Ghetto, in Police Community Relations: Images, Rules, Realities. Edited by Alvin Cohn and Emilio Viano. Philadelphia, Pa.: J.B. Lippincott Company. 1976.

Clinard, Marshall B. Anomie and Deviant Behavior. New York: The Free Press. 1964.

Cohn, Alvin W. and Emilio C. Viano. Police Community Relations: Images, Rules, Realities. Philadelphia, Pa.: J.B. Lippincott Company. 1976.

Festinger, Leon. A Theory of Cognitive Dissonance. Stanford, Ca.: Stanford University Press. 1957.

German, A.C., Frank Day and Robert Gallati. Introduction to Law Enforcement and Criminal Justice. Springfield, Ill.: Charles C. Thomas. 1973.

Guller, Irving B. "Higher Education and Policemen: Attitudinal Differences Between Fresh-
men and Senior Police College Students."
The Journal of Criminal Law, Criminology
and Police Science. Vol. 63, No. 4. 1972.

Lawrence, Richard A. The Measurement and Prediction of Police Job Stress, an unpub-
lished doctoral dissertation. Huntsville,
Tx.: Sam Houston State University, 1978.

Manning, Peter K. The Police, in Crime and
Justice in American Society, edited by
Jack D. Douglas. New York: Bobbs-Merrill
Company, 1969.

Manning, Peter K., and John Van Maanen.
Policing: A View from the Street. Santa
Monica, Ca.: Goodyear Publishing Company,
Inc, 1978.

Merton, Robert K. Social Theory and Social
Structure. New York: The Free Press, 1957.

Merton, Robert K., and Nisbet, Robert A. Social
Problems and Sociological Theory, in Contemporary Social Problems, edited by
Robert K. Merton. 2nd ed. New York: Har-
court, Brace, and World, Inc, 1966.

Merton, Robert K. Social Theory and Social
Structure. New York: The Free Press, 1968.

Niederhoffer, Arthur. Behind the Shield. Garden
City, New York: Doubleday and Co., Inc.,
1969.

Nettler, Gwynn. Explaining Crime. New York:
McGraw-Hill Book Company, 1974.

Radelett, Louis A. Police and the Community.
2nd ed. Encino, Ca.: Glenco Press, 1977.

Skolnick, Jerome H. *Justice Without Trial.*
New York: John Wiley and Sons, Inc., 1975.

Smith, N.B., B. Lock and A. Fenster. "Author-
itarianism in Policemen Who Are College
Graduates and Non-College Police." *The
Journal of Criminal Law, Criminology and
Police Science.*, Vol. 61, 1968.

Wilson, James Q. *Varieties of Police Behavior.*
New York: Atheneum Press, 1976.

Wolman, Benjamin B. *Dictionary of Behavioral
Science.* New York: Van Nostrand Reinhold
Company, 1973.

Wool, Harold. *National Manpower Survey of the
Criminal Justice System,* Vol. 2.
Washington: National Institute of Law
Enforcement and Criminal Justice, 1978.

Charles L. Johnson is an Assistant
Professor at the University of Arkansas at
Little Rock in the Department of Political
Science and Criminal Justice. He received
his B.S. and M.S.W. from Florida State
University and his Ph.D. in Criminal Justice
from Sam Houston State University.
Dr. Johnson has had extensive line and administrative experience in human services
agencies and his research efforts have pre-
dominently concentrated on human resource
issues in corrections and law enforcement.
Specifically his research includes a national
analysis of the initial security officer
position in state penal institutions, an
analysis of employment obstacles and their
effects upon university law enforcement
graduates, the impact of criminology courses
upon students' perceptions of etiology,
patterns of probation and parole organizations
in the United States, and the impact of
unionization on institutional and community
corrections. Prior to his current position
he was Project Manager for an LEAA funded
Manpower Planning Grant concerned with
developing an on-line data base for manpower planning in criminal justice.

84

Gary D. Copus obtained the Bachelor of Science from Georgia Tech in Biology, 1967. He received a Masters of Criminal Justice from Sam Houston State University in 1968, and the Ph.D. in Sociology from the University of Missouri, 1971. From 1971 to 1979, he was a member of the faculty of the Texas Criminal Justice Center, Sam Houston State University. In 1980, Dr. Copus joined the Criminal Justice Program at the University of Alaska, Fairbanks. His areas of concentration are program development, statistics, systems, and research.

The Continuing Cycle of Systemic
Police Corruption: A Prognosis
For New York City

Paul E. Murphy, Ph.D.
T. Kenneth Moran, Ph.D.

I. Introduction

Since just before the end of the last century, and up until the beginning of this decade,
the New York City Police Department has experienced five major corruption scandals in what
approximates twenty-year cycles. The first
important investigation uncovering corrupt
activities was conducted by the Lexow Committee
(1894), followed in turn by the Curran Committee
(1913) and the Seabury Investigation (1929); then
the Kefauver Committee unearthed the Gross
scandal (1950), and most recently, the Knapp
Commission (1970) found corruption once again to
be widespread throughout the department.[1]

Now the type of police misconduct referred
to here is not, of course, the independent and
isolated transgressions of individual officers
which occur from time to time as the opportunities
and inclinations present themselves --this type
can never be completely eradicated or prevented.
Rather, it is the pervasive, systematic misconduct that has plagued, at one time or another
and in one form or another, most major police
departments in this country. Some law enforcement agencies may rightly feel a serious organized
corruption problem does not exist in their
departments, or they may subscribe to the "rotten-
apple" theory.[2] However, the wise administrator
will recognize that, at the least, a real and
imminent threat of a serious corruption problem
does exist, and he will take appropriate preventive and corrective actions.

In the light of this history of cyclic
corruption, there are two questions that must

logically be asked: first, can we expect the cycle to continue? Second, if so, can we expect the police department to be shaken by yet another major corruption investigation within the next decade or so (ca. 1990)? Based simply on the evidence of history, the answers to both these questions would have to be in the affirmative.

The purpose then of this essay is to explore the liklihood of a reoccurrence and focus on several essential corrective measures, hopefully to break the cycle and end systemic corruption for good. Specifically we will first look briefly at the findings of the five investigative bodies mentioned above in an effort to discover what kind of environment prevailed that enabled corruption in each of these historical periods to take seed and flourish. If a common Sitz im Leben could be isolated, some light might be shed on how to break the samsara3 of corruption.

Secondly, if discovered, we will look closer at these common factors to determine why they so adversely affected police conduct.

Then, by examining the present situation, almost ten years after Knapp, we should be able to determine if the same environment prevails -- signposts along the road to corruption and scandal. For surely, if the cycle is to be broken, the destructive environs of unethical behavior must be identified, eliminated, and replaced by those that engender ethical conduct.

Finally we will examine the contributions of the professional law enforcement, educational and criminal justice organizations to end the dilemma of organized, cyclical police misconduct.

Now although this study will concentrate almost solely on the New York City Police Department, it is hoped that the conclusions and recommendations propounded in this essay are applicable to other departments. The studies

that have been done on typologies of corruption[4]
clearly indicate that although differences do
occur between agencies, there are great similarities in their corrupt behavior. It has often
been said that "police work is the same the
world over"-- so too can it be said of police
misconduct.

II. Cynicism: Cornerstone of Police Misconduct[5]

    Perhaps one of the best studies on the sub-
ject of police cynicism and its affect on the
individual police officer and the department,
and its interrelationship with public cynicism
has been that of Arthur Neiderhoffer[6] to which
we will refer often in this section. He treats
the concept of cynicism and its ultimate sequen-
tial stage of anomie, a term developed by
Emile Durkheim at the end of the last century,[7]
as counterproductive to police efficiency. Before
discussing these terms and their impact on
unethical police behavior, it would be best to
define[8] them along with another term, "skepticism," which is the initial stage and dis-
tinquishable from the other two.

    Skepticism is defined non-philosophically
as a doubting or incredulous state of mind; thus
a skeptic is one who by nature possesses a
disbelieving attitude, one who questions or doubts
what he hears, sees or reads. Cynicism, on the
other hand, is contemptuousness of or disbelief
in the virtues of others; a cynic is further
defined as a sarcastic, sneering, faultfinding
and distrusting person, especially, one who
believes that all men are motivated by selfish-
ness. And lastly, anomie is defined as an
anxious awareness that the prevailing values of
society have little or no personal relevance to
one's condition; also, as a condition of society
characterized by the relative absence of norms or
moral standards. It is derived from the Greek
word anomia, which means "lawlessness."

Niederhoffer does not distinguish between skepticism and cynicism in his treatise, nor does he even mention the former term; he may have felt that for his purposes the terms were either synonymous or the distinction was too subtle to mention and that the effect on personal attitudes and conduct was the same. However, although the distinction is subtle, it is nevertheless of great importance if we are to understand more completely the total sequence of which cynicism represents the median stage.

Both cynicism and anomie have pernicious, negative and counterproductive effects on police mentality and performance and must, therefore, be eradicated when found to exist and safeguarded against even when not actually identified. Such need not be the case however with skepticism which can be helpful and an asset to police efficiency. Every police officer knows he[9] must be somewhat suspicious in his relationship with the public -- especially the criminal element. He learns quickly to be alert constantly for the unexpected -- in fact, to expect the unexpected; never to be taken by surprise; and always to verify statements the average "trusting soul" would readily accept. This essential police mentality might be termed a "healthy skepticism." But, at the same time, he must never prejudge or sterotype; he must always keep an open mind, ever ready to change opinion or make concessions when the situation warrants. And here is precisely wherein the potential danger lies; if the officer is not constantly on guard to keep his skepticism within reasonable bounds -- if he allows it to become "unhealthy" -- he will soon find that his cautious mistrust has become a cynical mistrust. And in time, this attitude may become so much an integral part of his behavioral patterns as to become anomic.

Now the causes of police cynicism are various and Niederhoffer treats them at length. The new recruit usually enters the police academy with idealism; soon, however, the seeds of doubts and

90

disenchantment begin to take hold while he is yet
in training[10] - he is influenced by the cynicism
and "role conflict" of his instructors,[11] and the
"reality shock" of the street.[12] Police discretion, so essential to efficient police work is
also a source of cynicism. The police officer
soon learns that he cannot devote equal time
to all laws and ordinances, and at the same time
perform the service-oriented functions which
consume 85 to 90% of his time. Hence, these
laws must be selectively enforced --emphasis being
placed on only the most serious transgressions,
while the lesser laws are either overlooked
entirely or corrected through warnings and
admonitions. In short, he is a modern day Solo-
man --operating, at times, within certain well-
defined parameters --but, nevertheless, relying
upon his own discretion concerning arrests,
summons, referrals, warnings, admonitions and
outright non-involvements.

Now, it is in this discretionary capacity
that the police officer exercises his awesome
power which runs the gamut from mild reprimand,
to deprivation of liberty, and finally to the
taking of human life --no other public figure, or
indeed any other human being possesses greater
authority over personal destiny. A jury, after
a lengthy court trial and painful deliberation,
may find a defendant guilty of murder and
recommend the death penalty; the judge may respond
by invoking the death penalty after more painful
deliberation within his own conscience; and
finally, then the state may actually carry out
that execution --perhaps after a dozen or so years
of experiencing one appeal after another exhausted.
But, the police officer, in one split second,
without the benefit of law school or judicial
roles or legal appeals, acting as judge, jury and
executioner may accomplish the same final result.

Now if all this authority causes the officer
confusion, loss of respect for the law, or a
feeling that he is above the law, then cynicism
may result and become more entrenched as his

91

career develops. Neiderhoffer describes the
process as follows:

> Always searching for this tenuous and
> blurred dividing line in the behavior
> of others, the policeman frequently
> loses the ability to distinguish be-
> tween law and license in himself . . .
> the result of United States Supreme
> Court decisions . . . . have confused
> the averaged patrolman until he is
> often uncertain of the proper course
> of action. His ignorance dims the
> luster of the law because the policeman
> learns to manipulate the law in the
> name of expediency, and this loss of
> respect, in turn, breeds more cynicism.[13]

It is when the police officer is enslaved by
his cynical or "lawless" attitudes that he is
most susceptible to unethical behavior and
corruption - it is the cornerstone upon which a
sustained condition of corruption is built. This
is not to say that all corruption is primarily
caused by cynicism; indeed, this would be over-
simplistic; for, admittedly, there are variegated
causative factors involved in any type of
official misconduct. However, the contention is
made that corruption cannot long exist without
cynicism as an accompanying misanthropic factor.

The reason for this contention is simple --
idealism and professionalism are the opposites
of cynicism and anomie. If a police officer
possesses a high sense of professional pride in
conjunction with idealistic motivation, he could
not condone a corrupt officer. Idealism and professionalism inspire such a pride in and respect
for one's calling and such a dedication to public
service that serious misconduct (corruption)
would be, for the police officer, unsupportable.
And the degree of professionalism and idealism is
in direct proportion to the ethical conduct
resulting - the most idealistic officer, for
example, would probably not even accept a free

92

cup of coffee (which is unethical, but not necessarily corrupt). It is our assertion that it is our moral characters that keep us honest (forgetting, for the moment, the possible fear of getting caught, or of reprisal as motivating factors). What incentive, then, would the amoral or immoral officer have for being honest? Furthermore, would it not be a contradiction in terms to say the "lawless" (anomic) officer or one in the penultimate stage of lawlessness (cynic) is apt to be lawful (idealistically moral and ethical)?

The cynical police officer employs the "Golden Rule of Cynicism" as his credo --Do unto others before they do unto you! When confronted with a corrupting situation he also employs a warped and equally cynical rationalization --he may even convince himself that he is performing a worthwhile and honorable deed and to act otherwise would be wrong! This mentality can be seen in the following rationalizations:

1.) The public thinks every cop is a crook - so why try to be honest --"get the name, play the game!"

2.) The money is out there --if I don't take it someone else will!

3.) I'm only taking what's rightfully mine; if the City paid me a decent wage, I wouldn't have to get it on my own!

4.) I can use it--it's for a good cause -- my son needs an operation, or dental work, or tuition for medical school, or a new bicycle or . . . .

The reciprocity of cynicism between the police and the public nourishes itself in an unending cycle. The officer senses the cynicism of the public, most pronouncedly in the ghetto,

93

and retaliates in kind with his own cynicism -
this, in turn engenders increased cynical reaction from the public, and the sequence continues, unfortunately, in ever-worsening cyclic
progression. James Baldwin, the Black writer,
depicts this feeling of ghetto resentment of
the police most forcefully in the following oft-
quoted excerpt from his writings:

> ...the only way to police a ghetto is to
> be oppressive. None of the Police Com-
> missioner's men even with the best will
> in the world, have any way of under-
> standing the lives led by the people
> they swagger about in twos and threes
> controlling. Their very presence is
> an insult and it would be, even if they
> spent their day feeding gumdrops to
> children ...
> ...He (the policeman) is facing, daily
> and nightly, people who would gladly
> see him dead, and he knows it....
> There are few things under heaven more
> unnerving than the silent, accumulating
> contempt and hatred of a people. He
> moves through Harlem, therefore, like
> an occupying soldier in a bitterly
> hostile country; which is precisely
> what and where he is, and is the reason
> he walks in twos and threes. (Italics
> mine.)[14]

This commonly held view is not supported by
actual studies of black attitudes towards the
police. James Q. Wilson points out that the
general attitudes of both blacks and whites toward the police are positive, not negative. He
bases his assertions on a 1964 study of blacks
living in several large cities, including New
York City, which indicated that the majority of
those interviewed "thought the police treated
blacks 'very well' or 'fairly well.'"[15]

But whether Baldwin's assessment concerning

the attitudes of ghetto "people" toward the police is accurate is not the crucial question here; what is more important is that the relatively small percentage of black cynics and social miscreants who constantly run afoul of the law do feel as Baldwin describes. And these are the very people the police come in contact with --the silent majority of the law-abiding citizens have little contact with the police. So, the police officer experiences this "contempt and hatred," and it has a devastating affect on his morale, and hence on his attitudes and conduct. No wonder, then, he is easy prey to cynicism and develops what William A. Westley calls the "pariah feeling."

> He [the police officer] is regarded as corrupt and inefficient by, and meets with hostility and criticism from, the public. He regards the public as his enemy, feels his occupation to be in conflict with the community and regards himself to be a pariah.16

Michael Banton, likewise, employs the same imagery and, in so doing, links it with cynicism and alienation, and finally with the resultant subculture:

> ...individuals pursue their own ends with little regard for public morality, and the policeman sees the ugly under-side of outwardly respectable house-holds and businesses. Small wonder, then, that many American policemen are cynics....Couple this experience of the public with the policeman's feeling that in his social life he is a pariah, scorned by citizens who are more respectable but no more honest, and it need surprise no one that the policeman's loyalties to his depart-ment and his colleagues are often stronger than those to the wider society.17

III. The Blue Curtain of Secrecy

As a result of all this cynicism, low morale,
feelings of frustration, loss of self-respect
and alienation from society, police officers
tend to close ranks and retreat within the safe
confines of their subculture. This closed
fraternity phenomenon has been referred to in
such terms as: "isolation syndrome," the "we-
they syndrome," "blue curtain," "blue power,"
"police solidarity" or just plain "police
secrecy." The members are thus cemented together in a strong bond of interdependency for
self-protection. Their wagons formed in a
tight, impenetratable circle, they are now ready
to withstand the onslaught of the enemy --the
public.

So close is this bond of police solidarity
that in many departments across the country,
violators of the code of secrecy from within
the ranks are often looked upon contemptuously
as "stoolies" and shunned or even persecuted by
their fellow officers --sometimes, it is sad to
say, by entire departments as well. One does
not have to search far to determine if this is
true. Most departments have a rule that requires
an officer to report to his superior (or to a
separate internal unit charged with the responsibility of investigating police misconduct)
any breach of conduct or unlawful activity
committed by other police officers that he is
directly aware of or otherwise suspects. Police
officers unabashedly refer to this as the "rat
rule." It is unnecessary to comment further -
the mere appellation adequately expresses the
sentiments of the rank and file.

It is understandable, therefore, that in an
enviroment such as this, an investigation of
alleged police misconduct, whether internal or
external in origin, or even the mild inquisitive
probings of media representatives might meet
with organized resistance and/or a complete lack

96

of cooperation. Such sterotypical remarks as:
"the matter is still under investigation," or,
"I am not at liberty to divulge that information
at this time," or simply a "no comment,"
accompanied by a doleful smile are commonplace
responses to the inquirer.[18]

It has rightly been said that there is
nothing more detrimental to an investigation of
corruption, nor more apt to enhance the contin-
uance of corrupt activities than the presence
of the "blue curtain" obfuscating the police
and their activities. And police administrators
must be made aware that systemic corruption will
never be irradicated until they first recognize
the hazards of cynicism and take precautionary
and remedial steps to prevent its cancerous
growth. Secondly, the blue veil of secrecy must
be torn down allowing the light of understanding,
mutual respect and openness between police and
the public to enter and shine brightly. Communal respect is essential to police integrity
and efficiency, but it is not owed the police
by right --it must be earned.

So far our approach has been rather negative:
a preventative --avoidance of cynicism, and the
dissolution of the police subculture which
prevents police --community growth and understanding. Now the positive:

IV. Attitudinal Change: A Return to Idealism and
Professionalism

It would seem that the less difficult of
the two corruption-preventive tasks mentioned
above would be to put a check on cynicism.
Surely, a departmental educational campaign
could cause the needed self-awareness in the
individual officer to put him on guard so that
his skepticism would not become cynicism - the
remedy, therefore, is more on an individual basis.
Police secrecy, however, is more of an organi-

zational problem. For, even policemen who are not in the least cynical, but whose social needs for group identification, comradery and loyalty might cause him to succumb to the rule of secrecy out of a false or misplaced sense of loyalty, or, as one of our colleagues terms it --"a perverted esprit de corps." How then is this veil to be rent?

The traditional response to this problem is to attempt an 'end run around' the curtain of secrecy by establishing strong organizational control of the police working environment. This approach is typified by the following excerpt from an anti-corruption manual, "When a chief has defined, located and measured corruption, he has the basic information necessary to formulate or devise an anti-corruption policy. After he decides on a policy, it becomes necessary to establish operations to put this policy into action."[19] Sherman contends that the most effective mechanism for implementing organizational control of corrupt police practices is to utilize a number of social control devices which produce the types of threats that will hopefully act as a deterrent to the police department.[20] Implicit in this approach is the idea that the issue of police secrecy disappears if you remove corruption at its source; Sherman's discussion of the anticipated consequences of the various types of social control reflects this assumption. He defines three types of control: scandal, dismissals and the utilization of preventive and punitive internal policies each of which are designed to deter corruption through the deterrent effect of fear.[21]

The success of these programs turns on the ability of the police managers to motivate, lead and direct their field personnel. In truth, although it is not recognized as such, police commanders and managers have a very limited effect on their field personnel.[22] This poses an awkard problem for police organizations.

98

In such organizations, the structure is hierarchical and therefore the propensity for command and direction is from the top down. But in the case of secrecy and the toleration of corruption, the decision-making occurs at the bottom of the structure, which makes for a natural tension between police commanders and their line officers.

The differing views of management can cause patrol officers to feel that they are not backed up by their commanders. Indeed, Wilson states that under these types of circumstances, the relationship between patrol officers and their commanders is defined by the extent to which they themselves feel "backed up" by the latter.[23] Clearly, if an officer does not trust his department's leadership, the chances of the department breaking the veil of secrecy are significantly reduced.

Given the present way that our police do their jobs, it would seem that law enforcement is by its nature an informal process. This suggests that formal policy making will tend to experience limited success unless it takes cognizance of the tendency of the patrol officer to make his own street policy. That is, although anti-corruption programs at the command and middle management level are important the key to the problem of corruption is the policeman on the street. A change in his ethical standards (how he feels about secrecy and cynicism) will result in a change in police practices.

In the past, the rule of solidarity mandated that, right or wrong, policemen had to stick together and should never "rat" on each other -- cast in the mythical "honor among thieves" mentality. The revelations of the Knapp hearings, however, suggest that honest policemen owe no allegiance to the dishonest. There is a growing feeling that corrupt officers are "traitors in our midst" who are "out for all they can get"

and are not in the least concerned who gets
hurt so long as they remain unscathed. This
has led to the question: is a criminal any less
deserving of condemnation and police action merely
because he carries a shield? Police officers,
not only in New York, but across the nation, are
finally coming to the realization that the public
revelation of a single corrupt police officer in
Anytown, U.S.A. sullies the reputation and public
image of the police officer in Everytown, U.S.A.
Every policeman, no doubt, who has ever worn a
uniform has, at one time or another, been challenged with the absurd question, "Why are all
policemen dishonest?" As more police officers
come to believe that the corruption-bent officer,
deserves not one iota of coverup protection from
his fellow officers, there will be a significant
drop in corrupt police practices. Statistics
over the past few years have suggested that
there is some evidence of this change of
attitude on the part of New York City Police
Officers; i.e. the vast majority of complaints
against policemen for misconduct have been
initiated by the police officers themselves. It
is primarily through this mechanism that this
cancerous growth that saps the police of its
strength and efficiency can be cut out.

V. Contributions of the Professional Organizations

The emergence of a cadre of police officers
who are willing to stand up and fight for ethical
police practices is an encouraging, albeit recent,
phenomenon. Much is still to be done in order to
encourage this movement. Professional police
organizations can contribute to this movement.
While many of these organizations differ in
terms of   membership and directions, each
fosters the idea that the police service is an
honorable and vital organization, which can be
used to counter the "Golden Rule of Cynicism."

In addition, each organization incorporates

100

the ideal that corruption is antithetical to professionalism. The American Academy for Professional Law Enforcement (A.A.P.L.E.), one of the many professional organizations, has directly linked police professionalism with a willingness to break the code of silence on the subject of corruption. The Code of Ethics which was adopted unanimously by the board of directors deals with a wide range of police behavior. The following excerpt from the professional and legal standards section reflects a commitment to eradicate this problem:[24]

1. Unethical behaviors such as fabricating, altering, or withholding evidence to affect an arrest or gain a conviction as well as theft, graft and acceptance of bribes or gratuities cannot be tolerated.

2. No officer should by his acquiescence or approval support unethical, improper or unlawful behavior by a colleague.

3. If an officer observes seriously improper or unlawful behavior by a colleague, he is required to report the case to his immediate supervisor or to other designated organizational channels for investigation and action. If the officer's supervisor is involved in this seriously improper or unlawful behavior either by direct participation or by condoning its performance by another, the officer should follow the legally prescribed course of action for reporting the activity. When a department does not support officers who do take such action, an ethical officer should seriously consider his career potential in such an organization. (However, it should be recognized that ethical people have lived through

101

eras of widespread organizational
impropriety. In such instances the
need may be to concentrate strictly
on high quality performance and
personal non-involvement in impropriety.)

These standards represent a clear linkage
between the concept of police professionalism
and a commitment to take all necessary steps no
matter how painful, against unethical or
corrupt practices.

The authors are not so naive as to suggest
that the A.A.P.L.E. Code of Ethics spells the
end of police corruption. We all realize that
no one single factor can accomplish this. However, we feel that the adoption of this code
indicates an important further step in this
direction. For the first time, an officer can
look to a national organization of police officers
drawn from every rank for guidance and support in
the move toward the upgrading of the police service through, among other things, the reduction
of corruption.

Summary

Hence, it is the contention of the authors
that if the attack on police secrecy continues by
police professionals, accompanied by a continuous
awareness of the pernicious nature and detrimental effect of cynicism on the overall police
function, the prognosis for an end to systemic
corruption in New York City as elsewhere is good
for now we will have added two essential dimensions to the combat of corruption which have been
neglected in the past and which doomed to failure
any serious attempt at ending the recurrence of
systemic corruption.

It must again be remarked, however, that we
are concerned here only in the fundamental Sitz

im Leben which nurtures police misconduct.
The various combative techniques that have met
with varying degrees of success in the past must
still be applied and, indeed, new ones sought.
But they will have greater chance for lasting
effect if the two essentials for reform are present.

Footnotes

[1]Commission to Investigate Allegations of
Police Corruption and the City's Anti-Corruption
Procedures (New York City), Commission Report
(With Summary and Principal Recommendations,
Issued August 3, 1972), by Whitman Knapp, Chairman (New York: Bar Press, Inc., December 26,
1972), pp. 6-11. Hereafter referred to as Knapp,
Report. According to this theory, "any policeman found to be corrupt must promptly [sic]
be denounced as a rotten apple in an otherwise
clean barrel. It must never be admitted that his
individual corruption may be symptomatic of
underlying disease." p. 6.

[2]Ibid.

[3]A Sanskrit term referring to the Buddhist
concept of transmigration--the endless cycle of
birth, death and rebirth--or eternal being and
becoming.

[4]Thomas Barker and Julian B. Roebuck, An
Empirical Typology of Police Corruption: A Study
of Organized Deviance (Springfield, IL: Charles
C. Thomas, 1974) passim. See also Herman Goldstein,
Police Corruption: A Perspective on Its Nature
and Control, (Washington: Police Foundation, 1975),
pp. 16-22.

[5]For a more detailed treatment of this
subject, see the forthcoming monograph by co-author,
Dr. Paul E. Murphy entitled, Cynicism: Cornerstone of Unethical Police Conduct, soon to be
published by the John Jay Press, New York.

[6]Arthur Niederhoffer, Behind the Shield: The Police in Urban Society (New York: Anchor Books, 1969), pp. 9-10, 46-47, 63-65, 74-77, 95-108, 199-248 (Appendix), and passim.

[7]Emile Durkheim, The Division of Labor in Society, trans. George Simpson (New York: The Free Press, 1933), from the first (1893) and the fifth and last (1926) editions. Durkheim uses the term "anomie" in the Introduction to the first edition in which he describes the term as "the contradiction of all morality." See Simpson's translation, p. 431, note 21.

[8]The three terms in question are defined according to the Funk and Wagnalls Standard College Dictionary, 1973.

[9]The authors, lest they be falsely accused of chauvinism, happily recognize the fact that police officers are both male and female. However, purely for literary smoothness (to avoid the irksome "he/she," "him/her," and the preponderance of plural nouns so that "they" and "them" may be used with impunity), the masculine pronoun understood in its generic sense, will be employed throughout this essay.

[10]Niederhoffer, pp. 46-47.

[11]Ibid., pp. 49-50.

[12]Ibid., pp. 52-53.

[13]Ibid., pp. 64-65.

[14]James Baldwin, "Fifth Avenue, Uptown," in Man Alone: Alienation in Modern Society, ed. Eric Josephson and Mary Josephson (New York: Dell Publishing Co., Inc., 1963) p. 352. This is a reprint from his book, Nobody Knows My Name (Dell, 1962), pp. 65-67.

[15]James Q. Wilson, Thinking About Crime (New York: Vintage Book Edition, 1977), p. 110;

here, the author refers to the study of Angus Cambell and Howard Schuman, "Radical Attitudes if Fifteen Americans Cities," in Supplemental Studies for the National Advisory Commission on Civil Disorders (Washington, D. C.: U.S. Government Printing Office, 1968), pp. 41-45.

[16]It appears that this term was first used by William A. Westley, excerpted here from "The Police: A Sociological Study of Law, Custom and Morality," Ph.D. dissertation, University of Chicago, 1951. In more recent times, the same term has been used by James Q. Wilson in his discussion of the policeman's alienation and need to develop a sub-culture--"The Police and Their Problems: A Theory," Public Policy, Yearbook of the Harvard University Graduate School of Public Administration (Cambridge, 1963), pp. 192-93; see also, Louis A. Radelet, The Police and the Community (Eucino, CA: Glencoe Press, 1977), pp. 110 and 116.

[17]Michael Banton, The Policeman in the Community (New York: Basic Books, Inc., 1964), pp. 169-70.

[18]Even men who have been retired from the police service have on occasion experienced this lack of confidentiality and cooperation from their former colleagues. It seems that, in the view of certain active policemen, retirement places the separated officer in the ranks of the outsider and, therefore he is to be treated with a cautious distrust.

[19]Richard H. Ward and Robert McCormack, An Anti-Corruption Manual for Administrators in Law Enforcement (New York: John Jay Press, 1979), p. 65.

[20]Lawrence W. Sherman, Scandal and Reform (Berkley: University of California Press, 1978), pp. 202-203.

^{21}Ibid.

^{22}Kenneth Culp Davis, Police Discretion
(St. Paul: West Publishing Co., 1975), p. 38.

^{23}James Q. Wilson, Varieties of Police
Behavior (New York: Atheneum, 1975), p. 75.

^{24}American Academy for Professional Law
Enforcement, Ethical Standards in Law Enforcement
(444 W. 56th St., N.Y., N.Y.), p. 3.

Dr. Paul E. Murphy is an Associate Professor
in the Department of Law, Police Science, and
Criminal Justice Administration of the John Jay
College of Criminal Justice, City University of
New York, where he offers courses in a wide range
of Police Science and Criminal Justice subjects.
His specialties are Criminal Justice Ethics and
Criminalistics. In the field of Police Ethics,
Dr. Murphy is doubly qualified; as a pragmatist,
he was a highly decorated member of the New York
City Police Department and retired in 1974 with
the rank of Lieutenant after nearly twenty-three
years of service. His assignments included the
patrol and detective branches, advancing to
supervisory and command positions. As an
academician, besides a baccalaureate in the
physical sciences from Fordham College, he holds
a M.P.A. degree in police science from the City
University of New York, and M.A. and Ph.D.
degrees in Theology from Fordham University.
Professor Murphy has published several articles
on theological and police topics and has lectured
extensively in the United States on police
corruption and in the broader area of police
ethics. He is currently preparing his own text
in the field of Criminal Justice Ethics. In
January 1980 Dr. Murphy began a six months

exchange professorship at the Police Staff College, Bramshill House, near Basingstoke, England, where he is lecturing on American policing to the elite command officers of the United Kingdom's police constabularies.

T. Kenneth Moran is an associate professor of law and police science at John Jay College of Criminal Justice, and Executive Director of the American Academy for Professional Law Enforcement. He has had considerable managerial and research experience in both judicial and criminal justice administration. He received his Ph.D. in 1974 from the University of Connecticut.

Prosecutorial Ethics

John Jay Douglass, J.D.

> Obedience to the unenforceable has from
> time immemorial been the keynote to pro-
> blems involving legal ethics.[1]

American prosecutorial roles and functions
are not fully replicated in any other criminal
justice system in the world. The singular
nature of American prosecutors is made more so
by the ethical standards of conduct imposed
upon them. They have extremely broad authority
with they exercise largely on their own discretion; often, that broad discretionary authority
is effectively checked only by a personal code of
conduct. Because prosecutors are both public
officials and members of the legal profession,
their professional responsibility is ambivalent.
There is the constant pull and tug--the yin and
yang--of duties and responsibilities both as a
lawyer and as a public official, which makes
this position a difficult one. Much of what has
been written to guide prosecutorial conduct is
vague, and the conscientious prosecutor thus
must rely upon a personal code of ethics as the
guide to official actions. The written codes
and canons, philosophical discussions, statutory
admonitions, court rulings, and standards for the
prosecution function promulgated by numerous
bodies often fail to capture the nuances of a
particular fact situation to provide explicit
guidance.

In addition to the problems created by
vagueness, inadequacy, and lack of specificity in
ethical guidelines, the prosecutor most often is
required to make ethical decisions rapidly.
These decisions of conscience may have a long-
range effect on official functions from which it
is impossible later to withdraw. The requirement
for immediate reaction makes personal instincts

even more significant. The prosecutor's
personal instincts must arise from an in-depth
intuitive understanding of the ethical responsibilities demanded of a lawyer/prosecutor/public
official.

Concern for the ethical responsibilities of
prosecutors might not be so significant were it
not for the tremendous influence they exert.
In 1940, Attorney General Robert H. Jackson
addressed a conference of United States Attorneys.
The thoughts he expressed may well be appropriate
in 2040 or for as long as prosecutors are the
key figures in the system of American criminal
justice.

> The prosecutor has more control
> over life, liberty, and reputation than
> any other person in America. His discre-
> tion is tremendous. He can have citizens
> investigated and, if he is that kind of
> person, he can have this done to the tune
> of public statements and veiled or un-
> veiled intimations. Or the prosecutor may
> choose a more subtle course and simply
> have a citizen's friends interviewed.
> The prosecutor can order arrests, pre-
> sent cases to the grand jury in secret
> session, and on the basis of his one-
> sided presentation of the facts, can
> cause the citizen to be indicted and
> held for trial. He may dismiss the case
> before trial, in which case the defense
> never has a chance to be heard. Or he
> may go on with a public trial. If he
> obtains a conviction, the prosecutor
> can still make recommendations as to
> sentence, as to whether the prisoner
> should get probation or a suspended
> sentence, and after he is put away, as
> to whether he is a fit subject for
> parole. While the prosecutor at his
> best is one of the most beneficent
> forces in our society, when he acts
> from malice or other base motives, he

is one of the worst.[2]

The beginning and end rule for prosecution
has been expressed in the case law,[3] in the Code
of Professional Responsibility,[4] in the American
Bar Association Standards on the Prosecution
Function,[5] and in some state statutes, which
declare that the prosecutor's interest is not
that he shall win a case, but that justice shall
be done.[6] This rule appeared in the legal
literature and court decisions in the early part
of the nineteenth century, and it is not important
by whom or how it was first expressed. It is the
rule. It is this rule that so often makes
the prosecution role difficult. It is an unusual
rule of the adversary system in which the lawyer/
prosecutor has been trained. The best expression
of this rule is perhaps found in Berger v.
United States,[7] in an opinion delivered by
Mr. Justice Sutherland:

> That the United States prosecuting
> attorney overstepped the bounds of that
> propriety and fairness which should
> characterize the conduct of such an
> officer in the prosecution of a criminal
> offense is clearly shown by the record.
> He was guilty of misstating the facts
> in his crossexamination of witnesses;
> of putting into the mouths of such
> witnesses things which they had not
> said; of suggesting by his questions
> that statements had been made to him
> personally out of court, in respect
> of which no proof was offered; of
> pretending to understand that a wit-
> ness had said something which he had
> not said and persistently cross-
> examining the witness upon that basis;
> of assuming prejudicial facts not in
> evidence; of bullying and arguing
> with witnesses; and, in general, of
> conducting himself in a thoroughly
> indecorous and improper manner. It
> is impossible, however, without

reading the testimony at some length,
and thereby obtaining a knowledge of the
setting in which the objectionable matter
occurred, to appreciate fully the extent
of the misconduct. The trial judge, it
is true, sustained objections to some of
questions, insinuations and misstatements,
and instructed the jury to disregard
them. But the situation was one which
called for stern rebuke and repressive
messures and, perhaps, if these were
not successful, for the granting of a
mistrial. It is impossible to say
that the evil influence upon the jury
of these acts of misconduct was removed
by such mild judicial action as was
taken.

The United States Attorney is the
representative not of an ordinary party
to a controversy, but of a sovereignty
whose obligation to govern impartially
is as compelling as its obligation to
govern at all; and whose interest,
therefore, in a criminal prosecution
is not that it shall win a case, but
that justice shall be done. As such,
he is in a peculiar and very definite
sense the servant of the law, the two-
fold aim of which is that guilt shall
not escape or innocence suffer. He
may prosecute with earnestness and
vigor--indeed, he should do so. But,
while he may strike hard blows, he
is not at liberty to strike foul ones.
It is as much his duty to refrain from
improper methods calculated to produce a wrongful conviction as it is
to use every legitimate means to bring
about a just one.[8]

This philosophy that the prosecutor is "not
to convict but to see that justice is done" is
ordained by statute in some states. The Texas
Code provides:

Each district attorney shall
represent the state in all criminal
cases where he has been, before his
election, employed adversely. When
any criminal proceeding is had before
an examining court in his district or
before a judge upon habeas corpus,
and he is notified of the same, and is
at the same time within his district,
he shall represent the state therein,
unless prevented by other official
duties. It shall be the primary duty
of all prosecuting attorneys, including
any special prosecutors, not to convict, but to see that justice is done.
They shall not suppress facts or secrete
witnesses capable of establishing the
innocence of the accused.[9]

This guideline, this basic philosophy, this
statutory requirement, this motto for prosecutors
is defined in that indefinable term "justice,"
which may be variously interpreted by almost any
lawyer, including prosecutors. Some prosecutors
may choose to define justice as the end sought
in the "war against crime." As the noted Texas
criminal defense lawyer Richard "Racehorse"
Haynes said of police in a press interview,
"They more often than not believe that they are
engaged in a war, the war against crime, and, as
in love, all is fair. They do tend to justify
the means by the ends received."[10] Prosecutors,
too, tend to feel that they are in a war against
crime as well. Many feel responsibility for
maintaining public order and tend toward what
has been called the "white hat" syndrome.
However one may define justice, it is clear that
when one party enters an adversary proceeding
without having the same goal to win as does one's
opponent, one can feel frustrated and hampered
in the performance of one's duties.

The Code of Professional Responsibility
developed by the American Bar Association is
directed to the conduct of all lawyers. The Code

was adopted by the House of Delegates of the American Bar Association in 1969 and was amended in 1970, 1974, and 1975. The roots of the present Code can be traced to the Code of Ethics adopted by the Alabama Bar Association in 1887, taken from the lecture of Judge George Sharswood and originally published in 1854.[11]

The 1975 Preface to the Code of Professional Responsibility recognized the limitations on the Canons when it stated "The present Canons are not an effective teaching instrument and they fail to give guidance to lawyers. . . ."[12] Certainly this can be emphasized as it relates to the ethical problems faced by public prosecutors, for the Code is almost devoid of direct and explicit behavioral advice to this large group of lawyers. Prosecutors can look to Canon 7 and the Ethical Considerations amended thereto. What may be said for the Canons applies to a lesser extent even to the American Bar Association Project on Standards of Criminal Justice [hereinafter referred to as ABA Standards] and the National Prosecution Standards of the National District Attorneys Association[13] [hereinafter referred to as NDAA Standards] . Specifically, the ABA Standards define unprofessional conduct as "conduct which it is recommended be made subject to disciplinary sanctions."[14] The term is used in twenty-six instances throughout the Standards.[15] These instances are helpful in providing specific guidance to prosecutors and cover a broad spectrum of prosecutorial functions. The NDAA Standards in Chapter 25 treat professional ethics:

> To ensure the highest ethical conduct and maintain the integrity of prosecution and the legal system, the prosecutor shall be thoroughly acquainted with and shall adhere at all times to the Code of Professional Responsibility as promulgated by the American Bar Association and as adopted by the various

114

state bar associations.[16]

The NDAA Standards are unique in adding reference to finances:

Disclosure of financial holdings, liabilities, and interests is necessary to assure the public that no conflict of interest may affect the unbiased operation of the prosecution function.. ..

Financial disclosure should be made by all candidates for the office of prosecutor at the time of filing for election. Elected prosecutors should disclose financial information at those times required by state law, or annually.[17]

Throughout the twenty-seven chapters of NDAA Standards, there are many other specific references to prosecutorial action, and NDAA Standard 2.3 reaffirms that the "prosecutor has the duty to seek justice and improve the law, not merely to enforce the law."[18]

Because prosecutors, as other lawyers, are officers of the court, they find their greatest source of guidance on conduct as well as control from the trial and appellate courts. The ambience of the court can affect decorum of counsel and inhibit outward manifestations of improper conduct. More effective is the appellate review of a criminal trial. The effectiveness is multiplied because prosecutorial misconduct can be grounds for reversal and any misstep through the trial of a case by the prosecuting attorney becomes grounds for appeal. Chief Judge John Onion of the Texas Court of Criminal Appeals states that in 60% of the appeals in that court, there are allegations of prosecutorial misconduct.[19] Obviously, this is a fertile field for appellate defense attorneys to plow. From the opinions of the appellate

115

courts, the prosecutorial community receives guidance for ethical conduct across the whole field of prosecutorial activity from charging to relations with the grand jury, plea bargaining, discovery, relations with the press, and trial practices.

Disciplinary Action

It has been asserted that the professional conduct of lawyers in this country is inadequately supervised.[20] The disciplinary actions which have been taken over the years have not been sufficient to encourage widespread belief by the lay population that the rascals are being vigorously rooted out. The education of lawyers is spread over more than 150 law schools, the standards of admission are fixed by fifty states, and literally hundreds of state and local bar associations variously attempt to deal with complaints and discipline. Traditions of decorum have fallen into disuse. Moreover, standards of professional conduct are ill-defined.

Two sources of control and discipline are available. First, trial judges can enforce appropriate standards by insisting on compliance with proper conduct in the cases before them and imposing sanctions for improprieties. At the appellate level, the sanction of reversal of convictions is really not an effective penalty for miscreant prosecutors. The second source of control and discipline (largely neglected) is the power of the organized bar to deal with professional misconduct of its members. This power, however, is meaningful only in the unified or integrated bar association, which has official status either by judicial rule or legislative enactment. The lack of such authority in other states and in local bar associations is a grave and inherent weakness in the structure of the legal profession.

116

The traditional penalty for serious ethical violations by members of the bar has been disbarment or some lesser penalty imposed by a bar grievance committee or group. The NDAA Standards recognize the problem that may be presented by bar association control over the prosecutor who is an elected public official.

A mechanism should be established to enable the legislature or court of highest appellate jurisdiction to suspend, remove, or supersede a local prosecutor upon a demonstration, after reasonable notice and hearing, that the prosecutor is incapable of carrying out the duties of his office.

A. Disciplinary Initiation:
Such suspension, removal or superseder should be initiated by the appropriate professional body, in a proceeding designed to safeguard the right of the prosecutor.

B. Disciplinary Rationale:
Such proceedings should be initiated only for just and serious cause, including:
  1. Disbarment
  2. Conviction of a felony, or a crime involving public corruption
  3. Mental incompetency and/or physical disability which would prevent performance of the duties of prosecution
  4. Willful neglect of duty[21]

Most states provide expressly in the constitution or by statute for the control and removal of public officers. Even where the power to discipline prosecutors has been constitutionally delegated, such as the power of removal to the Governor of New York, the courts retain review authority.

The governor may remove any elective
sheriff, county clerk, district attorney
or register within the term for which he
shall have been elected; but before so
doing he shall give to such officer a
copy of the charges against him and an
opportunity of being heard in his defense.[22]

The statutes of many states provide for
discipline of lawyers by the state board and also
for removal of the prosecutor by state action.
California law provides:

The rules of professional conduct
adopted by the board, when approved by
the supreme court, are binding upon
all members of the state bar.

For a wilful breach of any of these
rules, the board has power to discipline
members of the state bar by reproval,
public or private, or to recommend to
the supreme court the suspension from
practice for a period not exceeding
three years of members of the state
bar. . . .[23]

An accusation in writing against
any officer of a district, county, or
city, including any member of the
governing board of a school district,
for wilful or corrupt misconduct in
office, may be presented by the grand
jury of the county for or in which
the officer accused is elected or
appointed. . . .[24]

The same proceedings may be had
on like grounds for the removal of
a district attorney, except that the
accusation shall be delivered by the
foreman of the grand jury to the
clerk, and by him to a judge of the
superior court of the county. . . .[25]

118

It would be somewhat anomalous for the state bar grievance committee to discipline a prosecutor to the extend of denying him the right to practice law. In effect a private body would be in the position of removing a public official from office in derogation of the statutory authority otherwise provided for the removal of public officials. This issue was addressed in Simpson v. Alabama State Bar[26] by the Alabama Supreme Court:

> The issue presented is whether a district attorney, while serving a term of office, can be disciplined by the Board of Commissioners of the Alabama State Bar for alleged violation of the Rules Governing the Conduct of Attorneys, which were in effect at the time of the commission of the act charged. . . .

> The Bar Association was without authority to discipline or disbar a district attorney during the term of his office under the rules of conduct in effect at the time involved here. In that narrow sense, we perceive no difference between a judge and a district attorney. Both, by mandate of the Constitution, must be lawyers; neither may practice law while holding office . . . .

> This court retains the power to approve or disapprove any rule adopted by the Board of Bar Commissioners governing the conduct of attorneys, to inquire into the merits of any disciplinary proceedings, and to take any action it sees fit in such matters. Ex parte Thompson, supra. But, at the time of the commission of the act complained of here, this court had not formulated or approved any rules governing the conduct of district attorneys, who are constitutional

officers. . . .

Insofar as the conduct of a district attorney is concerned, the Board of Bar Commissioners was, at the time of the act complained of, without authority to institute or conduct disciplinary proceedings of any kind under the then existing rules governing conduct of attorneys, where the only method of removal then existing was that which the Constitution provided. . . .

We do not mean to suggest that, by the holding herein, district attorneys should ever be held to a lesser degree of professional responsibility than is required of other attorneys or officers of courts. Nor do we condone the action of the district attorney in this case. All attorneys should maintain the highest ethical standards and owe to their profession and the office they hold the highest degree of professionalism. We simply hold that district attorneys were not subject to being disciplined as attorneys by the Board of Bar Commissioners for violation of the old rules governing the conduct of attorneys.

Further, as the trial court did, the Bar Association would make a distinction between "official" and "nonofficial" acts. The trial court found no authority in the statute prescribing the duties of a district attorney for calling news conferences and concluded, therefore, that such act necessarily was a "nonofficial" act, for which the Bar could discipline. We disagree with this conclusion, and would make no distinction between "official" and "nonofficial" acts, insofar as the Bar Association's authority to discipline a duly elected or appointed district

attorney under the old rules during
his term of office.[27]

The ultimate in court supervision is the
removal from office of a prosecutor. In <u>Attorney
General v. Tufts</u>[28] the Massachusetts Supreme
Court, after extensive hearings, took this
drastic action.

> The powers of a district attorney
> under our laws are very extensive. They
> affect to a high degree the liberty of
> the individual, the good order of society,
> and the safety of the community. His
> natural influence with the grand jury,
> and the confidence commonly reposed in
> his recommendations by judges, afford
> to the unscrupulous, the weak or the
> wicked incumbent of the office vast
> opportunity to oppress the innocent
> and to shield the guilty, to trouble
> his enemies and to protect his friends,
> and to make the interest of the public
> subservient to his personal desires,
> his individual ambitions and his pri-
> vate advantage. The authority vested
> in him by law to refuse on his own
> judgement alone to prosecute a com-
> plaint or indictment enables him to
> end any criminal proceeding without
> appeal and without the approval of
> another official. Powers so great
> impose responsibilities correspondingly
> grave. They demand character incor-
> ruptible, reputation unsullied, a
> high standard of professional ethics,
> and sound judgement of no mean order.
> Profound learning and unusual
> intellectual acumen, although eminently
> desirable, are less essential. A
> district attorney cannot treat that
> office as his selfish affair. It is a
> public trust. The office is not
> private property, but is to be held and
> administered wholly in the interests

of the people at large and with an eye
single to their welfare.

The removal of a district attorney
is a drastic act. The power of removal
is vested by the statute in the judicial
department of government. That circumstance implies from its very nature
that the cause for removal must be one
cognizable by courts in the exercise of
judicial attributes. The sole matter
for inquiry is the public welfare, as
affected by the moral, intellectual
and professional characteristics and
conduct of the man in question. Such
characteristics and conduct need not
be confined to his administration of the
office, nor to the period of his official
service. An isolated act of malfeasance
outside the present term of office or
having no relation to official duties,
not showing a corrupt or depraved
disposition, doubtless would be insuf-
ficient to warrant removal. Misdeeds
or lapses for which expiation has
been made by established uprightness
and integrity would hardly justify
removal. If his character is bad, his
sense of moral fitness blunted, or in
other respects his behavior is offensive
to the right minded, so that public
confidence in the purity and impartiality
of his official work is justly shaken,
then sufficient ground for removal is
shown.[29]

An example of the extent of investigation
that grievance committees take on allegations of
prosecutorial impropriety may be found in the
statement issued by the Illinois State Bar
Association, which investigated the charges
against the State's Attorney and his Special
Assistant in the case of People v. Miller.[30]
The Supreme Court in its opinion in Miller v.

122

Pate,[31] made serious charges against the prosecutors, which resulted in these proceedings.
The State Bar took the unusual step of issuing
a public statement noting in part that the Supreme
Court "had misapprehended the facts. . . ."[32]

In 1956, Lloyd Eldon Miller, Jr.
was tried and convicted in the Circuit
Court of Hancock County, Illinois of the
murder of an 8-year-old Canton, Illinois
girl, Janice May. On February 13, 1967,
the United States Supreme Court over-
turned the murder conviction on the ground
that the prosecution had knowingly used
false evidence to convict him by introducing into evidence a pair of undershorts
which it contended were stained with
blood. The Court based its decision on
testimony given seven years later at a
habeas corpus hearing in the U.S. District
Court in Chicago, to the effect that
the only stains on the shorts were paint
stains. In its opinion the Supreme Court
said that the prosecution at the original
trial had "deliberately misrepresented
the truth" in regard to the shorts.

In view of the serious implications
of such charges, the Grievance Committee
of the Illinois State Bar Association,
on its own motion, commenced an investigation in April of 1967 to determine
whether disciplinary action against the
prosecutors was warranted. The investigation extended over a period of approximately nine months. The voluminous
records in the case included the trans-
cripts of testimony at the original trial
and before the Pardon and Parole Board
and in the habeas corpus proceedings in
the U.S. District Court. Also reviewed
were the abstracts of record and the
briefs in the several appeals to the
Illinois Supreme Court, the U.S. Court of
Appeals and the United States Supreme

123

Court. These documents, all of which were minutely examined by the Committee, comprised some 3300 printed and typewritten pages. In addition, the Grievance Committee interrogated the attorneys who prosecuted and defended the case at the original trial, and in response to these questions received detailed answers concerning every area of possible misconduct on the part of the prosecutors.

It became apparent to the Committee early in its investigation that the United States Supreme Court had misapprehended the facts of the case.[33]

The Board discussed in detail the facts as found by them. In addition, the Board proceeded to evaluate various other charges which "if true, could have provided a basis for disciplinary action against the prosecutors," and concluded that there was no basis for disciplinary action against the prosecutors and dismissed the charges.[34]

Rules for Prosecutorial Conduct

The complaint is often made by younger lawyers that in the teaching of ethics or professional responsibility the rules for action are never specific but too often couched in generalities. This complaint can be made by prosecutors with even more justification. The rather unique responsibility of the prosecutor in the practice of law is all too frequently not even significantly referred to in the source books of lawyer ethics. Often the directives on conduct are not applicable or at least are not specific when placed against the general standard required of the prosecutor. The unusual nature of the prosecutorial services makes it difficult to relate to the canons, ethical considerations, and disciplinary rules designed for attorneys representing private parties.

124

Any prosecutor must be able to rely on his
own sense of duty and honor to resolve many of
the problems with which he is faced each day.
Too often the guidance comes after the fact when
a court or grievance committee judges an action
by hindsight without being able to understand the
environment in which the act may have been committed. No written record can recreate the
factual situation, the competing interests, the
heat of argument, or the emotional involvement
of the parties.

It is well to review the prosecutorial
roles and functions and analyze the prohibitions,
limitations, and requirements placed upon the
prosecutor in performing his role. These
restrictions arise out of court decisions,
custom, bar and association studies, and the
writings of authorities. There is no collected,
compiled, annotated, categorized black letter
publication, and perhaps it is not possible, as
standards for professional responsibility
within the prosecutorial community change and
evolve. Matters relating to decorum (or manners)
about which Chief Justice Burger has repeatedly
referred have been omitted as have references to
ex parte discussions with judges. The delicate
question of prompting perjury by the method of
interviewing witnesses or suggesting "facts"
after the style of Anatomy of a Murder[35] would
require far more space than is available, and
any discussion would provide little specificity.
No consideration is given on the issue of cross-
examination of a witness whose testimony is
believed to be truthful by the cross-examiner.
This matter is omitted based on the reasoning
in the ABA Standards which state in part:

> There was a consensus among the
> experts consulted, and one shared by
> the Advisory Committee, that the dif-
> ficult and delicate decisions presented
> by the wide range and variety of
> situations cannot be made the subject

of rigid standards. There was general agreement that cross-examination is perhaps the best known device for ascertaining truth and revealing falsehood. Essentially an "invention" of the common law system, the power to cross-examine adverse witnesses is a monopoly of lawyers and ought not be misused for destroying known truth. The power to cross-examine is a power vested in a lawyer by virtue of his being an officer of the court.[36]

The Part-Time Prosecutor and Conflicts of Interest

In modern times, there has come more and more the realization that the criminal justice system should not be served by the part-time (or partially-compensated) prosecutor. This phenomenon arose out of the concept of the local elected prosecutor in each county. The population of some jurisdictions has increased tremendously while others have remained relatively stable (and small). The situation has developed where some prosecutors have infinitely greater caseloads than those in adjoining counties. The solution to this problem has taken various turns. In some jurisdictions, the elected prosecutor has been permitted to hire assistants. In some cases the assistants, too, are part-time. In many the part-time county attorney has been assisted by full-time assistants, which, by the nature of things, has resulted in the subordinates being paid more (and in some cases much more) than the elected official. The solution elsewhere was to create roughly equal districts by combining jurisdictions and setting up one full-time position where several existed. The problem has not been resolved and part-time prosecutors are the rule across the nation and include the largest and most populated states as well as smaller. The issue of changing to a district system has become a political issue in many states.

126

The significance of the problem as it relates to prosecutor ethics can be placed under two rubrics. First, a part-time prosecutor (even by part-time standards) is commonly underpaid, and to achieve an income comparable to other lawyers in the community must devote much time to private practice. As a result, in some communities, the position is passed from lawyer to lawyer as a duty (pro bono) or is reserved for a young lawyer in the community to sustain him until he builds a private practice.

The second ethical problem is the conflict of duties arising out of either law partnerships or arising out of conflicting legal interests of private clients.

The Code of Professional Responsibility, the ABA Standards, and the NDAA Standards all address the problems of conflicts of interests as they face the prosecutor. Canon 9 of the Code of Professional Responsibilities declares,"A lawyer should avoid even the appearance of professional impropriety,"[37] and the Canon is amplified in the Disciplinary Rules: "A lawyer shall not accept private employment in a matter in which he had substantial responsibility while he was a public employee."[38]

Two of the ABA Standards relate to the problem of the part-time prosecutor and are quite explicit:

1.2 Conflicts of Interest:
(A) A prosecutor should avoid the appearance or reality of a conflict of interest with respect to his official duties.

(B) A conflict of interest may arise when, for example,
  (I) A law partner or other lawyer professionally associated with the prosecutor or a relative appears as, or of, counsel for

127

a defendant;

(II) A business partner or associate or a relative has any interest in a criminal case, either as a complaining witness, a party or as counsel;

(III) A former client or associate is a defendant in a criminal case.[39]

2.3 Assuring High Standards of Professional Skill:

(B) The offices of chief prosecutor and his staff should be full time occupations.

Commentary

b. Full-time occupation
An important step in achieving the goal of professionalism is to make the position of prosecutor a full time occupation for its holder. At present, a large number of prosecutors, including some in urban areas, devote only a portion of their professional effort to the duties of their office. Many undesirable problems arise from this situation. Apart from the problem of conflict of interests, which raises ethical problems, there is a great risk that the part-time prosecutor will not give sufficient energy and attention to his official duties.[40]

The NDAA Standards look at the problem from a career point of view: "The office of prosecutor shall be approached as a career position."[41]

The complexity of today's criminal law practice requires that all prosecutors devote their full efforts to their roles as prosecuting attorneys. Part-time law practice is inconsistent with the type of commitment the community has a right to expect of its prosecutor.

128

In smaller jurisdictions the majority of prosecutors serve part-time, either for financial reasons, or because of lack of need for a full-time prosecutor in a small district, or simply because the prosecutor in that area has always served only part-time. This practice of part-time prosecutorial service may face the problem of conflicts of interest:

While direct conflicts of interest between the prosecutor's public and his private practice are clearly unlawful and, we may assume, rare, there are many indirect conflicts that almost invariably arise. The attorneys he deals with as a public officer are the same ones with whom he is expected to maintain a less formal and more accommodating relationship as counsel to private clients. Similar problems may arise in the prosecutor's dealings with his private clients whose activities may come to his official attention.

It is undesirable to place a prosecutor in a position in which he must always be conscious of this potential for conflict and be careful to avoid improprieties or the appearance of conflict.

Even where no conflict of interest arises a potential for difficulty exists:
. . . .there is a great risk that the part-time prosecutor will not give sufficient energy and attention to his official duties. Since his salary is a fixed amount, and his total earnings depend on what he can derive from his private practice, there is continuing temptation to [42] give priority to private clients.

129

The President's Commission on Law Enforcement and Administration of Justice in its Task Force Report on the Courts[43] noted that one of the obstacles to effective prosecution was the part-time nature of the position in many cases. This, the Commission attributed to low salaries paid prosecutors and noted that a talented attorney could not expect to remain long in the office if it was his only source of income, no matter how dedicated.[44] Six years later, the National Advisory Commission on Criminal Justice Standards and Goals in its volume on courts noted the low salaries and recommended:

> The complexities and demands of the prosecution function require that the prosecutor be a full-time, skilled professional selected on the basis of demonstrated ability and high personal integrity. The prosecutor should be authorized to serve a minimum term of four years at an annual salary no less than that of the presiding judge of the trial court of general jurisdiction.
>
> In order to meet these standards, the jurisdiction of every prosecutor's office should be designed so that population, caseload and other relevant factors warrant at least one full-time prosecutor.[45]

Some jurisdictions have sought to eliminate the problem of the part-time prosecutor by statutory limitations. For example, New York provides:

> The district attorney of a county having a population of more than one hundred thousand according to the last federal census shall give his whole time to his duties and shall not engage in the practice of law, act as an arbitrator, referee or compensated

mediator in any action or proceeding
or matter or engage in the conduct of
any other profession or business which
interferes with the performance of his
duties as district attorney.[46]

The Oklahoma legislature early recognized
the problem and prohibited the private practice
of law by statute.[47] This statutory provision
was contested very shortly thereafter and
upheld by the Supreme Court of that state. The
decision of the court was bottomed on the unfair
influence on the court which might be exerted
by the county attorney shifting to a private
capacity.[48]

If the salary paid the part time prosecutor
is not sufficient for a living wage (and generally
it is not, for the full-time prosecutor's salary
is often less than that of his counterpart outside government), he will then be required to
supplement his income by private practice.
And this private endeavor will be more than
moonlighting. He will seek to supplement his
public income and in fact the private portion
may become the main source of his income. Excluding the possibility of conflicts, the outside
practice will take time. It the "squeaky wheel"
proverb means anything, it will apply to the
paying client.

From the ethics standpoint, the more difficult problem for the part-time prosecutor is
the possibility of a conflict of interest.
Experience indicates that most part-time prosecutors are extremely dedicated and do not shirk
their public responsibilities but, on the contrary,
devote far more time, energy, and interest than
the public deserves for its tax money. But the
opportunities for conflict are many because of
the nature of the situation.

Prof. Uviller comments:

. . . .the prosecutor may be expected

131

to shun financial interests which might
be affected by matters within his office.
Perhaps, little of the local prosecutor's
work alters the financial condition of
any enterprise in which he is likely to
own a share. Yet, it is surely well to
advise prosecutors to avoid investment
(for example) in taverns or construction
and maintenance firms contracting with
the local government for we would not
want his investigative or prosecutorial
ardor cooled by the prospect of financial
loss.

But let us not fall into the sweet
naivete of the economists' uncluttered
view of human motivation. Man is not
moved by bread alone. Is not the ideal
of personal detachment from the cause
as seriously jeopardized by the prosecutor's relationship, friendship, or
prior association with victim, witness,
defendant, or adverse counsel? The
litigating bar of most communities is
small and frequently friendly. The prosecutor (particularly if well chosen) is
likely to be associated professionally
or socially with some of the others in
the group. The bar prides itself that
friends can be diligent adversaries.
But now one of the friendly combatants
is a public official besides. Should
we be concerned that his duty may conflict
with the interests of friendship or the
residue of prior association?[49]

Most part-time prosecutors are associated
with other lawyers who are not bound by ethical
considerations to refuse to accept clients who
may be charged and prosecuted. Significantly,
the new "conflicts" statutes coming into vogue
tend to add the taint of conflicts to the members
of a firm joined by a former government official.
In cases where the potential conflict appears,

132

the part time (or any) prosecutor can and should recuse himself.

An interesting situation sometimes develops where part-time prosecutors are called upon to serve as defense attorneys in criminal cases in adjoining jurisdictions. Clearly in no wise could a public prosecutor perform as a criminal defense attorney in his own jurisdiction. There are instances where judges have appointed prosecutors from outside the jurisdiction as court-appointed counsel. The theory is that who is better than a prosecutor to defend in a criminal case. Opinions of the American Bar Association prohibit such representation even in another state.[50] In the United States, the state is a party to a criminal case and the lawyer for the state owes first and total fealty to that client. Further the very fact that if an accused is defended by a prosecutor from another jurisdiction, the court and jury cannot help but be influenced by the position of such a "defense" attorney and perhaps give undue weight thereto.

Media

The most obvious and perhaps most blatant ethical errors committed by those in the field of prosecution are extrajudicial statements made to the media. Notwithstanding the continued warnings, cautions, directions, and court orders, some prosecutors seem to be constitutionally unable to refuse comments to the press about on-going trials. The reasons vary from the personal vanity of seeing one's name in print to the almost violent demands of the media for some statement, even if it is not newsworthy. In this heyday of the investigative reporter, it becomes almost impossible for a public official to refuse to issue a statement on any subject. This is dangerous in the area of providing a fair trial and justice. Granted, to refrain from comment when queried is not easy for a public official,

133

particularly an elected official, who is daily reminded of the right of a free press. All too frequently a simple statement of facts would suffice, but the prosecutor being questioned cannot resist going beyond the guidelines and cannot resist the temptation to answer the free speech commentary of defense counsel. Though there has been discussion ad nauseum in the area of fair trial/free press for a number of years, the issues of preventive orders, gag rules, and precensorship have all stirred media emotions with little recognition or concern for the fairness of the trial or the responsibility of the members of the bar. Prosecutors caught in the middle of this battle have been torn by the stand expected of them.

The ethical responsibilities of the prosecutor in dealing with the press finds this official attempting to strike a delicate balance between the right of a fair trial for the accused and the opposing constitutional guarantee of a free press. The guidelines appear to be quite explicit in what may and may not be provided. However, these guidelines cannot anticipate the atmosphere of a particular trial in which inexperienced assistant district attorneys find themselves. If there is any area of professional responsibility where the question is one not solely of prohibitions and legalities, it is this area of media relations in which so much depends on individual judgement of the prosecutor. Though in public statements the prosecutor is enjoined "not to exploit his office by means of personal publicity," [51] he is expected to make available to the press that information which is necessary to a public understanding of the problems of criminal justice. Nor is the prosecutor "to make public comments critical of the verdict," [52] even though the verdict becomes a matter of public discussion by the media and occasionally by his adversary from the recent trial. If this were not difficult enough, the prosecutor should familiarize the local police agencies with the case

134

law concerning fair trial and free press and
encourage them to adopt policies to protect
the rights of the individual.[53] Again, one is
confronted by a strange double standard in the
adversary system. Dean Freedman states that
"because the prosecutor should be barred from
speaking publicly about the case before trial,
does not mean that the defendant or the defense
counsel should or can constitutionally be
similarly restricted."[54]

Investigation and Charging

The initial duty of the prosecutor is to
review the evidence and make the charging decision.
The actions taken at this stage of the process
usually determine all future actions in a case.
It is at the charging stage that the overwhelming
discretionary authority of the prosecutor
arises. The authority may be exercised in error
and likewise it may be tainted with ethical
misconduct. Either through errors of judgment
or failure to observe the standards of professionalism, the case may be so tainted that it
cannot be saved. The charging discretion of the
prosecutor may be used to charge, to undercharge,
to overcharge, or to refuse to charge at all.

Allied to the responsibility for charging
is the correlative investigative function. This
duty is not always performed by the prosecutor
and is more generally considered to be a police
function. It is not surprising to learn that the
immunity customarily applied to prosecutorial
functions does not inure to the investigation
function when performed by the prosecutor. As an
investigator, the prosecutor is held to the
standard of good faith and reasonableness
required of the police.

Recognizing that the prosecutor may be
required to undertake additional investigation,
the ABA Standards are usually specific in setting

guidelines for prosecutorial actions in this area. The ABA Standards provide:

> (B) It is unprofessional conduct for a prosecutor to use illegal means to obtain evidence or to employ or instruct or encourage others to use such means.

> (C) A prosecutor should not obstruct communication between prospective witnesses and defense counsel. It is unprofessional conduct to advise any person to decline to give information to the defense.

> (D) It is unprofessional conduct for a prosecutor to secure the attendance of persons for interviews by use of any communication which has the appearance or color of a subpoena or similar judicial process unless he is authorized by law to do so.

> (E) It is unprofessional conduct for a prosecutor to promise not to prosecute for prospective criminal activity, except where such activity is part of an officially supervised investigative and enforcement program.

> (F) The prosecutor should avoid interviewing a prospective witness except in the presence of a third person unless the prosecutor is prepared to forego impeachment of a witness by the prosecutor's own testimony as to what the witness stated in an interview or to seek leave to withdraw from the case in order to present his impeaching testimony.

Commentary

Prospective witnesses are not partisans; they should be regarded as

136

impartial spokesmen for the facts as they see them. Because witnesses do not "belong" to either party, it is improper for a prosecutor, defense counsel, or anyone acting for either to suggest to a witness that he not submit to a interview by opposing counsel. It is not only proper but it may be the duty of the prosecutor and defense counsel to interview any person who may be called as a witness in the case (except that the prosecutor is not entitled to interview a defendant represented by counsel).

A prosecutor may not grant "dispensation" for criminal conduct because the actor is cooperating with the prosecutor in other areas of law enforcement. However, the need for and propriety of the use of informants in law enforcement is universally recognized and accepted, so long as they are not used to instigate criminal activity. Accordingly, this standard recognizes that it is not improper for a prosecutor to promise not to prosecute an informant for specific criminal activity in which the informant may engage as part of a supervised effort to obtain evidence of crime committed by other principal actors.[55]

The NDAA Standards devote a chapter to the investigative function recognizing that "Too frequently there is a need to supplement police investigative work, and the prosecutor must have the financial and manpower resources to do so."[56] The Standards also emphasize the need for tight control over the investigative function at top level.[57]

In People v. Green,[58] the accused in a capital murder case expressed a desire to talk,

137

and after being fully advised of his rights, waived appearance of his appointed counsel. A detective and an assistant prosecutor interviewed the accused and did not communicate with his counsel. The court held that

> . . . while this defendant's initiative and willingness to speak and the lack of overreaching by the assistant prosecuting attorney are factors to be considered in mitigating, they do not excuse compliance with the standard of professional conduct prescribed by DR 7-104 (A) (1).[59]

This disciplinary rule provides that a lawyer shall not "communicate. . . on the subject of a representation with a party he knows to be represented by a lawyer in that matter unless he has the prior consent of the lawyer representing such other party."[60]

Because the charging function is so fundamental to the role of the prosecutor, considerable attention has been directed to this matter. The Code of Professional Responsibility provides "A public prosecutor or other government lawyer shall not institute or cause to be instituted criminal charges when he knows or it is obvious that the charges are not supported by probable cause."[61]

Both the NDAA Standards and the ABA Standards list the factors to be considered by the prosecutor in determining whether to charge and what to charge. Both are firm in stating that it is improper to charge when it is known that the charges are not supported by probable cause. Both agree that it is part of the prosecutor's discretionary authority to refuse to charge or present all charges which the evidence may support.[62]

Two major ethical concerns in the charging function are the possibility of using the charge either to harass individuals or for a vindictive purpose. Harassment is possible because the law books are filled with such a vast assortment of crimes that it is a poor prosecutor who cannot find at least a technical violation of some statute which can be charged against almost anyone. As Judge Breitel has so eloquently put it in his discussion of discretionary authority, "If every policeman, every prosecutor, every court and every agency performed his responsibility in strict accordance with the rule of law, precisely and narrowly laid down, the criminal law would be ordered but intolerable."63 Prosecutors are justified in making discretionary judgments on charging, but as Justice Jackson said:

> If the prosecutor is obligated to choose his cases, it follows that he can choose his defendants. Therein is the most dangerous power of the prosecutor: that he will pick people that he thinks he should get, rather than pick cases that need to be prosecuted. In such a case, it is not a question of discovering the commission of a crime and then looking for the man who has committed it, it is a question of picking the man and then searching the law books, or putting investigators to work, to pin some offense on him. It is in this realm-- in which the prosecutor picks some person whom he dislikes or desires to embarrass, or selects some group of unpopular persons and then looks for an offense, that the greatest danger of abuse of prosecuting power lies. It is here that law enforcement be- comes personal.64

When any prosecutor brings repeated charges on a single individual, there is always that underlying current of suspicion that this is harassment. The late Robert Kennedy's reputation still suffers from the allegation that as a prosecutor he sought to find a charge to bring against Jimmy Hoffa. Less easily distinguished are single charges brought against individuals to harass, as the Nixon administration was alleged to have done with its IRS "hit list." If there is any part of the prosecution function that must rely on the personal code of conduct of a prosecutor, it is here. Other than for the admonition to refrain from personal prosecution, it is difficult for courts or others to restrain prosecutors in their discretionary authority.

Clearly allied to harassment and perhaps indistinguishable is vindictiveness of the prosecutor. The Supreme Court has pursued this matter of vindictiveness in the criminal justice system through the Pearce,[65] Colten,[66] and Chaffin[67] cases to Blackledge v. Perry,[68] which was specifically directed at the prosecutorial authority to charge. In Blackledge, the accused had a right to a trial de novo on a misdemeanor charge by taking the case to the superior court. The prosecutor substituted a felony charge for the original misdemeanor charge. The opinion states in part:

> A prosecutor clearly has a considerable stake in discouraging convicted misdemeanants from appealing and thus obtaining a trial de novo in the Superior Court, since such an appeal will clearly require increased expenditure of prosecutorial resources before the defendant's conviction becomes final and may even result in a formerly convicted defendant going free. And if the prosecutor has the means readily at hand to discourage such appeals by "upping the ante" through a felony indictment whenever a convicted misdemeanant pursues his statutory appellant remedy the State can insure that only the most hardy defendants will brave the hazard of a de novo trial.[69]

140

The use of the grand jury in the charging
process is not universal throughout the fifty
states. Even where it is a viable part of the
process, the prosecutor's role is not uniform.
Nonetheless, when the prosecutor does relate
to the grand jury, the action must be in accord
with the ethical responsibilities expected in
other prosecution functions. Recently, the
literature has been critical of the grand jury
system as a "tool" of the prosecutor. As a
consequence there is increasing pressure to open
the grand jury to defense counsel. The NDAA
Standards provide:

> The prosecutor should not make
> statements or arguments in an effort
> to influence grand jury action in a
> manner which would be impermissible at
> trial before a petit jury.

Commentary

> In situations where the prosecutor
> must prosecute an indictment returned
> by a grand jury, it is especially im-
> portant that he be free to express his
> opinion.

> A prosecutor should not, however,
> take advantage of his role as the
> ex parte representative of the state
> before the grand jury to unduly or
> unfairly influence it in voting upon
> charges brought before it. In general,
> he should be guided by the standards
> governing and defining the proper
> presentation of the state's case in an
> adversary trial before a petit jury.[70]

Discovery

In recent years there has been ever greater
emphasis on discovery practices in criminal cases.
These efforts have included permissive discovery

141

procedures as well as court-required discovery. Though there is no "open file" system (other than in military practice), both by court rule and decision the prosecutor is facing greater requirements to reveal his files, witnesses, and records to the accused. Brady v. Maryland[71] and Jencks v. United States[72] were landmarks in forcing prosecutorial disclosure of evidence. The efforts to encourage omnibus hearings have not usually been welcomed, but disclosure has moved toward that process. For a number of years, the requirement for automatic and unrequested prosecutorial disclosure was in a confused state, but United States v. Agurs[73] provides considerable guidance. The most vexing problem facing the prosecutor concerns the matters not in his file but of evidence he may suspect to be available which may negate the guilt of the accused or mitigate the crime. How far is the prosecutor required to go and what should he do ethically to pursue additional evidence of value to the defense?

Since Chief Justice John Marshall in United States v. Burr[74] first ordered a letter turned over by President Jefferson to the defendant Aaron Burr, the concept of providing the accused with knowledge of evidence against him has been growing and is emphasized by one of the more specific black-letter requirements of the Code of Professional Responsibility.

> A public prosecutor or other govern-
> ment lawyer in criminal litigation shall
> make timely disclosure to counsel for the
> defendant, or to the defendant if he has
> no counsel, of the existence of evidence,
> known to the prosecutor or other govern-
> ment lawyer, that tends to negate the
> guilt of the accused, mitigate the degree
> of the offense, or reduce the punishment.[75]

This rule is further expanded by the ABA Standards:

(A) It is unprofessional conduct for

142

a prosecutor to fail to disclose to the defense at the earliest feasible opportunity evidence which would tend to negate the guilt of the accused or mitigate the degree of the offense or reduce the punishment.

(B) The prosecutor should comply in good faith with discovery procedures under the applicable law.

(C) It is unprofessional conduct for a prosecutor intentionally to avoid pursuit of evidence because he believes it will damage the prosecution's case or aid the accused.[76]

The NDAA Standards are equally specific:

In order to provide adequate information for informed pleas, expedite trials, minimize surprise, afford opportunity for effective cross-examination and meet the requirements of due process, discovery prior to trial should be as full and free as possible.[77]

If, prior to or during a hearing or trial, a party discovers additional evidence or material previously requested or ordered which is subject to disclosure or inspection, or the identity of an additional witness, the other party or his counsel or the court shall be promptly notified of the existence of the additional material or witness.[78]

It is an interesting footnote to the NDAA Standards that they "do not anticipate reciprocity, they demand it."[79]

In Agurs the Court seems to say that, while full disclosure would be helpful to the system, it is not constitutionally required and, if it

143

is to come, it will be by statutory reform. _Agurs_ appears not to weigh the motive or bad faith of the prosecutor but tends to look at the nature of any request for information and the materiality of the evidence known to the prosecutor. Clearly, the Court in _Agurs_ said, the failure of prosecutor to disclose unrequested evidence is not a denial of due process unless the undisclosed information creates a reasonable doubt of guilt.[80]

Plea Bargaining

Plea bargaining is an essential component of the administration of justice. Properly administered, it is to be encouraged. . . .

It leads to prompt and largely final disposition of most criminal cases.[81]

Plea negotiation or plea bargaining has continued to come under attack from all sides. The National Advisory Commission on Criminal Justice Standards and Goals recommended that all negotiations be abolished by 1978.[82] Defense attorneys, prosecutors, judges, and academicians all write at length of the need to reform, eliminate, change, or reevaluate plea negotiation, but it continues to be a major element in the criminal justice process and has in the past few years been sustained by the United States Supreme Court as a necessary part of the system. Though statistics are not clear, it is apparent that a major portion of the felony cases (in urban areas at least) are disposed by plea negotiations.

Much of the criticism of the plea bargaining process is directed at the use of the powerful discretionary authority of the prosecutor. The criticisms cover excessive charging, use of weak evidentiary cases, use as a substitute for case preparation, discriminatory use of discretionary authority, greatly reduced sentences and on and on.

This area of the prosecutor's role no less than others is governed by ethical standards. In light of the fact that so much of the plea negotiation process is conducted out of court and is not totally a matter of record, it is important that the negotiations be conducted on a high ethical level.

Both the ABA Standards and the NDAA Standards deal with this subject at length.

4.1 Availability for plea discussions
(A) The prosecutor should make known a general policy of willingness to consult with defense counsel concerning disposition of charges by plea.

(B) It is unprofessional conduct for a prosecutor to engage in plea discussions directly with an accused who is represented by counsel, except with counsel's approval. If the accused refuses to be represented by counsel, the prosecutor may properly discuss disposition of the charges directly with the accused; the prosecutor would be well advised, however, to request that a lawyer be designated by the court or some appropriate central agency, such as a legal aid or defender office or bar association, to be present at such discussions.

(C) It is unprofessional conduct for a prosecutor knowingly to make false statements or representations in the course of plea discussions with defense counsel or the accused.

Commentary

"Intentionally deceiving opposing counsel is ground for disciplinary action."

145

Monroe v. State Bar, 55 Cal. 2d 145, 358
P.2d 529, 533, 10 Cal. Rptr. 257 (1961).
Although the prosecutor is under no
obligation to reveal any evidence to
defense counsel in the course of plea
discussion, truth is required in the
presentation of facts relating to the
case or any mitigating facts to the
defense counsel. The prosecutor's
basic duty to seek a just result as
well as his obligation to eschew the
use of deception in dealing with the
evidence also forbids his misrepresent-
ing the law or sentencing practices of
the court in his plea discussions. Not
only does misrepresentation reflect
upon the integrity of the prosecutor
but it severely handicaps his ability
to effect just disposition by pleas of
guilty since lawyers will understandably
be reluctant to negotiate with a prosecutor who cannot be trusted.[83]

4.2   Plea disposition when accused
      maintains innocence.
      A prosecutor may not properly
participate in a disposition by plea of
guilty if he is aware that the accused
persists in denying guilt or the factual
basis for the plea, without disclosure
of the court.[84]

4.3   Fulfillment of plea discussions.
(A)   It is unprofessional conduct for
a prosecutor to make any promise or
commitment concerning the sentence
which will be imposed or concerning a
suspension of sentence; he may properly advise the defense what position
he will take concerning disposition.

Commentary

a. Misrepresentation of power or intention.

146

It is essential to pleas discussions that the guilty pleas are entered understandingly and voluntarily. To achieve this the Advisory Committee on the Criminal Trial has recommended that the process be entirely open and that the court make careful inquiry into what representation, if any, was made by the prosecution as well as by the defense counsel. ABA Standards, Pleas of Guilty § 1.5 (Approved Draft, 1968). A plea entered as the result of a prosecutor's promising concessions beyond his power to fulfill is involuntary and the defendant is entitled to withdraw it. <u>Machibroda</u> v. <u>United States</u>, 368 U.S. 487 (1962). It is therefore important that the prosecutor make clear to the defense that he is not able to assure the judicial consequence of a guilty plea. Any intentional deception of the defense by the prosecution, on the other hand, is unprofessional conduct.[85]

The NDAA Standards place more emphasis on procedure, authority, and records than on the ethical considerations.

Standard 16.1
Propriety of plea discussions and plea arguments
A. Where it appears that the interest of the State in the effective administration of criminal justice will be served, the prosecutor, while under no obligation to negotiate any criminal charges, may engage in plea negotiations for the purpose of reaching an appropriate plea agreement. This should be done only through defense counsel, except when the accused is not eligible for or does not desire appointment of counsel and has not retained counsel.

Standard 16.2

147

Availability for plea discussions
A. The prosecutor should make known a general policy of willingness to consult with defense counsel concerning disposition charges by plea, and should set aside times and places for plea discussions, in addition to pretrial hearings.

B. The prosecutor should always be vigilant for the case where the accused may be innocent of the offense charged.[87]

Standard 16.4
Fulfillment of plea discussions
A. A prosecutor should not make any promise concerning the sentence which will be imposed or concerning a suspension of sentence; the prosecutor may properly advise the accused of the position prosecution will take concerning disposition.

B. A prosecutor should avoid implying a greater power to influence the disposition of a case than prosecution actually possesses.

C. If the prosecutor is unable to fulfill an understanding previously agreed upon in plea negotiations, the prosecutor should give notice promptly to the accused and cooperate in securing leave of the court for the accused to withdraw any plea and take such other steps as would be appropriate to restore the accused and the state to the position they were in before the understanding was reached or plea made.

Commentary

Judicial guidelines for prosecutors concerning a voluntary plea are less clear except for a small group of cases

148

in which a guilty plea was induced by
actual or threatened physical force.
Most cases involving the voluntariness
of a guilty plea, whether induced by the
prosecutor or the judge, require examination of two propositions. First,
consideration must be given to the
possibility of threat to a defendant
who feels a not guilty plea will result
in an unfair trial. For example, he
may be led to believe that the judge
will be prejudiced or that perjured
testimony will be introduced. Secondly,
there may be a threat to the defendant
that he will be subjected to a more severe
punishment upon conviction at trial rather
than simply submitting a plea of guilt.
By avoiding the aforementioned threats,
the prosecutor may encourage the
defendant to plead voluntarily.[88]

The Supreme Court of Oregon, acting in its
supervisory authority over the bar, discussed the
refusal of a district attorney to open plea
negotiations with defendants represented by
specific defense counsel while at the same time
negotiating with other defendants in the same
case represented by other counsel.

Mr. Ringle (defense) asked Mr. Rook
(prosecutor) whether the offer made to
Mr. Sturgeon's client was available to
the defendants represented by him and
Mr. Thom. Mr. Rook told Mr. Ringle
that the offer was not available to their
fifteen clients so long as they were
represented by Messrs. Ringle and Thom
or by anyone associated with or sharing
offices with either of them. Mr. Rook
added that if Messrs. Ringle and Thom
were to withdraw from the case and obtain
other counsel, the offer of bail for-
feiture would be available to the defendants through their new attorneys. When
Mr. Ringle asked Mr. Rook to explain his

149

position, Mr. Rook stated that Mr. Thom was involved in 'organized crime' and that he was upset with Mr. Ringle for saying "bad things" about him.

After this meeting, the pending trial was postponed, and Messrs. Ringle and Thom withdrew as counsel for the fifteen defendants. . . . Within a few days thereafter, the accused allowed the fifteen defendants previously represented by Messrs. Ringle and Thom to forfeit $50 bail and dismissed the criminal charges against them. . . .

We fully recognize, as contended by the accused and as a general proposition, that in order to discharge the duties of his office it is of importance that a prosecuting attorney be able to act "with independence and without fear of consequences." As recognized by the accused, however, "that is not to say that a prosecutor is not answerable for unethical conduct. . . ."

We also recognize, as contended by the accused, that disciplinary proceedings against an elected public official who is also an attorney must be supported by "clear and convincing evidence. . . ."

In agreeing with that conclusion we need not decide whether, as contended by the accused, a district attorney is under no mandatory duty to engage in plea bargaining with any defendant in any criminal case. . . .

To approve of the conduct of the accused in this case would be to approve of a practice under which a prosecuting attorney would decide for himself, in cases involving more than one criminal

150

defendant, which criminal defense attorneys
he would deal with and which criminal
defense attorneys he would refuse to deal
with. He could enforce such a practice
by the simple expedient of offering a plea
bargain to one defendant and refusing to
offer the same plea bargain to other
"similarly situated defendants" represented by other attorneys unless they
discharged such attorneys.[89]

The most common criticism of the prosecutor
in the plea negotiation process is the charge
that prosecutors consistently overcharge in order
to facilitate the plea. Dean Freedman, a critic
generally of prosecutors, indicates such procedure becomes coercive and may be especially
damaging to an innocent accused who pleads in the
face of strong charges.

> One method of assuring a sufficient
> number of pleas is to overcharge, that
> is, to charge a more serious offense
> or an accumulation of offenses and there-
> by "set the stage for subsequent bar-
> gaining." Commonly, cases are drawn up
> as felonies, with the prosecutor noting
> that a plea for some misdemeanor should
> be accepted. Thus, the prosecutor
> consciously coerces the defendant into
> foregoing the constitutional right to
> trial by jury. As noted in the Depart-
> ment of Justice report: "Negotiation
> in such cases is a formality." Although
> the reason for this practice--"the great
> volume of business at the court"--is a
> serious practical problem, it does not
> justify the unethical practical effect
> of impairing a constitutional right by
> a combination of duress and trickery.

> In fact, the situation is often
> far worse than that, because the prose-
> cutor is knowingly participating with
> unscrupulous defense counsel in misleading

151

the defendant into believing that a
real plea bargain has been made, when
in fact both attorneys know that the
defendant was overcharged in the first
instance.[90]

Shupe v. Sigler[91] faced the question of
coercion of a guilty plea and the effect of
discussion of such a plea with defendant in the
absence of his counsel. The issue was one of
right to counsel:

> Leaving out comment on the fact
> that statements were taken from
> petitioner on the operating table when
> not entirely conscious and recorded
> by the court reporter, it is undisputed
> that the prosecutor had several con-
> versations with the petitioner in the
> absence of his counsel. Admittedly,
> he endeavored to persuade petitioner
> that he had no defense and that he
> should plead guilty and save the prose-
> cutor trouble of trial. Admittedly,
> bargaining took place in the absence
> of counsel as to the sentence to be
> imposed. . . .
>
> The court concludes that for a
> prosecuting attorney to talk with the
> defendant in the absence of his counsel
> and attempt to have him change a plea
> of not guilty to a plea of guilty and in
> the absence of counsel to reach an
> agreement as to the length of his
> sentence, whether made with or without
> authority of the court, is to deprive
> the defendant of the effective assistance
> of counsel at a time when it was needed.[92]

The Supreme Court in Santobello v. New York[93]
sustained the plea negotiation concept but insisted
that the bargain of the prosecutor must be kept.
In Brockman v. State,[94] the court set out the
rationale of giving the accused the benefit of

152

his bargain."

We should note that the State's
attempt at rescission does not appear
so much as "bad faith," as it was "bad
timing." The prosecutor's recognition
of his "obligation to society," appears
to have come during his hallway medi-
tation just before concluding the
disposition. "All foreseeable consequences" of (the) plea bargain should
have been considered by counsel before
the initial offer was made identically
to both defendants. Even at that point,
as we indicated in Wynn, the prosecutor
was not bound (as may have been so in
contract law) by the mere acceptance
of the offer. It was the State's
passively permitting if not overtly
leading appellant to a position of
prejudice that foreclosed the option of
turning back.[95]

Forensic Impropriety

(1) General

The literature is abundant in setting out
causes for the unprofessional or unethical acts
committed by prosecutors. These are better
subsumed under the rubric of myths including
political ambition, emotional involvement or
"white hat" syndrome, ignorance or inadvertence.
Whatever the reasons for individual incidents,
most of those that gain attention occur in the
trial arena. Here the prosecutor is in a goldfish
bowl observed by the judiciary, the bar, and the
public. Additionally, the written record of
trial may come back to haunt the prosecutor either
in or out of context.

It is in this arena that prosecutorial misconduct is more likely to result in retrial or
dismissal or at least in a judicial reprimand of

153

counsel. Quite probably, many in-trial errors could and should be cured by instructions from the trial judge. Most trial practitioners are aware, however, that what may be obvious in the record is not so clear during trial. What appears obvious in the cold written record to the hindsight of appellate review may have been quite acceptable as the trial progressed.

The essence of prosecutorial trial behavior (or any counsel's behavior) is honesty in the submission of evidence and the recognition that counsel is not a witness and should not express an opinion or state as fact personal knowledge. To these requirements are to be added the requirement that counsel show respect for the court by behavior and decorum. Courtroom behavior includes such virtues as courtesy, dignity, and punctuality. Decorum does not mean the sterility implied by Justice Frankfurter in his dissent in Sacher v. United States[96] when he declared:

> Criminal justice is concerned with the pathology of the body politic. . . . A criminal trial, it has well been said, should have the atmosphere of an operating room.[97]

Other commentators have been more realistic and recognize that there remains even in the more sedate courtroom of today some opportunity for flights of forensic eloquence.

(2) Voir dire

Juror selection is a matter of high priority for the prosecutor. Dozens of articles and hundreds of lectures have been presented on the methodology for insuring a proper jury panel. The importance of this trial function cannot but lead to the opportunity for improprieties. More significantly, the relationship can provide the appearance of impropriety when none exists, and prosecutors are wise to deal at arms length with those called for jury duty. The relationships should preclude any unnecessary or improper communication. Counsel should be careful to prevent the harassment of the venireman. Specifically forbidden are attempts to improperly influence the jurors in their decision by actions prior to or during the pendency of the trial.

The ABA Standards are direct and explicit on the relationship with jurors and prospective jurors and it is noted in the commentary that "in smaller communities where the prosecutor is more apt to be acquainted with the jurors, he must politely decline to engage in conversation with them."[98]

An interesting case arose in the Oklahoma courts where the accused complained of a denial of right to trial by an impartial jury where one juryman was the husband of the secretary of the district attorney. The voir dire included questions which should have elicited this relationship.

In _Manuel v. State_,[99] the Court states:

> . . . .since defense counsel was not informed of the relationship after he had manifested his interest therein by specific interrogatories incorporated into a more general examination at a time when the veniremen and most probably the prosecution were knowledgeable thereof, he was effectively deprived of an opportunity to fully explore this area as a potential foundation for a challenge for cause. Additionally, the defendant was at the very least deprived of knowledge upon which he could intelligently exercise a premptory challenge, for we do not doubt that any juror with such a kinship to an employee of his adversary when, as here, circumstances otherwise permit.[100]

(3)   Argument

Opening statements and closing arguments are opportunities for appeals to emotion, bias, and prejudice more than at any other stage of trial. It is at this point that counsel tends to stray from the evidence and into the realm of fantasy and vivid imagination. While the days of forensic oratory may be only a remnant of the past, some prosecutors still seem to get carried away with the sound of their own voices and as a result create errors that can reverse an otherwise valid decision of the court.

The ABA Standards address separately opening argument and final jury argument.

5.5 Opening statement.
In his opening statement, the prosecutor should confine his remarks to evidence he intends to offer which he believes in good faith will be available and admissible and a brief statement of the issues in the case. It is unprofessional conduct to allude to any evidence unless there is a good faith and reasonable basis for believing that such evidence will be tendered and admitted in evidence.[101]

5.8 Argument to the jury.
(A) The prosecutor may argue all reasonable inferences from evidence in the record. It is unprofessional conduct for the prosecutor intentionally to misstate the evidence or mislead the jury as to the inferences it may draw.

(B) It is unprofessional conduct for the prosecutor to express his personal belief or opinion as to the truth or falsity of any testimony or evidence of the guilt of the defendant.

(C) The prosecutor should not use arguments calculated to inflame the passions or prejudices of the jury.

(D) The prosecutor should refrain from argument which would divert the jury from its duty to decide the case on the evidence, by injecting issues broader than the guilt or innocence of the accused under the controlling law, or by making predictions of the consequences of the jury's verdict.

Commentary

a. Argument of reasonable inferences: misrepresentation
     The most elementary rule governing the limits of argument is that it must be confined to the record evidence and the inferences which can reasonably and fairly be drawn therefrom. Assertions of fact not proved amount to unsworn testimony of the advocate, not subject to cross-examination.

b. Expressions of personal belief
     Such expressions by the prosecutor are a form of unsworn, unchecked testimony and tend to exploit the influence of his office and undermine the objective detachment which should separate a lawyer from the cause for which he argues.[102]

5.9 Facts outside the record
It is unprofessional conduct for the prosecutor intentionally to refer to or argue on the basis of facts outside the record whether at trial or on appeal, unless such facts are matters of common public knowledge based on ordinary human experience or matters of which the court may take judicial notice.[103]

On this matter, there is great similarity between the NDAA Standards and the ABA Standards. In the commentary of the NDAA Standards, there appears the following:

The opening statement, which provides the trier of facts with his or her first opportunity to hear the issues and facts to be resolved, should be presented in a manner consistent with the prosecutor's obligations as a representative of the sovereignty. While the prosecutor's remarks should be motivated by impartiality and good faith, such statements ought to be inspired by the ultimate goal sought to be achieved at trial: the innocent should be granted their freedom, but the guilty should not be allowed to escape justice.

The limitations on prosecutorial argument are designed to leave in the hands of the jury the determination of guilt or innocence based upon the evidence validly presented to them. The limitations are to prelude decision making by the jury based upon emotion or references of evidence which is not before them.[104]

The reports are filled with cases of excesses in argument. In People v. Hoffman,[105] the court noted:

The State's Attorney went too far, however, and his language was, at times, too violent. His lack of restraint and his apparent violence of language were not of the type to be desired in an officer of the court. In his argument at one point he stated, "If I had one slightest reasonable doubt about Stanley Hoffman's guilt upon my words as a man and as an American, as a father and grandfather, I would say I do not believe he is guilty and I would dismiss this case. But, I know all the facts in this case as you know various people." This was an expression of his own

158

individual opinion and the State's Attorney should have been more restrained.[106]

And in _Volkmor v. United States_,[107] the court found the statements intentionally abusive.

> Admitting that these statements were wholly unjustifiable--as indeed must be done--the government contends that, as defendant failed to ask for exceptions, the error is not available. In the first place, there was no adverse ruling on the objections, and in that situation an exception was a matter of dubious propriety. But, even if there had been no objections, it was the duty of the court, on its own motion, to reprove counsel and to instruct the jury to disregard the remarks. This is not a case of inadvertence of statement, but of intentional abuse.[108]

The courts do seem to recognize that prosecutors, too, are human and become wrapped up in their presentations. In _State v. Gonzales_,[109] the court said:

> In the closing argument, excessive and emotional language is the bread and butter weapon of counsel's forensic arsenal, limited by the principle that attorneys are not permitted to introduce or comment upon evidence which has not previously been offered and placed before the jury.[110]

Perhaps the admonition was done in a more expressive way over one hundred years earlier by Judge Lumpkin in _Berry v. Georgia_[111] when he said:

> . . . .giving reins to their imagination, they may permit the spirit of their heated enthusiasm to swing and sweep beyond the flaming bounds of space

and time - _extra_ _flammanoia_ _moenia_
mundi. But let nothing tempt them
to pervert the testimony, or sur-
reptitiously array before the
jury, facts which, whether true or
not have not been proven.[112]

(4) Evidence

The use of false or manufactured evidence
to assist in the conviction of an accused is so
repugnant to the concept of justice that it
does not seem to warrant rising to the level of
a Supreme Court decision. Nonetheless, there
seem to be isolated instances of the use of
such evidence in criminal trials. At least as
reprehensible but far more likely to occur is
the surreptitious offer of improper evidence
by placing it in the view of the jury or even
offering it in evidence when its admission is
known to be improper. These attempts to influence
the jury are perhaps more insidious, for there is
little likelihood of reversal for such tactics.
Few are the lawyers who cannot relate an anecdote
of the forbidden item ostentatiously placed on
counsel table for "viewing."

The Code of Professional Responsibility is
explicit as to all attorneys.

    (A) In his representation of a client,
        a lawyer shall not:
        (1) Knowingly use perjured testimony
            or false evidence.
        (2) Participate in the creation or
            preservation of evidence when he
            knows or it is obvious that the
            evidence is false.[113]

The ABA Standards leave little doubt as to
the requirements placed upon the prosecution.

    (A) It is unprofessional conduct for a
    prosecutor knowingly to offer false
    evidence, whether by documents, tangible

160

evidence, or the testimony of witnesses.

(B) It is unprofessional conduct for a prosecutor knowingly and for the purpose of bringing inadmissible matter to the attention of the judge or jury to offer inadmissible evidence, ask legally objectionable questions, or make other impermissible comments or arguments in the presence of the judge or jury.

(C) It is unprofessional conduct for a prosecutor to permit any tangible evidence to be displayed in the view of the judge or jury which would tend to prejudice fair consideration by the judge or jury until such time as a good faith tender of such evidence is made.

(D) It is unprofessional conduct to tender tangible evidence in the view of the judge or jury if it would tend to prejudice fair consideration by the judge or jury unless there is a reasonable basis for its admission in evidence. When there is any doubt about the admissibility of such evidence, it should be tendered by an offer of proof and a ruling obtained.

Commentary

a. Presenting inadmissible evidence.
   A prosecutor should exercise great care in deciding what evidence to use; he should avoid jeopardizing a strong case by introducing evidence which is essentially cumulative but which may bring about a reversal. In the period when confessions were generally under attack many cases were reversed because confessions, which were not needed to make a case, had been introduced "to strengthen the case." Not surprisingly, prosecutors, as with all lawyers, sought to make "assurance

doubly sure," even when eyewitnesses
and other evidence made out a strong
case.[114]

The Supreme Court through Chief Justice
Burger in Giglio v. United States [115] addressed
the problem of attributing the act of one member
of the prosecutor's office to the state's case
generally:

> Moreover, whether the nondisclosure
> was a result of negligence or design,
> it is the responsibility of the prosecutor.
> The prosecutor's office is an entity
> and as such it is the spokesman for the
> Government. A promise made by one attorney
> must be attributed, for these purposes,
> to the Government. See Restatement
> (Second) of Agency § 272. See also
> American Bar Association, Project on
> Standards for Criminal Justice, Discovery
> and Procedure Before Trial § 2.1 (d). To
> the extent that this places a burden on
> the large prosecution offices, procedures
> and regulations can be established to
> carry that burden and to insure communi-
> cation of all relevant information on
> each case to every lawyer who deals with
> it.[116]

Dean Freedman notes a collateral problem--
the allegation of manufacture of evidence by
police known or unknown to the prosecutor:

> Another important area of unprofessional
> conduct by prosecutors relates to con-
> doning and covering up police abuses,
> such as brutality, perjury, unlawful
> arrests, unlawful searches and seizures,
> and unlawful interrogation. Again,
> there is a practical difficulty
> at the root of the problem. The prose-
> cutor must maintain a close working
> relationship with the police. The prose-
> cutor's job can be made extremely onerous

162

if there is not willing cooperation
from the police, both in investigating
and in presenting evidence in court.
As a consequence, the prosecutor sometimes is under considerable compulsion
either to present charges against
members of the police department for
unlawful conduct, which impairs cooperation, or to condone or cover up police
crime.

The problem is a serious one. As
stated by Judge Irving Younger (formerly
a prosecutor and now a Professor of Law
at Cornell University): "Every lawyer
who practices in the criminal courts
knows that police perjury is commonplace."
Similarly, Professor Uviller has noted
that prosecutors have become so concerned about police perjury regarding
unlawful searches in narcotics cases,
that the New York County District
Attorney recently joined with defense
counsel in an unsuccessful attempt to
have the New York Court of Appeals shift
the burden of proof to the state when
abandonment by the defendant is asserted
in reply to a motion to suppress contra-
band.[117]

The landmark case of recent years is Miller
v. Pate,[118] in which the court charged that the
prosecutor in a murder case had knowingly
presented underclothing into evidence as blood-
stained when, in fact, the stains were paint
stains. Justice Stewart declared in his opinion
"the prosecutor deliberately misrepresented the
truth."[119] The court proceeded:

More than 30 years ago this Court held
that the Fourteenth Amendment cannot
tolerate a state criminal conviction
obtained by the knowing use of false
evidence. There has been no deviation
from that established principle. There

can be no retreat from that principle here.[120]

As noted earlier, subsequent investigation by the Illinois Bar totally disagreed with the interpretation of facts of this case by the Supreme Court.

(5) Examination of Witnesses

The nature of the adversary system of criminal trial requires that the essence of the case comes to the judge and jury through the examination of witnesses. Examination of witnesses is thus under the scrutiny of the court, and the relationship of the attorney to witnesses--and particularly of a prosecutor--must be above reproach. The professional approach to witnesses is not limited to those witnesses brought to the stand by the prosecutor but of defense witnesses as well. It should be noted that silence of a witness may be as significant as what is said, and the comment by the prosecutor on such silence, especially that of the defendant, is limited.

The ABA Standards provide some help to the prosecutor.

> (B) The prosecutor's belief that the witness is telling the truth does not necessarily preclude appropriate cross-examination in all circumstances, but may affect the method and scope of cross-examination. He should not misuse the power of cross-examination or impeachment to discredit or undermine a witness if he knows the witness is testifying truthfully.

> (C) It is unprofessional conduct for a prosecutor to call a witness who he knows will claim a valid privilege not to testify, for the purpose of impressing upon the jury the fact of the claim

164

of privilege.

(D) It is unprofessional conduct to ask a question which implies the existence of a factual predicate which the examiner cannot support by evidence.

In modern criminal trials, the use of expert witnesses is common, and often the case may become a battle of experts. To protect the integrity of the expert, the ABA Standards provide:

> It is unprofessional conduct for a prosecutor to pay an excessive fee for the purpose of influencing the expert's testimony or to fix the amount of the fee contingent upon the testimony he will give or the result in the case.

Commentary

b. Fees to experts
It is important that the fee paid to an expert not operate as an inducement to influence the character of the expert's testimony. To avoid both the existence and the appearance of influence, the fee should not be made contingent on a favorable opinion or result in the case, and the amount of the fee should be reasonable. See ABA Code DR 7-109 (C) (3).[122]

The whole problem of fees for witnesses is a difficult one and the ABA Standards raise it to an ethical level.

> It is unprofessional conduct to compensate a witness, other than an expert, for giving testimony, but it is not improper to reimburse an ordinary witness for the reasonable expenses of attendance upon court, including transportation and loss of income, provided

165

there is no attempt to conceal the
fact of reimbursement.

Commentary

a. Compensation of witnesses
     Because of the risk of encouraging
perjury, or appearing to do so, witnesses
may not be compensated by parties for
their testimony but may be paid ordinary
witness fees.[123]

     Ethical considerations in examination of
witnesses relate not only to the substance of
the testimony but also to the impressions that
may be given by testimony. In Alcorta v. State
of Texas,[124] the accused was charged with the
murder of his wife and relied on a Texas statute
that treated killing under influence of a
"sudden passion" as murder without malice.
Castilleja, the key eyewitness, in answer to
inquiries by the prosecutor about his relationship with the deceased said he had driven
her home from work and the relationship had been
only a casual one. On direct examination he
denied he was in love with the deceased or had
ever talked of love with her. This was inconsistent with the accused's claim that he had
come upon his wife kissing Castilleja in a parked
car.

     In a subsequent petition for habeas corpus,
Castilleja testified he had in fact been the lover
and paramour of the deceased. This was known to
the prosecutor, who told the witness not to
volunteer any information about intercourse
although if specifically asked to answer truthfully.

     The court concluded:

          It cannot seriously be disputed that
     Castilleja's testimony taken as a whole,
     gave the jury the false impression that
     his relationship with petitioner's wife

166

was nothing more than that of casual
friendship. This testimony was elicited
by the prosecutor who knew of the illicit
intercourse between Castilleja and
petitioner's wife. If Castilleja's
relationship with petitioner's wife had
been truthfully portrayed to the jury,
it would have, apart from impeaching
his credibility, tended to corroborate
petitioner's contention that he had
found his wife embracing Castilleja. If
petitioner's defense had been accepted
by the jury, as it might well have been
if Castilleja had not been allowed to
testify falsely, to the knowledge of the
prosecutor, his offense would have been
reduced to "murder without malice"
precluding the death penalty now imposed
upon him.[125]

Similarly, the courts have indicated that,
as well as direct evidence and false impressions,
the requirement of truth applies to the
credibility of the witness. In Napue v.
Illinois,[126] a key witness falsely testified
that no consideration had been given for his
testimony. Chief Justice Warren wrote:

> The principle that a State may
> not knowingly use false evidence, including
> false testimony, to obtain a tainted
> conviction, implicit in any concept
> of ordered liberty, does not cease to
> apply merely because the false testimony
> goes only to the credibility of the
> witness. The jury's estimate of the
> truthfulness and reliability of a given
> witness may well be determinative of
> guilt or innocence, and it is upon such
> subtle factors as the possible interest
> of the witness in testifying falsely
> that a defendant's life or liberty may
> depend.[127]

167

Conclusion

The role of the prosecutor is not an easy one in an adversary system. The prosecutor must be constantly alert to withstand the "win syndrome" and maintain a concern for justice. Often he is aware of facts that are inadmissible; often he becomes emotionally concerned for the victim; often he is pressured by the media and public to take a stronger stand in law enforcement; often the trials are fraught with emotion. These factors may operate to encourage conviction.

The guidelines discussed above are in many cases quite specific and in other instances vague and of little assistance. Prosecutors of long experience know the rules and when delicate situations arise are quite capable of adjusting and remaining with the Code. The more usual situation in prosecutors' offices is to find lawyers with fewer years of experience on the firing line day after day with little time for determination of the proper ethical action.

The reports continue to be filled with allegations of prosecutorial misconduct. Few reach the heights achieved by the Assistant United States Attorney in United States v. Bourg,[128] in which Justice Gee of the Fifth Circuit described his acts as follows:

> Although we find the evidence sufficient to convict them, the convictions of Bourg, Thibodeaux, Duvigneaud and Glorioso must be reversed and their cases remanded for a new trial. This disposition is necessitated by the trial conduct of the prosecutor--conduct that was at best merely unprofessional and at worst uncontrollable and highly prejudicial to the defense. We would, perhaps, be convinced by the government's argument on appeal that the prosecutor's unnecessary and improper conduct was

168

harmless error if the misconduct were
confined to a few isolated instances
over the course of the seven-day trial.
This is not the case, however, the
record is filled with examples of
behavior inappropriate for an officer
of the court. We could not possibly
detail in this brief opinion all of the
incidents in which the Assistant United
States Attorney overstepped the bounds
of fairness. It is enough to say that
he continually interrupted and cut off
defendants' counsel in their attempts
to object and argue on behalf of their
clients, he disobeyed clear admonitions
from the bench, he ridiculed defense
counsels' objections and implied that their
efforts to protect their clients' rights
were frivolous, he made insulting
remarks to opposing counsel, and he was
arrogant and impertinent in his conduct
toward all other participants in the
trial, including the trial judge. At
one point Judge Mitchell apologized to
Bourg's counsel for the prosecutor's
deportment, saying, "I tried to control
him, but I can't very well do it." The
judge then reprimanded the prosecutor
and said, "I'm astounded sometimes at
some of the things you do." So are
we. . . .

We are unimpressed, in the face of
conduct designed to demean defense
counsel and their legitimate efforts
to present such defenses as they had,
by arguments that the sufficiency of
the evidence cured the misconduct.
We realize that a trial is not a tea
party, and we do not decry zeal, but its
manifestations here far exceeded such
conduct as unprejudicial.[129]

Whatever the experience factor, the courts,
in their proper concern for the rights of the

accused, keep a very careful eye on the prosecutor. Appellate hindsight comes from the
record and the problem is well described in
Donnelly v. DeChristoforo[130] by Justice
Rehnquist:

> Isolated passages of a prosecutor's
> argument, billed in advanced to the jury
> as a matter of opinion not of evidence,
> do not reach the same proportions. Such
> arguments, like all closing arguments
> of counsel,are seldom carefully constructed
> in toto before the event; improvisation
> frequently results in syntax left imper-
> fect and meaning less than crystal clear.
> While these general observations in no
> way justify prosecutorial misconduct,
> they do suggest that a court should not
> lightly infer that a prosecutor intends
> an ambiguous remark to have its most
> damaging meaning or that a jury, sitting
> through lengthy exhortation, will draw
> that meaning from the plethora of less
> damaging interpretations.[131]

Courts seek to curb prosecutorial misconduct
by reprimand, by requiring retrial or at the
extreme, dismissal which appears to punish
society along with the erring prosecutor. Few
have gone as far as Nevada Chief Justice Funderson
threatened in Moser v. State,[132] when he noted
that unprofessional conduct by prosecutors
results in raising appellate issues, sometimes
results in new trials and erodes confidence
in the system. As a solution he declared:

> Accordingly, in cases tried after
> this date, where the trial transcript
> discloses improper argument, I under-
> stand that this court will consider
> referring the offending attorney to
> the local administrative committee for
> determination of an appropriate penalty.
> Where a retrial is necessitated, I
> suggest the penalty might properly

170

include payment of court costs to the
state, and an appropriate assessment to
cover the cost of public or private
defense counsel.

More than a century of admonitions
had failed to engender in all who serve
as prosecutors that instinct for propriety and fairness which their public
duty obviously demands. Manifestly,
another approach is indicated.[133]

Surely such drastic steps should not be
required. In the alternative the prosecutorial
community would be well advised to become
familiar with the guidelines and develop a
strong personal code of conduct. The requirement was recognized in the 1704 Connecticut
statute which provided for appointment of the
first prosecutor in America:

Henceforth there shall be in every
countie a sober, discreet, and religious
person appointed by the countie courts,
to be atturney for the Queen to prosecute
and implead in the lawe all criminals
and to doe all other things necessary or
convenient as an atturney to supproose
vice and immoralitie.[134]

Justice Jackson summed it up when he said
that "the qualities of a good prosecutor are as
illusive and as impossible to define as those
which mark a gentleman. . . . the citizen's
safety lies in the prosecutor who tempers zeal
with human kindness, who seeks truth and not
victims, who serves the law and not factional
purposes, and who approaches his task with
humility."[135]

SOURCES

1. National College of District Attorneys, *Ethical Considerations in Prosecution* (1977).

2. Address by Robert H. Jackson, *The Federal Prosecutor*, to the Second Annual Conference of the United States Attorneys, in Washington, D.C. (1940).

3. E.g., *Berger v. United States*, 295 U.S. 98 (1935).

4. American Bar Association Code of Professional Responsibility and Code of Judicial Conduct (as amended 1978) [hereinafter cited as ABA Code] .

5. American Bar Association Project on Standards for Criminal Justice, Standards Relating to the Prosecution Function and the Defense Function (Approved Draft, 1971) [hereinafter cited as ABA Standards].

6. E.g., Tex. Crim. Proc. Code Ann. art. 2.01 (Vernon).

7. *Berger v. United States*, 295 U.S. 78 (1935).

8. Id. at 88.

9. Tex. Crim. Proc. Code Ann. art 2.01 (Vernon).

10. Quoted in Douglass, *The Ethical Role of the Prosecutor*, Virginia Law Weekly, April 28, 1978, at 3.

11. Judge George Shamswood, *Professional Ethics* (lectures published 1854).

12. ABA Code (1975 edition).

13. National Prosecution Standards, National District Attorneys Association (1977) [hereinafter cited as NDAA Standards].

14. ABA Standard 1.1.

15. NDAA Standards 2.8(a) Relations with the courts and the bar; 2.9 (a)(c) Prompt disposition of criminal charges; 3.1(b)(c)(d)(e) Investigative function of prosecutor; 3.2(a) Relations with prospective witnesses; 3.3(b) Relations with expert witnesses; 3.11(a)(c) Disclosure of evidence by the prosecutor; 4.1(b)(c) Availability for plea discussions; 4.3(a) Fulfillment of plea discussions; 5.2(c) Courtroom decorum; 5.4(a) Relations with jury; 5.5 Opening statement; 5.6 (a)(b)(c)(d) Presentation of evidence; 5.7 (c)(d) Examination of witnesses; 5.8(a)(b) Argument to the jury; 5.9 Facts outside the record.

16. NDAA Standard 25.1.

17. NDAA Standard 25.2(a),(c).

18. NDAA Standard 2.3.

19. Interview with John F. Onion, Presiding Judge, Texas Court of Criminal Appeals (May 5, 1971).

20. Special Committee on Evaluation of Disciplinary Enforcement [Clark Committee], Problems in Disciplinary Enforcement (American Bar Association, 1970).

21. NDAA Standard 1.5.

22. N.Y. Const. art. 13.

23. Cal. Bus. & Prof. Code §6077 (West).

24. Cal. Bus. & Prof. Code § 3060 (West).

25. Cal. Bus. & Prof. Code § 3073 (West).

26. Simpson v. Alabama State Bar, 311 S. 2d 307 (1975).

27. Id. at 308-10.

28. Attorney General v. Tufts, 132 N.E. 322 (Mass. 1921).

29. Id. at 326.

30. People v. Miller, 13 111.2d 84, 148 N.E.2d 455 (1958).

31. Miller v. Pate, 386 U.S. 1 (1967).

32. Statement of the Grievance Committee of the Illinois State Bar Association in the Matter of the Prosecution of the Case of People of the State of Illinois v. Lloyd Eldon Miller, Jr. (May 14, 1968).

33. Id.

34. Id.

35. R. Traver, Anatomy of a Murder (1958).

36. ABA Standard 5.7(b) (Commentary).

37. ABA Code, Canon 9.

38. ABA Code, DR 9-101(B).

39. ABA Standard 1.2.

40. ABA Standard 2.3.

41. NDAA Standard 1.1(c).

42. Id. at 12 (footnotes omitted).

43. President's Commission on Law Enforcement and Administration, Task Force Report on the Courts (1967).

44. Id. at 74.

45. National Advisory Commission on Criminal Justice Standards and Goals, Standard 12.1 (1973).

46. N.Y. County Law § 700 (McKinney).

47. Okla. Stat. § 1557 (Rev. Laws 1910).

48. Aldridge v. Capps, 156 P. 624 (Okla. 1916).

49. Uviller, The Virtuous Prosecutor in Quest of an Ethical Standard: Guidance From the ABA, 71 Mich. L. Rev. 1145, 1161 (1973).

50. ABA Opinion 30 (1931).

51. ABA Standard 1.3.

52. ABA Standards Relating to Fair Trial and Free Press, Standard 1.1 (1968).

53. NDAA Standard 26.3.

54. Freedman, Lawyer's Ethics in an Adversary System (1975).

55. ABA Standard 3.1.

56. NDAA Standards, Chapter 7, p. 108.

57. Id.

58. People v. Green, 274 N.W.2d 448 (Mich. 1979).

59. Id. at 453.

60. ABA Code, DR 7-104(A)(1).

61. ABA Code, DR 7-103(A).

62. NDAA Standard 9.3 and ABA Standard 3.9.

63. Breitel, _Controls in Criminal Law Enforcement_, 27 U. Chi. L. Rev. 427 (1960).

64. Address by Robert H. Jackson, _supra_ note 2.

65. _North Carolina v. Pearce_, 395 U.S. 711 (1969).

66. _Colten v. Kentucky_, 407 U.S. 104 (1972).

67. _Chaffin v. Stynchcombe_, 412 U.S. 17 (1973).

68. _Blackledge v. Perry_, 417 U.S. 21 (1974).

69. Id. at 27.

70. NDAA Standard 14.4(B).

71. _Brady v. Maryland_, 373 U.S. 83 (1963).

72. _Jencks v. United States_, 353 U.S. 657 (1957).

73. _United States v. Agurs_, 427 U.S. 97 (1976).

74. _United States v. Burr_, 8 U.S. (1 Cranch) 470 (1808).

75. ABA Code, DR 7-103(B).

76. ABA Standard 3.11.

77. NDAA Standard 13.1.

78. NDAA Standard 13.4.

79. Id. (Commentary).

80. _United States v. Agurs_, 427 U.S. 97 (1976).

81. _Santobellow v. New York_, 404 U.S. 257,260 (1971).

82. National Advisory Commission on Criminal Justice Standards and Goals, Task Force on Courts (1973).

83. ABA Standard 4.1.

84. ABA Standard 4.2.

85. ABA Standard 4.3.

86. NDAA Standard 16.1.

87. NDAA Standard 16.2.

88. NDAA Standard 16.4 (Footnotes omitted).

89. Complaint of Rook, 556 P.2d 1351 (Ore. 1976).

90. Freedman, Lawyer's Ethics in an Adversary System 88 (1975).

91. Shupe v. Sigler, 230 F. Supp. 601 (D.C. Neb. 1964).

92. Id. at 605-06.

93. Santobello v. New York, 404 U.S. 257 (1971).

94. Brockman v. State, 27 Md. App. 682, 341 A 2d 849 (1975).

95. Id. at 688; 856.

96. Sacher v. United States, 343 U.S. 1 (1952).

97. Id. at 37.

98. ABA Standard 5.4.

99. Manuel v. State, 541 P.2d 233 (Okla. Crim. App. 1975).

100. Id. at 236-37.

101. ABA Standard 5.5.

102. ABA Standard 5.8.

103. ABA Standard 5.9.

104. NDAA Standard 17.5.

105. People v. Hoffman, 399 Ill. 57, 77 N.E.2d 195 (1948).

106. Id. at 65.

107. Volkmor v. United States, 13 F.2d 594 (6th Cir. 1926).

108. Id. at 595.

109. State v. Gonzalez, 105 Ariz. 434, 466 P.2d 388 (1970).

110. Id. at 437.

111. Berry v. Georgia, 10 Ga. 511 (1851).

112. Id. at 523.

113. ABA Code, DR 7-102 (A).

114. ABA Standard 5.6.

115. Giglio v. United States, 405 U.S. 150 (1972).

116. Id. at 154.

117. Freedman, Lawyer's Ethics in an Adversary System (1975).

118. Miller v. Pate, 386 U.S. 1 (1967).

119. Id. at 6.

120. Id. at 7 (citations omitted).

121. ABA Standard 5.7.

122. ABA Standard 3.3.

123. ABA Standard 3.2.

124. Alcorta v. Texas, 355 U.S. 28 (1957).

125. Id. at 31.

126. Napue v. Illinois, 360 U.S. 264 (1959).

127. Id. at 269.

128. United States v. Bourg, 598 F.2d 445 (1979).

129. Id. at 449.

130. Donelly v. DeChristoforo, 416 U.S. 637 (1974).

131. Id. at 646.

132. Moser v. State, 544 P.2d 424 (1975).

133. Id. at 428.

134. Report on Prosecution, Wickersham Commission Reports No. 4, at p.7 (1931).

135. Address by Robert H. Jackson, supra note 2.

John Jay Douglass is Professor of Law at the University of Houston, and Dean of the National College of District Attorneys. The College is jointly sponsored by the National District Attorneys Association, the American Bar Association, the American College of Trial Lawyers and the International Academy of Trial Lawyers. Dean Douglass has also served as Dean of the Army's graduate law school. He received his J.D. from the University of Michigan, and LL.M. from the University of Virginia.

The author wishes to express his appreciation to Michael E. McGown, editorial associate, and Norman Stein, research assistant, for their contributions throughout the preparation of this chapter.

Correctional Ethics: The Janus View

Carolynne H. Stevens

Introduction: In Search of Half a Twist and a Bit of Glue

As children, which of us has not pondered the Mobius strip?

Take a strip of paper, give it half a twist, and glue the ends together. The resulting creation has a strange, undulate beauty of its own. Its fascination lies, however, in its disturbing disruptions of old expectations about familiar plane surfaces. A single, continuous line can now be drawn on both "sides" of the paper. Cutting along its middle, parallel to an edge, does not split it into two rings but creates one ring half the width and twice the diameter. And moving a "right profile" figure along the surface transforms it into a "left profile" figure.

Just half a twist and a bit of glue have wrought a miracle. What were two planes have become one surface. What was separated has now achieved integrity. Inside and outside have become one side, bringing left and right orientations inexorably together. A flowing twisting circle has become something that cannot be split, something that, if splitting is attempted, only grows larger to encompass more area.

The equivalent of half a twist and a bit of glue has eluded the field of corrections throughout its history. As practitioners we remain deeply divided about our goals and our roles. Chasms separate insiders from outsiders, the left from the right. Whatever circles we occasionally form are easily split and rarely large enough to encompass very many ideas at once.

181

We have frantically sought this elusive wholeness, a union with--or at least a respect from--both our clients, the public and the offenders. The search has led us down some twisted paths, but none with the admirable characteristics of the Mobius strip. Consider one such search.

Early in 1979 the documentary, "Scared Straight," was shown on television stations around the nation. Filmed at Rahway Prison in New Jersey, it described an inmate-run program aimed at deterring further criminality in juvenile delinquents. The inmates, all serious offenders with long sentences, attempted to strip the youths of whatever romanticized illusions they were presumed to entertain about crime. Also attacked were any "macho" images the youths held of themselves or of "big time" offenders. Most of all, the inmates tried to show the children the reality of prison existence as they experienced it. Their method was raw confrontation: verbal abuse, threats, steady violations of normal psychological space, and obscenely graphic descriptions of the horrors of imprisonment.

Inmate murders, suicides, rapes, sexual exploitation, individual and gang bullying, and casual violence were presented as daily punctuations in a stultifying routine of boredom, regulation, and social isolation.

The film reported claims of high success for the method. Public and professional reactions were predictably enthusiastic and immediate, spawning many such programs across the country. After all, as one newspaper columnist later expressed it, "Let's suppose they are only ten percent successful. That means they have straightened out more than 1,300 kids of the 13,600 who have gone through their program. AND THEY HAVEN'T COST THE STATE A DAMN DIME FOR DOING THIS. Can the sociologists who have spent

182

hundreds of thousands of dollars on their questionable studies equal this record?"[1] Indeed, the Rahway program seemed to fulfill all the requirements for a perfect panacea--cheap, effective, allying inmates and correctional personnel in a common mission which the public supported.

In a shorter time than is usually the case, however, research and evaluating seriously challenged the efficacy and the safety of the method.[2] By mid-year the newsclippings were less one-sided, and correctional personnel were lining up on both sides of the question. By then more people were commenting on some things that had not appeared in the filmed presentation. In that film, no one had expressed shock, dismay, or outrage about the prison conditions. Inmates, criminal justice personnel, juveniles, and the interviewer had appeared to view these as regrettably normal prison conditions that had suddenly acquired a social value in that they were reputed to scare children out of criminal careers. Moreover, in the first wave of editorials and articles, this aspect of the presentation was only infrequently mentioned. In fact, it was so ignored that one feared that the program's popularity might lead to a demand that prison conditions be made even worse in order to increase their deterrent effect on delinquency.

This initial near-absence of condemnation of these prison conditions, which are not unique to Rahway, underscores the incredible ethical insensitivity that exists in corrections and in society.

The entire "Scared Straight" phenomenon also raises for correctional managers many questions about their ethical responsibilities in the development of treatment programs. Should programs be established or promoted that have not first demonstrated efficacy and safety under reasonable pilot or experimental condition? Is bargain-basement, poor quality treatment better than no treatment at all--or worse than no

183

organized treatment attempt? What clinical supervision should be required to protect participants from potential harm in lay-directed treatment programs? Consider this question in view of the following descriptions of Rahway-type programs:

1.   "Alabama and Louisiana have instituted Rahway-style programs. At Alabama's Kilby and Louisiana's Angola prisons, inmates place heavy emphasis on deglamorizing their lives. Kilby deputy warden James Murphy frequently invites a 19-year-old prisoner who was gang-raped in a county jail. 'Sometimes he can talk about it and sometimes he can't,' Murphy says. 'When he can talk about it, it's real effective.'"[3]

2.   "There were some occurrences during the film at Rahway which could have been instructive with reference to continued operation of the project. For example, one youngster was told by the lifers' (sic) to read a list of offenses for which some of the lifers had been incarcerated. The youngster refused to do so, and as a result was made to stand with his nose against the wall for 20 minutes. What was not made clear was that this youngster had dyslexia and was unable to read-- for which condition he was disgraced in front of the group."[4]

It is the function of all managers, regardless of their fields, to provide the moral and ethical leadership for the firm, to define the contours of its social responsibilities and to hold the firm fast to those responsibilities in every facet of daily practice. More than most, correctional managers must begin to view themselves as working in an ethical mine-field.

Ethical issues begin as questions that have no easy answers, and sometimes no answers at all:

What standards of efficacy and safety should apply in correctional programming?

Does an offender have a right to reject attempts to change behavior, or does society have a right to insist that that the offender submit to such efforts?

What are the rights and dignity to be accorded participants in treatment programs?

Should correctional managers assume responsibility for shaping, even resisting, public policy toward offenders, or is it merely their responsibility to implement public policy?

What special responsibilities should correctional managers assume for the psychological well-being of staff working in what is widely conceded to be an inherently stressful and corrosive environment?

These and hundreds of equally demanding questions should constantly bedevil any serious practitioner in corrections. It is disturbing that such questions seldom surface or, if they do, are frequently dismissed as philosophical niceties that cannot be addressed by harried managers. And what is diverting their attention from ethical considerations? Too many inmates in antiquated facilities that contribute to inmate disturbances, grievances, and suits that take still more time to handle. A frightened and angry public that demands longer sentences, resists community alternatives, and balks at the price tag on the extensive incarceration it

185

demanded. Staff who are often as demoralized,
resentful, and frustrated as the inmates--and
sometimes for the same reasons.

Half a twist and a bit of glue. . . . Is
there an equivalent for corrections? It isn't
that we did not seek such magic. We have probably chased every theoretical rainbow that ever
remotely promised to reveal a panacea: genetic
theories, social justice theories, economic
theories, psychoanalytic theories, learning
theories, biochemical theories, operant conditioning theories. . . . The list is nearly
endless. The results, almost always a bitter
disappointment to their proponents. Seldom was
that disappointment with the theoretical constructs and methodologies any more justified
than was the rampant zeal that hailed their
"discovery." We expected too much. We mis-used
the techniques. We applied the same "solution"
to everyone, irrespective of offenders' individual needs and differences. We put the
techniques in unskilled (also cheaper) hands, in
watered-down versions of programs grafted onto
institutional environments that were patently
unprepared to support any serious treatment effort.
We failed to keep good records or to subject
programs to evaluation. We aborted programs that
needed longer to mature. We clung to programs
that were poor but popular. And too often, we
failed to make any moral judgments about either
our treatment goals or our treatment methods.

Moreover, we failed to address the most
fundamental issue of all: whether corrections is
seriously intended to be a treatment and rehabilitation system as opposed to a system for incapacitation, retribution, and deterrence.
Correctional personnel have long decried the
organizational dysfunction inherent in our
severely conflicted goals and roles. We have
not, however, expended commensurate energy to
develop any altered process tactics to extricate
ourselves and both our clients (offenders and the
public) from the resulting quagmire.

186

Perhaps we have generally avoided any deep examination of these kinds of ethical, philosophical, and political issues because they seemed hopeless to resolve and too painful to confront on any sustained basis. But a callus grown too thick begins to create its own pain. The deep ethical calluses in corrections are now creating their own pressures. Given the magnificent complexity of human behavior and the comparatively humble state of correctional technology, it is neither surprising nor to our particular discredit that we do "fail" with many offenders, although current technology more intelligently applied could undoubtedly yield fewer failures and retrogressions. We must begin to judge ourselves far more harshly, however, on why and how we fail, on our motives, our methods, our processes, our human interactions with both our clients. If we are to use responsibly our present knowledge, and the awesome technology we can already glimpse on the behavioral sciences' horizon of the 21st Century, we must first heal our ethical calluses.

In view of the nature of the problems and choices that correctional practitioners must ever confront, it may be that the only substantial comfort we can offer either the public or the offenders is the assurance that we are committed to examine those choices openly, collaboratively, and in an ethically responsible manner. We have made demands of both our clients, but it is time to reverse the process. Our attention, our moral demands must first be on ourselves. It remains to be tested whether such a new self-consciousness, such a self-imposed requirement for increased ethical sensitivity might constitute our half a twist with a bit of glue, but the remainder of the article will consider that possibility.

187

In Search of Corns and Calluses

The Long War

One of the most striking characteristics of our approach to criminal justice is the extent to which its traditions and conceptualizations are militaristic and adversarial in nature. Although the military model, being very efficient in some respects, is detectable in most large organizations, it is especially prominent in criminal justice. We are predisposed by our history to assume that justice, moral rightness, and combat are normal bedfellows; government traces its orgins to successful warriors who linked their personal success to the favor of the prevailing deity. We are culturally predisposed to accept war as a legitimate means of conflict resolution. Warfare conceptualizations and simulations abound in our everyday language and interactions, casting a win-or-lose expectation on many situations where this is neither a necessary nor a useful outcome. Such militaristic conceptualizations must influence how problems are approached as well as how the ethical demands of various situations are perceived. Peculiar things happen to human ethics and relationships when a state of war exists and survival is perceived as threatened. Truth gives way to propaganda. Reason gives way to force. Open dealings give way to secrecy and spying. Trust vanishes. Cooperative, democratic interactions are curtailed--even among allies. And, most relevant to this discussion, sensitivity to individual needs and differences must give way to a derogation of masses of people lumped into the percept, "enemy." To a certain extent, the same dehumanization of one's allies occurs--their immediate utility to the task of winning or surviving becomes more important than their individual needs and differences. Since the criminal justice system is so heavily imbued with warfare conceptualizations, we might consider how this has affected its professional and ethical development.

188

The effects and characteristics are not the same across the system. The legal profession is deeply imbedded in a trial-by-verbal-combat, adversarial paradigm, but it is generally conceded to be a true profession with a fairly mature system of ethics--a perception not widely accorded to law enforcement and corrections. The legal profession, although not without a share of unethical members, does make a concerted effort to establish and enforce a strong code of ethics.[5] Its wars are also different, consisting of a series of discrete battles in a well-defined role against one clearly defined adversary who is bound by the same strictly enforced rules of combat. In contrast, the wars of police and correctional personnel are continual and less civilized skirmishes against frequently unknown adversaries who are not bound by the same combat rules. Moreover, both police and correctional personnel have more complex and conflicted roles (authority-enforcer, public protector, and helper) while the attorney is much freer to concentrate on client advocacy, whether the client is an individual or the state.

Whereas the attorney has no need to organize except for financial advantage, police and correctional personnel must work in an organized structure. Both selected a heavily paramilitary organization. Why? The immediate assumption might be that this was a very logical model since they are armed and their duties frequently require precise tactical teamwork. But which is cause and which is effect? Are reciprocal or synergistic forces at work? Perhaps police construe themselves as an army because the society chose to construe its offenders as aliens, as public enemies who have transgressed against the people collectively as well as the victim(s) individually. Perhaps some offenders behave differently because they are so regarded, incorporating this sense of alien-ness and enmity once they identify themselves as having committed an offense. Perhaps some citizens become offenders chiefly because they already view themselves as unjustly excluded from full social membership. To what extent have all of us been trapped within the boundaries of the conceptualizations and linguistic associations we use to describe and to structure the inter- actions among citizens who find themselves in a victim-offender relationship? In a guard- prisoner relationship? In an enmity relation- ship? The constraints of the conceptualization may be directing the prescribed and proscribed interactions of our relationships. Is a more useful conceptualization available?

Compare adult corrections, where the para- military structure and traditions are strong, with juvenile corrections where, despite its vestiges of military style discipline, the prevailing structure and terminology are dif- ferent. Even though the children are frequently called "wards," a word rooted in the concept of guarding (cf. warden), the word has assumed a protective connotation (cf. guard and guardian). "Ward" is not reserved in usage to delinquent children and is less denigrating than the adult equivalent, "prisoner." Juvenile corrections personnel, who are seldom uniformed, let alone armed, are usually called supervisors, house- parents, or simply staff, rather than guards, sergeants, captains, correctional officers. They are clearly expected to establish an advisor role with children and to maintain their authority while interacting with the children in a manner that would often be considered dangerous "frater- nization" in an adult correctional facility, i.e., guards are not even to acknowledge "brotherhood" with prisoners but staff are in a quasi-familial relationship with wards.

Although one cannot survey the juvenile correctional scene without being aware of its own serious problems, failures, often excessive authoritarianism, and abuses, neither can one fail to perceive that the gulf between wards and staff is typically neither as wide nor as bitter as

190

that between correctional officers and prisoners.
It is likely that some of this difference is
attributable to society's different conceptualization of its relationship with its juvenile
offenders. Public attitudes toward problem
children and delinquents do cycle, but society
does not conceptualize itself as being at war
with delinquent children in the same way that
it is with adult criminals. Juvenile proceedings
are civil rather than criminal in nature and,
despite the admixture with punishment, disap-
proval, and public protection, the avowed primary
purpose of the juvenile justice system is to
provide treatment and reintegration, not punishment and revenge. This puts a very different
construction on service development and inter-
personal relationships. The argument that the
natural differences between children and adults
(e.g., size, aggressiveness, experience, degree
of threat posed, etc.) fully account for the
difference in societal conceptualization is not
convincing. Most practitioners believe that
only a minority of persons incarcerated in either
system is clearly vicious or dangerous. The
major difference appears to be in the eye of the
beholder. Society is willing to assume that
most children can change, can respond to treatment.
It is also willing to assume that most adult
offenders are implacable enemies for whom
incapacitation is prudent, punishment is
justified, and rehabilitation is a fantasy grudg-
ingly, pessimistically, and ineptly pursued.
However, the fact that the juvenile correctional
system exists in its present form and is, at
worst, no more dysfunctional than the adult
system, proves that there is an alternative to
the warfare approach society has chosen for corrections.

Whether there is yet sufficient motivation
to enter into a different model for societal-
offender relationships is a question that needs
to be tested. Since, later in this article,
we will be considering ways to facilitate a
reconceptualization of societal and correctional

relationships with offenders, it might be appropriate to acknowledge here that warfare
obviously has enough positive reinforcements
to have assured its popularity as a conflict
resolution device throughout history. Among its
more obvious satisfactions are: excitement; the
chance to prove skill and valor and to earn
public esteem; the chance to overcome a personal
or ideological adversary; the opportunity to
prosper in a wartime economy; the avoidance of
ambiguity because sides are made clear and complex issues are reduced to something that can
be "resolved" in combat; and the sense, or at
least the illusion, of moving positively toward
a safer and more defined future condition.
The equivalents of these satisfactions would
have to exist in any serious attempt to put
criminal justice on a peace-time footing.
Robert Sommer suggested that we consider the
uses of "amnesty"[6] as a means to stop a war
nobody is winning, but the first task is to
find our way to a truce table.

By the time people have reached a state of war,
it is virtually impossible to sort out truth
from fiction, or good from evil, or to assess
each other's responsibility for the hostilities.
Humankind is only beginning to realize the full
significance of interdependence on an international scale, or to perceive how decision-
making processes and actions taken by one or
more nations may contribute to a chain of events
that enhances the probability of war elsewhere
on the globe. Such an awareness of chained events
does not justify war any more than an awareness
that many criminals have experienced hardship
and social injustice can justify their criminality. Persons, nations, and yes, even correctional organizations must be held morally
and socially accountable for how they solve their
problems as well as for how they contribute to
them. An awareness of the interconnectedness of
people and the events in their collective past
is useful only to the extent that it is used to
identify options for solving or for preventing

192

relationships with offenders, it might be appropriate to acknowledge here that warfare
obviously has enough positive reinforcements
to have assured its popularity as a conflict
resolution device throughout history. Among its
more obvious satisfactions are: excitement; the
chance to prove skill and valor and to earn
public esteem; the chance to overcome a personal
or ideological adversary; the opportunity to
prosper in a wartime economy; the avoidance of
ambiguity because sides are made clear and complex issues are reduced to something that can
be "resolved" in combat; and the sense, or at
least the illusion, of moving positively toward
a safer and more defined future condition.
The equivalents of these satisfactions would
have to exist in any serious attempt to put
criminal justice on a peace-time footing.
Robert Sommer suggested that we consider the
uses of "amnesty"[6] as a means to stop a war
nobody is winning, but the first task is to
find our way to a truce table.

By the time people reached a state of war,
it is virtually impossible to sort out truth
from fiction, or good from evil, or to assess
each other's responsibility for the hostilities.
Humankind is only beginning to realize the full
significance of interdependence on an international scale, or to perceive how decision-
making processes and actions taken by one or
more nations may contribute to a chain of events
that enhances the probability of war elsewhere
on the globe. Such an awareness of chained events
does not justify war any more than an awareness
that many criminals have experienced hardship
and social injustice can justify their criminality. Persons, nations, and, yes, even correctional organizations must be held morally
and socially accountable for how they solve their
problems as well as for how they contribute to
them. An awareness of the interconnectedness of
people and the events in their collective past
is useful only to the extent that it is used to
identify options for solving or for preventing

problems. Ultimately, combativeness, whether between individuals, between classes, or between nations, is most likely to be rejected as a means of resolving conflict when: an interdependence is recognized; when mutual needs are perceived as more important than conflicting needs; and when these insights force the development of consonant methods of conflict resolution.

No examination of correctional ethics can ignore the extent to which our warfare mind-set has a corrosive effect on the human sensitivity that is required for the development of ethically responsible behavior:

> Does an offender attack the guard to prove valor to his comrads?

> Does a guard turn his head at the critical moment because it is "only the enemy fighting among themselves"?

> Does the offender shun involvement with the treatment process because he fears becoming a "turncoat" whom neither "side" would see as reliable?

To behave in an ethically responsible manner toward another requires: that we be able to identify ourselves as having basic kinship with him; that we respect his rights as much as our own; that we are vigilant in assessing the effects of our behavior on him; and that we care about the other's well-being as a matter of conviction that his well-being is irrevocably connected to our own. Thus, a continuation of the warfare conceptualization of the relationship between offenders, as one of our clients, and their society, as the other of our clients, is clearly inimical to the development of a satisfactory system of professional ethics. It is also inimical to the process of growth for both our clients and ourselves.

Corrections is a profession that never developed, despite some moves in the direction of professionalization. Kruetzer states that a profession evolves from a religious or ethical belief system and commits the professional to serve humanity rather than self or affiliates.[7] Williams and Thomas confirmed a positive relationship between the expression of humanitarian service ideals and the level of professionalization among correctional workers--as well as a corresponding slight negative relationship between self-gain motivations and professionalism.[8] Logically, the warfare conceptualization would inhibit the development of a broad ethical or humanitarian commitment since war inherently serves self and affiliates in opposition to the welfare of others. Lentini lists the characteristics of a profession as: "(1) a recognized body of knowledge for which an institution of higher learning will award a degree, (2) high standardized entrance qualifications throughout the profession, (3) minimum levels of acceptable professional practice, (4) a code of ethics enforced by: (5) a national governing body, (6) members are licensed to practice, (7) mobility, (8) public recognition."[9] Clearly, neither correctional nor police personnel can qualify as professionals by these criteria, although the criteria do suggest a casual chain between the warfare conceptualization and the severe problems we experience in clarifying our goals and ethical responsibilities.

The normal developmental course of professionalism begins with that general ethical-humanitarian orientation which gives rise to a sense of duty expressed in the context of a special body of knowledge and applied skills--a discipline. A profession emerges as that knowledge becomes more complex and requires increasingly formalized transmission. The profession assumes responsibility for focusing the duty into prescribed and proscribed practices.

It also assumes responsibility for giving specificity to the overall ethical orientation within the practice of the discipline--that is, it develops and enforces a professional code of ethics.

Corrections, however, took a detour through the land mines of the war zone. The general humanitarian orientation of the legal profession, from which corrections emerged as a subsidiary function, might be expressed as the desire to assure equal justice for all men before the law and to protect individual rights from the power of the state--an obviously unfulfilled ideal since prisoners are hardly representative of lawbreakers in general. Correctional purposes became entangled, however, in the punitive, warfare conceptualization that separated the interests of society at large from the interests of the offender, i.e., corrections became the instrument of a philosophy that devalued some people in comparison to other people. At that juncture, any general ethical integrity or general commitment to humanity became unattainable. Later efforts to re-inject a broadly humanitarian mission--to include treatment and rehabilitation goals aimed at restoring the offender to his society in an acceptable condition--failed primarily because these programs were erected over what was still an ethically flawed philosophy that resisted change. The result was a stalemate that fixated the correctional field in a state of hopelessly conflicting goals and strategies.

Without an ethical and humanitarian imperative, and further handicapped by conflicted purposes that prevented the development of any coherent body of knowledge, the development of true professionalism was doomed. Public respect, which is accorded true professions, was not only withheld but grew closer to public animosity. The contempt stemmed from the fact that corrections pleased neither the punishment adherents nor the treatment adherents. Our response to that disfavor with the several segments of the public who insist on antithetical goals and strategies has only made matters worse. If a man has promised each of many creditors to devote half his income to repayment, he generally tries to avoid them--and goes to even greater lengths to assure that they do not meet to compare notes! Likewise, in its efforts to appease its divided publics, corrections has made foolish, conflicting promises, these have led to furtive, reclusive behavior as we tend to keep the public at arm's length so its factions will not see our deceptions, our failures, our shufflings between irreconcilable goals. Ethical behavior does not develop in dark places, in restricted places where others are not available to help one to see how he affects the life of another. Professionalism is not built on deceptions of self and others, no matter how much others may want to hear reassuring fantasies, simplistic "solutions," or other untruths. And the public cannot re-evaluate its criminal justice policies as long as we cooperate to prevent a direct public confrontation with all of the effects of the current policy confusion.

There is more evidence that there is no correctional profession. There is no generic term for us, one that umbrellas our practice and sub-specialties in the same way that lawyer, teacher, doctor describe the generic practice of those professions. Corrections is still an uneasy alliance of people who came from many occupations, professions, and educational backgrounds and who try to maintain that professional identification while they work in correctional settings. Not surprisingly, such disparate groups assembled into an already goal-conflicted setting rarely cohere into an effective team. Nassi points out that prison psychiatrists and psychologists, entering with a well-defined treatment orientation and clear ethical obligations, adapt in one of four ways: permitting the use of their skills in the service of punitive and/or custodial objectives; accepting the futility of

197

the situation and retreating into perfunctory service; quitting; or confrontive resistance.[10] Non-professionals who enter corrections either in security or support service occupations often have no philosophical base from which to perceive underlying issues in staff conflict, predisposing them to attribute clashes with treatment staff to the latters' orneriness. Line staff are also typically given little training or supervision concerning the ethical decision-making requirements of their roles.

The problems created by our lack of professional status go beyond contributing to staff discord within institutional settings. Certainly we are rarely regarded as an esteemed partner by the rest of the criminal justice system. Even worse, we are seen as something of a pariah by most of the helping professions who appear to assume that we must be louts and brutes to tolerate conditions in the correctional field. More than wounded pride is at stake in our need to be regarded as professional equals by our peers. Corrections cannot secure specialized services for offenders, nor plan effective community-based alternatives until it can establish a professional relationship with allied agencies, a relationship in which our objectives and our judgments are not automatically discounted as incompetent or self-serving. The other helping professions, if they saw us as respectable partners and if they could be persuaded to assume their share of responsibility for offenders as a multi-faceted client group, might become powerful allies in the critical task of advocating public reconsideration of correctional policies.

Our detour has led us to a Tower of Babel where we cannot communicate effectively with either of our clients, where we cannot share the difficult pilgrimage of others who would serve mankind, and where we cannot even make sense of what we say to each other. To extricate ourselves from our predicaments we must seek another environment, an open environment where rational communi-

cation and problem solving can take place,
where professional and ethical maturation can
be facilitated, and where we can see a common
purpose that will permit our fragmented members
to be welded into the strength of their rich
diversity.

Pathfinding

The Games Dilemmas Play

How can we find our way out of the conceptual minefields and philosophical wilderness?
We have followed correctional rainbows, trying
(however well or poorly) every intervention any
theoretical construct could suggest. We have
leapt confidently into massive implementations
of bold new ideas. The penitentiary model and
the concepts of probation and parole were once
that new and promising. More recently, combined
War on Poverty and Safe Streets funding were
hailed as a sure solution. Still we have not
solved the problem of crime--and all our solutions
have brought their own problems. Chief among
those solution-derived problems in a growing,
cynical despair of finding any answers. In
truth, there may not be any good answers for
crime. Certainly, there will be no simple
answers to a multivariate problem that may have
causal links to some deeply cherished social
values.

What to do with the offender, singly or in
the aggregate, is always a moral dilemma, a
question with no clear, right-or-wrong answer.
The human reaction to a moral dilemma is usually
either to beg the question, where that is possible,
or to try to force-fit the question into some
established, pre-arranged, pre-judged value
system that will permit a quicker, less painful
decision. For example, it is much easier to
adopt the simplified position that all murder
should be punished by death or by long imprisonment. Such a response suppresses such elements

of the moral dilemma as:

> Is the taking of life inherently wrong,
> or is it acceptable for the state?
> Is long incarceration more humane
> than capital punishment or is it
> more akin to a death sentence of
> the human spirit?

> Are some murders more justifiable than
> others and therefore deserving of
> lesser punishment?

> What happens to the cherished principles
> of fairness, equal justice, and rule-
> by-law when such individual differ-
> ences and circumstances are taken in-
> to account?

> What happens to the equally cherished
> principles of proportionality, of
> tempering justice with mercy, and
> of respecting individual differ-
> ences when these different circum-
> stances are not taken into account?

> Do our sentencing policies and practices
> deter or breed violence? How could
> we study all their effects?

The worst result of avoiding moral dilemmas
through simplistic, prejudged responses is not
that it turns us into moral cowards who buy our
peace of mind by suppressing the other sides of
the question. The most insidious result is that
this inevitably leads to the suppression of, or
selective inattention to, research or observation
that might have answered those unasked questions.
When we are busy avoiding a moral dilemma we are
necessarily busy fending off any facts or
experiences that might undermine our tidy, pre-
packaged solutions or re-introduce the terrible
questions we are trying to escape. Moral cowardice leads to intellectual cowardice.

This is essentially the desperate game that we have been playing in our society. The public at large does not want to face the pain and anguish of the moral dilemmas posed by crime and corrections any more than do those of us in the field. But it is when we refuse to feel that pain and to struggle knowingly with those terrible questions that we become ethically calloused and, eventually, ideologically stagnant. If there are any better solutions, we will find them only through experiencing our dilemmas, not through a stiff numbness to everything that is around us. Likewise, we must insist that the public know and share our ethical burdens, our pain, and that of the offenders.

The Process Proposition

Traditionally, we have approached corrections as if it were like any other business-with attainable goals. This is not a tenable approach. Unlike other businesses, our goals are, at best, conflicted and, at worst, unattainable. We have no assurance that there is any "cure" for crime. At least, we have no assurance that we can eradicate crime without resorting to currently insupportable revisions in our social values and structures. Corrections may be more akin to a pure research operation than to a functioning business. Perhaps we should pattern ourselves after the early chemists and physicists whose successes in discovering knowledge depends on scrupulous adherence to the scientific methods of observation and experimentation. For them, the outcomes were so unknown that only the integrity of their processes allowed them to develop a true profession that, in time, contributed something of value.

Perhaps we, too, are at a place where we can develop professionally and contribute something of value only if we forsake the illusion of seeking ends in favor of paying strict attention

201

to the means. Just as the early physical
scientists had to develop their research methods,
so will we have to define our search processes.
Because we are human beings trying to effect a
reconciliation of other human beings among themselves, we must develop a process that is as
insistent on ethical sensitivity as is the
scientific method insistent on intellectual
honesty and objective accuracy. Our clients are
at war with each other, and with us. If we are
to act as peacemakers, there must be no question
of our integrity.

There is no guarantee that by shifting our
primary objective from searching for a solution
in favor of developing an ethical search process
we will ever "solve" the problem of crime. On
the other hand, it is reasonable to suppose that
insistence on ethical process may actually
improve system performance, at least with certain
groups of offenders. For example, modeling
theory, which has its roots in the process of
incorporation-identification emphasized in
analytically oriented theories, suggests that the
effectiveness of the change agent is improved
by overt display of the desired behaviors. The
work of Yochelson and Samenow[11] is directly
based on the theory that established criminal
thinking patterns must be surfaced and re-
trained. However, one is struck by what appears
to have been a very nearly obsessive quality of
the ethical modeling that the therapists presented and then taught the offenders to use in
a technique they termed "moral inventory."
Apparently, being in contact with a human being
of unmistakable ethical and moral integrity is,
in itself, a powerful emotional experience even
for, perhaps especially for, the habitual criminal. But, then, leading by example is not
really a new concept.

Premises

If we determine to undertake an objective of ethical means, ethical pathfinding, we should consider certain logically derived beliefs and premises that may suggest a few of the problems we should plan to address along the way. The first premise is that if our search process becomes more ethically sensitive, we are likely to consider more options. At least, process insensitivity appears to account for the fact that some of our ends-oriented solutions have done more harm than good. This implies that we must prepare ourselves and the public to accept or reject ideas on rational rather than emotional or political grounds.

Another premise is that our ethical sensitivity cannot increase until we improve the amount and diversity of viewpoints available to examine correctional decision-making. It is the current nature of corrections to wield enormous power over the daily lives of offenders and to do so without immediate benefit of other judgments. We cannot defend a continuation of this practice when we know the moral corruption and abuses that unwatched power breeds. We have been disgraced repeatedly in courts when customary correctional practices were adjudged unfair, abusive, illegal. Could we devise citizen participation processes that would not only spare us some of the expense and professional humiliation of those court scenes but also spare offenders the additional damage or embitterment that such abuses of power inflict? Would effective involvement of citizens, including offender family representatives, in ethical oversight functions help to demonstrate to more offenders that society and correctional staff do respect their personhood, do respect the same laws and principles that the offenders were punished for violating? It is for us to decide whether we honor these principles because the offender "deserves" it, or because otherwise we, ourselves, are lost. Perhaps both are true.

The second premise leads logically to the third: we can no longer tolerate, let alone tacitly encourage, public alienation from the operational and policy formulation burdens and dilemmas of corrections. Corrections is the public's business even more than it is ours. Some of corrections' failures have their roots in public neglect and projection of blame onto the correctional system when, in fact, the system could not possibly fulfill conflicting, irrational, and unsystematized objectives. Some corollary beliefs are that: (1) the public will not necessarily welcome this degree of involvement because we will not bring them tidy, comfortable problems; (2) correctional personnel must be willing to face their ethical issues both before and after they seek a new partnership with the public; (3) the public is capable of constructive involvement in the search for ethically responsible and reasonably effective solutions provided it is given good information, intelligent technical assistance, and the time and support to assimilate these.

Another premise is that the present political process as applied to corrections is not a satisfactory means of achieving a broad-based, ownership-level sense of public responsibility for its correctional system. Most correctional systems do, of course, have one or more mechanisms for submitting correctional action plans to citizens boards or councils before these are submitted to the legislature for funding. Such plans may even have been generated with advice from non-agency people. Most correctional planning processes, however, pay scant attention to the philosophies and values underlying the action alternatives, and pay inadequate attention to the reciprocal effects of ideologically conflicted policies or practices. The political action process as usually practiced does not provide a proper vehicle to assure that

the ideological differences in our society
with respect to the proper goals of corrections
are fully surfaced and seriously debated by
society or by policy planning and decision-making
authorities. As a consequence, most plans and
code revisions tend to become a new configuration
of hodge-podge, designed to include enough of
everything to pacify all philosophical factions.
Sadly, most "debate" and opinion formulation
about corrections, and far too many decisions
that impact corrections, are made on the basis
of rhetoric, simplistic sloganeering, and appeals
to non-rational thought. ("Lock them all up."
"Tear down the prisons." "Don't forget the
victims." "Offenders are political prisoners,
oppressed minorities.") We must find ways to
immunize more people against such shallow non-
sense. We must find new processes to assure a
complex, emotion-laden subject the careful and,
above all, sustained thought it demands. We must
seek a public partnership process that will
eventually culminate in the enunciation of whatever societal values, beliefs, and philosophy
corrections is expected to use to guide the
development of services.

While this degree of involvement is years
away even under the most favorable conditions and
the most aggressive efforts, clarification of
public philosophy is the prerequisite for
resolving the issue of conflicting correctional
mandates. Only when the public assumes the
ownership-partnership role will it realize that
the system cannot address punishment, rehabilitation, and deterrence all at once with all
offenders. Society would then have to decide
whether it wants to retain all of the currently
attempted goals or not. If all were retained,
then the choice would be whether all apply to all
offenders, or some apply to some offenders, until
the basis for rational sentencing and classification could be determined. Other options could
be identified--such as retaining the conflicted
goals but segmenting and sequencing them in such

a way that offenders and correctional personnel alike would always know what the programs were expected to achieve at any given time. Merely to arrive at a clearly segmented approach to the conflict might have a beneficial effect on program development, ethical integrity, and offender morale. The point, however, is that real problem-solving will not occur until there is (1) a more widespread recognition of the issues; (2) a more broadly accepted or shared definition of the problem(s) in more operationally useful conceptualizations; and (3) a base of support to work forward toward acceptable solutions on a sustained basis. Thus, seeking out more effective public involvement processes is a necessary step for improving either our ethical performance or our professional effectiveness.

A final premise here is that corrections has a responsibility to take a leadership role to facilitate public reconsideration of its role, both with respect to offenders and in relationship to the formal correctional system. Correctional systems vary in the extent to which they are politically and administratively free to engage in direct public education and outreach. (Correctional public outreach has too often degenerated into self-serving lobbying or side-taking, thereby bringing on such controls.) Most systems do, however, have some degree of freedom to seek public help and support. The view taken here is that correctional managers have the duty to try to engage the public and the equal duty to do so responsibly. They have special knowledge and vantage points that must be used to establish and maintain a public involvement process.

The Pathfinder Style of Management

The immediate problem is that correctional administrators, managers, and planners have no established technology or experience to use as a

comprehensive model for creating effective
public involvement processes. So . . . what
would any good pathfinder do in such a situation?
First of all, he would not be particularly dis-
turbed that he had no "model." Pathfinders,
being explorers, expect to depend on their ability
to improvise passages with enough creativity
and judgment to survive, and to enable others to
survive, in a wilderness. Pathfinders always
study the terrain, and they study their traveling
companions so as to tailor the passage to their
weaknesses. Two pathfinders would not necessarily take the same route even though they might
eventually arrive at approximately the same
place. Similarly, correctional pathfinders must
expect to design public involvement processes
that are uniquely attuned to their own situations,
to set a pace that is reasonable for their companions, to take advantage of the skills and
contributions those companions have to offer on
the journey.

Any good pathfinder packs only what is
necessary--and does not encumber himself with
garments and equipment that serve no current
purpose. Even if he is a military pathfinder, he
does not travel in full-dress uniform, for
example! Likewise, the correctional pathfinder
may need to weigh the usefulness of his
paramilitary organizational structure, modifying
it to meet changing needs. For example, that
structure is best suited for conditions wherein
large numbers of people must work together on a
clear function or mission without benefit of
many other social or ideological ties. Its
strength becomes its weakness under different
conditions, however, in that it also inhibits the
development of additional social or ideological
ties within the group. It tends to "listen"
according to rank, not according to the merits
of what is said. It tends to discourage the
questioning of established goals or methods. It
tends to limit participation in problem-solving.
The correctional pathfinder must consider whether

207

his organizational traditions and prevailing management style are appropriate for what is essentially a research firm in search of its own morality and in search of public partnership.

Most of all, any good explorer observes for signs, noting where other explorers, even wild-life, succeeded or failed in their passages. Therefore, the most important thing a correc-tional pathfinder can do is to study history, beginning with the earliest roots of the community and the mechanisms conceptualized for effecting social change. Closer to our own time, a great deal has been learned from the successes and failures in the social engineering, community development, and race-relations work emphasized in the Sixties. We have also learned some things about culture analysis, group dynamics, and group behavior, as well as about the processes that facilitate a linking of cognitive and affective learning, values clarification strategies, and conflict resolution within and among groups. The field of management, which in the past twenty years has given considerable attention to welding the processes of scientific planning and problem resolution to the science of unleashing human creativity, has much to offer the conceptualization of a public partici-pation process. The fields of marketing, communications, and adult education will prove rich resources of theory and strategy for public involvement tasks. The growing literature in the developmental aspects of problem-solving, sociali-zation, and moral reasoning can help us to forge realistic differential strategies for reaching people who have distinctly different world-views.

In short, although the correctional path-finder will not have a roadmap across his wilder-ness, he does have relevant technology, experi-ences and conceptualizations available to be combined in new ways for his unique journey. These can help him to conceptualize his problems more usefully, as well as suggest fairly specific

208

strategies to consider for particular inter-
actional situations.

The correctional pathfinders must be responsible for choosing, from among unlimited possibilities, the courses they will set to educate
the public, to stimulate concern, to cause moral
re-examination--to bring the public into corrections. These pathfinders must choose the
timing and the rhythms of change. They must
decide how to select the most talented and committed persons and groups for the most difficult
tasks--and how to incorporate people whose contributions may be more mundane but nonetheless
critical to the overall task.

They will need to find ways to help staff,
offenders, and public to find a common language
so that each can describe the landscape that
he alone can see. Offenders have a private
language. The public often speaks in cliches.
And staff have built such a wall of jargon that
a psychoanalytically-trained psychologist can
barely talk to a behaviorally-oriented psycho-
logist--and neither may make much sense to
offenders or the public. Actually, all theoretical constructs are attempting to describe
essentially the same things, or different aspects
of those things; they only use different terminology, different metaphors in describing or in
ascribing causality. We might do ourselves an
enormous favor if we simply agreed to promote
one of these "languages" as a sort of conceptual
esperanto that we could use when communicating
technical material to those not trained in the
originating professional language. One such
esperanto candidate might be economics theory,
which views criminal behavior in terms of the
pecuniary and non-pecuniary (psychic) costs and
benefits of the criminal activity.[12] This
particular metaphor may sound less grand and
"professional" than some of the arcane terminology
we have invented, but money concepts are familiar
and might serve well our need to make correctional

theory and research findings more comprehensible to the general public. This terminology might also provide some interim relief to staff, lending a wider conceptual umbrella to reduce the ideological conflict among them. For example, the writer was previously employed in a correctional agency that spans from primary delinquency prevention staff to maximum security staff guarding inmates who are under death sentence. Economics theory terminology would not alter the fact that the former operate from a prevention and reintegration mandate while the latter operate from a retribution mandate. It would, however, make more comprehensible the fact that they are under the same organizational roof, with one working on benefit strategies and the other on cost strategies. More important, it would give them a common tongue, some potential to talk to each other more supportively about their vastly different roles and ethical choices. But whether or not the pathfinders find or create a correctional esperanto, it is important for them to select terminology that is as free as possible from destructive linguistic associations and that is less conceptually confining than some of our present terminology.

Whether our correctional pathfinders can lead us to some utopian destination is far from assured. All that is clear is that we do have some choices about whether the journey itself shall become a more ethical process and a more intellectually honest process. That journey will be filled with its own hazards, pains, problems. But our new pains and problems should, at least, be healthier pains and problems than those we now endure and inflict. It will be a journey into a mutual education process. Who can say that this mutual education might not prove to be the end as well as the means to the art and science of corrections? We can only hope that corrections has grown too wise to seek rainbows for their illusions of gold. We can also hope that it has grown wise enough to seek rainbows because they

evoke a sense of awe about the universe and
why we are in it.

Glimpses on the Horizon

The human species is struggling to end its
terrible infancy and darker adolescence. If we
survive these, an outcome still in considerable
doubt, a galaxy beckons us into new environments
where we shall establish our kind amidst new
challenges. What shall we have learned in our
earthly cradle that is worthy to spread among
the stars? The answer to that question will
greatly depend on what we do in the behavioral
sciences in the next fifty years.

In the last twenty-five years we have seen
a near-explosion in the development of behavioral
sciences technology: behavioral and cognitive
behavioral therapies, reality therapies, community mental health models, communication
therapies, family therapies, an extensive phar-
macopoeia of psychoactive drugs, the demysti-
fication of hypnosis, some strides in unraveling
the impact of physiological and biochemical
states on behavior. . . . All this, and more,
has come on the scene in that time. A burgeoning
computer technology is making the tasks of
learning, of solving problems, and of understanding ourselves through research a little easier.
It is also rapidly moving us toward a time when
we may have bio-interactive computer technology
that would expand the human mental capacity
beyond what we can now imagine. Bio-genetic
engineering may emerge to give us the power to
un-handicap some of our mentally and physically
handicapped members--or to create a new mutation
against which all of us now would seem handicapped.

We have not seen commensurate development of
the wisdom to use our current technology, let
alone the vast new technology we expect. All
knowledge carries new problems and new opportunities to use it for base purposes. Consider

the abuses of drugs, operant conditioning techniques, and psychosurgery that have occured in both prisons and mental institutions. Consider the ethical crises that the medical profession experienced when limited dialysis equipment forced it to choose which patients might live. Other life-prolongation techniques have caused the medical profession to re-define death and to wrestle with the ethical and legal questions of whether and when to assign or to remove a patient from such equipment. One response of the medical community has been to try to educate its members to the existence and demands of these new ethical dilemmas. Another response has been to reach out to the community, as well as to those with special training in ethical decision-making, establishing a process to involve such persons in the hard ethical choices technology forced on the profession.

There are "incorrigible," dangerous prisoners in our institutions who, even with present technology, might be made safe to release if we were free to use all that we know about behavioral alteration. But who shall identify these people? And should society ever unleash techniques that have such potential to degenerate into sadism or into abuse for political purposes? Or, on the other hand, is it more unethical to withhold that technology, dooming the offender instead to years of dehumanizing confinement while also running the risk that he will hurt or kill others?

These are the kinds of ethical dilemmas that are already commonplace, though generally ignored, in corrections. They go to the very heart of our foundations of government. It is imperative that our society, our lawmakers, and correctional practitioners begin to establish more effective forums that can continually address the problem of defining the rights of the individual as these conflict with the rights of society. The criminal justice system is intended to protect the fragile

institution of a free society by means of the
exercise of enormous power over citizens. An
extraordinary means of overseeing the ethical
use of that power is absolutely essential if
the avowed ideals of the society are to survive.
Our exploding technology will soon demand that we
become either more human or less human. That
choice--if we reach for our humanity--may prove
to be our Mobius strip, and, if we should reach
also to the stars, our legacy to them.

NOTES

1. K. Carolan. Above and to the Right: Pseudo
    Research. The Trentonian, Trenton, New
    Jersey, May 16, 1979.

2. J. Finckenauer. Juvenile Awareness Project:
    Evaluation Report No. 2. Rutgers Univer-
    sity, April 18, 1979.

3. Justice: Does Scaring Work? Newsweek.
    May 14, 1979.

4. G. Miller and H. Hoelter. Testimony Before
    the House Subcommittee on Human Resources,
    June 4, 1979. Available from: National
    Center on Institutions and Alternatives,
    1337 22nd St., N.W., Washington, D.C.,
    20037.

5. American Bar Association Code of Professional
    Responsibility with Amendments to Febru-
    ary 17, 1976. Black's Law Dictionary,
    Revised 4th ed., 17th printing, 1977.
    St. Paul, Minn: West Publishing Co., 1968,
    LVII-LXX.

6. R. Sommer. The End of Imprisonment. New York:
    Oxford University Press, 1976, 188-195.

7. W. Kreutzer. The Elusive Professionalization
    That Police Officers Seek. The Police
    Chief. August, 1968, 26-31.

8. J.S. Williams and C.W. Thomas. Attitudinal Correlates of Professionalism: The Correctional Worker. Criminal Justice Review, 120-125.

9. J. Lentini. Police Professionalism: A Plan for the Future. Law and Order, May 1973, 46-51.

10. A Nassi. Therapy of the Absurd: A Study of Punishment and Treatment in California Prisons and the Roles of Psychiatrists and Psychologists. Corrective and Social Psychiatry and Journal of Behavior Technology Methods and Therapy. Vol. 21, No. 4, Oct. 1975, 21-27.

11. S. Yochelson and S. Samenow. The Criminal Personality, Vol. II: The Change Process. New York: Jason Aronson, 1977.

12. J. Palmer. Economic Analyses of the Deterrent Effect of Punishment: A Review. Journal of Research in Crime and Delinquency, Jan. 1977.

Carolynne H Stevens graduated from Meredith College in Raleigh, North Carolina in 1957 and, in 1960, received a master's degree in psychology from East Carolina University. From 1957-1961 she was a teacher and later a principal in educational programs for institutionalized mentally retarded students in North Carolina and Tennessee.

In 1961 she entered the field of juvenile corrections in Virginia, serving as a staff psychologist until 1966 when she assumed directorship of the clinical program. From 1968-1978 she was an Assistant Director of the Division of Youth Services and administered a cluster of technical support services that included clinical

214

programs, reception and placement operations, delinquency prevention services, and staff development programs. For the next two years she was in the central offices of the Virginia Department of Corrections, engaged in system-wide planning in the areas of personnel management, service development for special offenders, and design of clinical support services for community-based operations.

In 1980 she joined the Virginia Department of Welfare where she is Director, Division of Licensing, the regulatory agency responsible for licensure of residential and day care services for children and aged, infirm, or disabled adults. This office will shortly encompass, as well, multiagency certification of public and private residential facilities for children, returning her to some involvement with juvenile correctional facilities in Virginia.

Mrs. Stevens resides in Richmond with her husband and their two school-age children.

The Questions of Ethics in Prison
Systems in America

David B. Miller Ph.D.
Mostafa M. Noury Ph.D.
Joseph J. Tobia

Letter to the Editor:
    Why should we find it so strange that
General Grijorenko (June 4) was considered insane
by Soviet psychiatrists? Every society sets its
own standards for "normalcy" and anyone who
deviates is sick. It happens in the U.S. all the
time, and no one is alarmed. In Iran, the
Ayatollah Khomeini is presently quite sane as he
orders political murder in the name of justice.
Sanity is relative.

                                    Wm. E. Wilson
                                    East Peoria, Ill.
                                    Time Magazine
                                    June 25, 1979

Americana

Wear It in Good Health
    The policeman's softball team in Jacksonville
is raising money to play in a tournament in New
Orleans by selling for $5 each, pastel T-shirts
decorated with a drawing of "old sparky," the
Florida electric chair, and bearing the legend
1 Down, 133 To Go. The reference is to the
recent execution of John Spenkelink and the 133
people left on death row in Florida. So far,
2,500 T-shirts have been sold and orders -
including some from lawyers and judges - have
come in from all 50 states and from as far away
as Australia.

                                    Time Magazine
                                    July 25, 1979

217

Introduction

In 1764 Cesare Beccaria wrote, <u>Dei delitti e delle pene</u>, a treatise which has had lasting influence on criminal reform in countries throughout the world. Becarria's major contention was that the arbitrariness and whimsicality of punishment must be removed from penal codes. Punishment should be made to fit the crime. He believed the basic principle that should guide legislation and indeed form its backbone is the greatest happiness to be shared by the greatest number of people, an idea in which he and several of his contemporaries, especially Jeremy Bentham, agreed.

Bentham elaborated the idea, now recognized as utilitarianism or the Principle of Utility, in his famous work, <u>Introduction to Principles of Morals, Legislation</u>.

Beccaria's most important contribution to posterity is that of making the law impartial. REID:110 All men should be equal under the law. When pain to the wrongdoer exceeds the pleasure he got out of committing the wrong the ends of justice would be served-- the offender would be deterred by his punishment and the rest of society's members would be deterred by the example of his punishment-- "crime doesn't pay."

Bentham's stated objectives of punishment were in every way in agreement with Beccaria's: 1) to prevent all offenses, 2) to prevent the worst offenses, 3) to keep down mischief, 4) to act at the least expense. Both Bentham and Beccaria did not believe that victimless crimes should be punished nor should vengeance be sought against the criminal. GEIS: 54

Because of Beccaria, Bentham and other profound thinkers of the 18th century, the arbitrary powers of judges were replaced by a firm and inflexible system of penalties. Understandably,

218

however, in the 19th century (the century in which most social sciences were ushered in) a reaction to rigid penalties occurred. REID:59 The reaction was due to a severe and all-encompassing code that did not allow for extenuating circumstances --such as physical, mental or environmental factors, nor mitigating ones --such as nonage and mental illnesses.

The philosophical provisions leading to the mitigating and extenuating circumstances in legal thought can be traced to the "moralization" of the sentiment of justice in the writings of John Stuart Mill, a follower of Bentham. While Mill retained and developed Bentham's principle of utility --the greatest good of the greatest number --he flexed Bentham's doctrinaire utilitarianism into a more intellectual and communal relativism through the investigation of the relations of justice, utility, individual and community interests.

Mill's perception of the complex relation between justice and utility allowed for extenuating circumstances which made Bentham's prevailing, psychological determinism relative and flexible. Mill attempted resolution between justice and utility, individual and collective interests through an application of individual discretion in the feelings of "right" in the individual. These feelings-- "the sentiment of justice" were "moralized" into a larger, communal interest, evanescing from a righteous "degree" of individual utility to a righteous "kind" of justice for all. According to Mill's perceptive and brilliant stroke, "the difference in degree became a real difference in kind." GOROVITZ:42-57 While maintaining its characteristic "calculus of pleasure," utilitarianism was transformed from an egoistic, psychological hedonism under Bentham into an ethical, altruistic hedonism under Mill.

Positivist, or realist legal theories

consider law as necessarily determined by the
subject matter, the content, the empirical.
Metaphysical, or idealist, legal theories deduce
the law from first principles based on an ethical
and rational being. Mill saw that Bentham, as
a positivist, derided the abstract concept of
justice per se, where maximizing individual
utility would indirectly achieve justice.
Accordingly, Bentham failed to reconcile individual and collective interests, focusing instead
on the positivist nature of law as a means of protection for individual freedom and initiative
in the pursuit of property and enterprise, sub-
sistence, abundance and security.

Although it was Mill who had intellectualized
the ethical "sentiment" for these reforms,
Rudolph Von Ihering clearly established the
sociological base for them. Ihering, to whom
Friedman accords singularity when he identifies
him as "the father of modern sociological
jurisprudence," insisted that the content of the
law must be infinitely various and must adapt its
regulations to the varying conditions of people,
according to the degree of civilization and the
needs of the time:

> The idea that law must always be the
> same is no whit better than that medi-
> cal treatment should be the same for
> all people. FRIEDMAN:324

Consequently, exceptions to the law were
legislated which modified responsibility and
lessened punitive severity. A concomitant
development was the admission of expert testimony
to help in determining one's responsibility
before the law. The net effect was that jurors
were given some discretion in determining the
question of guilt or innocence and maximum and
minumum sentences were introduced. VOLD:25

Today the paramount argument used in the
Western world for punishing law violators is that

of attempting to correct their wayward behavior. In effect, punishment normally implies treatment, giving some justification to the use of the terms "correction programs" and "correction systems."

Correction systems take many forms ranging from foster or group homes to half-way houses to intensive community treatment programs. On the one hand, such community approaches to corrections offer greater supervision and guidance than do programs of probation and parole. On the other hand, they are without the pervasively disruptive effect of total confinement.

The majority of social scientists today are of the opinion that community correction is the best answer we now have for curbing or containing crime in America. They reason that the traditional system of corrections based on quarantine and incarceration have simply not worked in effecting rehabilitation or checking rates of recidivism.

Even though incarceration is usually denigrated by the scientific community as serving no useful function beyond punishment and quarantine--i.e., not serving a corrective func- tion--there is a large conservative element supporting it in America. Indeed a case can be made that a conservative trend toward corrections is gaining an increased following of "average Americans." If so, and should the trend continue for any protracted period of time, it could cast us back into the very prison system from which we are presently trying to retreat.

The basic conservative scenario about the criminal and the justification of imprisonment for crimes committed follows: the criminal is too often coddled. Any miscreant should pay dearly for his misdeeds--man cherishes his freedom and is significantly dissuaded from crime due to the fear of incarceration. Imprisonment is not only a punishment for the criminal but a pro-

tection for society. Because an offender loses
his freedom upon confinement he will want to
"go straight" upon release or he will be sent
back for even more punishment. Thus, he the
criminal is deterred from committing more crimes
due to fear of further confinement.

Such a simple solution about turning
society's misfits around seems compelling on the
surface. In the present paper we have tried to
indicate the reasons why imprisonment does not
nor cannot normally, in se, correct criminal
behavior due to the inherent organizational
make up of the prison system at the onset. A
brief look at the ethical foundation supporting
current, competing theories of justice will
serve to clarify our position and to illuminate
our direction regarding imprisonment and its
effectiveness.

John Rawls in his impressive book, A Theory
of Justice, identifies utilitarianism as "the
predominant systematic theory. . . during much
of modern moral philosophy." He notes that
although critics have, over the years, found
incongruities between utilitarian implications
and "our moral sentiments," they failed to construct a workable moral conception to oppose it.
Rawls' "justice as fairness" is an attempt to
construct an alternate theory based on the
principles of equal political liberty for all
and on a distribution of goods such that any
inequalities of goods--power, wealth, income--
will be to the advantage of the least privileged
in the society. These two principles, says Rawls,
are "principles governing our moral powers, or
more specifically, our sense of justice." RAWLS:
51

Rawls makes it clear that principles justifying penal sanctions can be derived from the
principle of liberty since the principle of
responsibility grows out of liberty and not on
the idea that punishment is primarily retributive
or denunciatory. It is this view of responsi-

222

bility, contends Rawls, which enables an explanation of "most of the excuses and defenses recognized by the criminal law under the heading of
mens rea[1] and that it can serve as a guide to
legal reform." RAWLS:241 Rawls suggests, in a
footnote, that he follows the thinking of H.L.A.
Hart on these matters.

These excusing conditions provide common
ground of agreement between Rawls and Hart. Hart
suggests "that the purpose of a system of criminal
law not totally based on strict liability, and
the freedom of the choice of the individual, can
be preserved by a system of 'excusing conditions
to criminal responsibility.'" FRIEDMAN:65 These
conditions include the usual defenses such as
accident, provocation and insanity.

Ronald Dworkin, another contemporary moral
philosopher, is concerned about mental defenses
to the extent that they relate to his primary
focus which is the preservation of individual
rights. Like Rawls and Hart, Dworkin sees
mental defenses and other excusing conditions as
a means of preserving individual liberties. It
is important to note, however, that Dworkin--
contrary to Hart--is opposed to utilitarianism
based on the utilitarian's preoccupation with
the benefits of the greater number in the
society often to the disadvantage or denial of
individual rights. DWORKIN:274-5

The distinction which Dworkin makes between
liberty as license and liberty as independence,
"that is the status of a person as independent and
equal rather than subservient," is a useful
insight to our present day concern about the
liberal position regarding treatment of prisoners.

Dworkin asks: "does the use of unadvised
confessions, or preventive detention, contradict
the moral principles underlying the established

[1]Literally, "guilty mind."

doctrines?" (Like the doctrines that no man may be forced to condemn himself, and that a man is presumed innocent until proved guilty.) "I think they do, replies Dworkin, but it remains for jurisprudence to construct the bridges between legal and moral theory that support that claim." DWORKIN:13

Dworkin's question regarding the use of unadvised confessions and preventive detention, we feel, can be extended. The extended question asks whether imprisonment and the abrogation of basic individual rights contradict the moral principles underlying a society's comprehensive system of ethics?

We believe the following discussion clearly answers this question.

Prison: A Total Institution

Total institutions are places where in Goffman's terms "a large number of like situated individuals, cut off from the wider society for an appreciable period of time, together lead an enclosed, formally administered way of life." Such institutions range from hospitals and rest homes to military and prison systems. They epitomize the general tendencies of all bureaucracies. First relationships are coerced, the incarcerated lose virtually all control over their lives. Once admitted, inmates are deprived of most of their personal possessions--those items and attributes that help determine identity-- uniforms are issued, standardized behavior is demanded. Meaningless tasks are required, unreasonable commands are commonplace; so are physical and verbal abuses. Privacy, both physical and social, is non-existent excepting perhaps in one's dreams, for during the wake hours showering, eating, working and resting are shared activities. Continuous surveillance is, of course, a _sine qua non_ of control.

224

All these activities are contrived to disabuse people of their feelings of self-worth and force them into submissiveness, regression, helplessness and institutional dependence. LIGHT AND KELLER:278 When this occurs they are commonly believed to be very disposed toward accepting new roles--those the prison designs. However, in reality, significant contraforces exist.

We Group and They Group

At the first part of this century William Graham Sumner used the terms "in-group" and "out-group" to describe the feelings created by group membership. "In-groups" develop a sense of "we-ness" or consciousness of kind as a result of sharing common experiences. The feeling of belongingness in the "in-group" is enhanced by an elaborate system of controls, which are designed to keep outsiders from securing information about the group activities.

In contrast, an "out-group" is a circle of people a person feels he does not belong to. To paraphrase Sumner, groups are defined as much by a consciousness of the differences between insiders and outsiders as by a consciousness of the likenesses among members.

Almost anything can be used as a social boundary to distinguish "in" from "out," "us" from "them." One of the most effective is through conflict with outsiders; a common enemy draws people together. LIGHT AND KELLER:169 The greater the conflict with outsiders, the tighter the internal cohesion is likely to be. Emotional attachments are very important in maintaining in-group boundaries. (It perhaps is unnecessary to say that inmates consider themselves a we-group.)

The Prison Community: Fitting In

Society cannot endure unless there is agreement among the bulk of its members about moral ways of thinking, behaving, and responding. This means taking on appropriate norms, values, attitudes and behavior.

Through socialization, individuals develop the social character which enables them to function as they are expected to in society. The process is life long. All societies, for example, expect individuals to act like they should in specified age categories. Complex societies with rapid, technological, social, and cultural changes place ongoing demands on individuals to either change as society changes or become social anachronisms. The process by which societal influences bring about character changes in adulthood is called adult socialization.

The most dramatic form of any of the socialization processes is referred to as resocialization. It can occur at any juncture in life's course beyond the time when an infant internalizes culture; however, usually it denotes a rapid and extreme personality change in adulthood. Often imposed on individuals, it involves the relinquishment of one way of life and the acceptance of another one which is antithetical and incompatible with the one relinquished.

Six common elements seem to be involved with the resocialization phenomenon according to Horton and Hunt: (a) the removal of prior identifications and loyalities--induced or introduced dependency; (b) humiliation and assignment of unimportant and often meaningless tasks; (c) taking away feelings of identity and self worth; (d) having overseers who have seemingly unbounded authority; (e) being punished and controlled in numerous ways from social isolation and ridicule to physical abuse and debasement; (f) the exertion of peer pressures to conform. HORTON AND HUNT: 270

How the prison system hampers rather than facilitates rehabilitation was reported by Donald Clemner almost forty years ago. The work, The

226

Prison Community is as relevant today as it was
then. In it the term "prisonization" was coined
to refer to a resocialization process whereby
the norms, customs and symbols of prison culture
are acquired or sustained. Relevant factors
which Clemner identified that influence the degree
to which an inmate internalizes the ideology
of the prison community are personal characteristics, past and present relationships with the
outside community, whether there are primary
group involvements in prison, place in prison and
commitment to the dogmas and codes of the prison
culture.

Cogent insights into why a prison community
evolves are given by Gresham Sykes who believes
that one of the worst deprivations man can suffer
is loss of liberty. This is even more true when
society takes freedom away from one of its
members because he is a wrong-doer.

The moral rejection is a threat to an inmate's
very self concept--to his soul. Not only is he
deprived of material possessions he until then
accepts as given, his heterosexual relationships
are essentially terminated and his personal
security is in a very equivocal state. He faces
continual threats to his safety and health along
with considerable indignity due to the inordinate
social control wielded by his custodians.

An inmate's status is at least tarnished, or
worst nullified, for he has no autonomy, can show
no initiative. For the above reasons a prison
subculture emerges--one which is largely at odds
with society's standards of moral behavior based
on a code of ethics.

Inmate Codes

Maxims are bound up in inmate codes signified
by loyalty to other inmates, keeping one's "cool,"
not using force or fraud on other inmates, taking

227

what is handed out "like a man" and not siding
with "screws" who are the enemy. REID:593

Sykes and Messinger (1960) believe that a
system develops in prison which protects inmates;
as the prison population moves toward unity the
pains of imprisonment become less severe. Self
enhancement begins as inmates reassert their
male roles by recapturing characteristics of
dignity, composure, courage, the ability to "take
it" and "hand it out"--macho traits emphasized by
the inmate social system.[2]

Another important factor that affects prison
unity is the degree of resentment prisoners hold
toward society due to the treatment they have
been accorded by society. Factors that tilt
the scale of justice one way or the other include
color, wealth, age, sex, appearance, the
geographical location of the courts and the
whims, biases, quirks and the philosophy of
the judges.

This is especially frightening when one
realizes that the United States is the only
country in the free world without a form of
appeal and review of criminal sentences. Furthermore, and what is more disquieting is that as
many as nine out of ten defendents in jurisdictions across the country cop pleas of guilty
before trial commences and when this happens
they are ipso facto forced to accept the omni-
potent, decision of the judge. (Subsequently,
prisoners know about the prejudices, weaknesses,
and strength in the character of judges almost
as well as they know about the faults and virtues
of members of their own families.)

Many prisoners are convinced that correction
procedures are mainly determined by economic
reality not penal philosophy. When prison space

[2]The argument is impressive since similar systems exist in prisons all over the world.

228

is available judges are inclined to incarcerate. However, when prisons are full judges become more lenient in sentencing--probation becomes more commonplace.

Philip Zimbardo (1972) concludes from his research findings that brutality and submissiveness in prison are determined much more by the institutional structure than by the personalities of either the guards or prisoners. (It would appear that as guards become more calloused in attitude due to the positions of custodial authority they hold, prisoners become more submissive even servile.)

An offender in a federal institution spends about eight hours sleeping, five hours working, two hours eating and two hours in some type of program. He has seven hours free time per day.[3] In most state systems he has much more. Inside prison "time on one's hands" is a way of life.

Why? Even before the twentieth century began in America there was significant opposition to the products of prison labor competing with those of private enterprise. Acts were passed which virtually eliminated the interstate shipment of prison products. In the Great Depression the trend "mushroomed" leading thirty-three states to prohibit the sale of prison produced materials. In consequence, the teaching of meaningful vocational skills which prisoners could use in the "outside world" largely came to an end. ALLEN:58

[3]The mid-nineteenth century when prison industries provided extensive work for convicts, was a time of few riots. As prison industries died out, riots became more frequent occurrences. (When prisoners have time on their hands they often show each other the tools of their respective, criminal, trades.) ALLEN:465

An Inmate's Degree of Commitment
to the Prison Community

The functioning of the inmates social system
is reflected in its characteristic social roles.
Presumably, an inmate's role describes his own
personality and his modes of adjustment to the
prison environment. Certain inmate types represent deviance from inmate norms. SYKES:84-85
Some center on violence. Gorillas coerce and
intimidate so they get life's amenities including
sex and deference. Toughs are volatile and non-
predictable, exploding against fellow prisoners
while being deferent toward guards. Hipsters
"badger" the weak for the acceptance of the
strong.

Another role centers on economic and
political manipulation. The Merchant, through
trading in stolen goods from prison supplies,
through gambling,chicanery and gaining "ins" with
prison officials, perverts prison policies to
his advantage.

The Rats and the Square John violate the
inmate prohibitions against too close intimacy
with officialdom. The Rat carries secrets to
prison officials while the Square John allies
himself with the officials. The role centers on
sincere self-identification with the rehabilitative goals of the officials, which are not
approved by the inmate social system. He
actually shares the guard view. The Ding cannot
adjust to prison norms due to mental deficiency,
psychoses, or religious fanaticism.

Then there are the roles that surround sex.
The Wolf is the sexual aggressor who rapes inmates
but does it for relief not physical attraction
and thereby escaping the charge of effeminancy.
The Fag accepts a passive role. Paradoxically, he
is believed to be the enticer by use of his female
mannerisms. The Punk submits out of fear, and
this is a direct sacrifice of his manhood.

230

The ideal role model for prisoners is the
Right Guy who endures confinement with dignity
and self control, complies with inmate norms
and does not abuse weaker inmates. He fools
officials when he can, keeps his promises and
fights when he must.

In sum, the traits of a Right Guy qualify a
prisoner for leadership. Other desired qualities
for a leader are a large store of knowledge about
criminal techniques, demonstrable sophistication
in female matters, participation in spectacular
crimes, physical prowess, attitudes, gambling
suavity and the possession of money with which
to dispense luxuries to friends.

Prison--"Subculture" or "Contra-Culture": The Distinction

A subculture refers to those members inside a
dominant culture who possess a group of norms,
values and attitudes which gives them a marked
distinctiveness. Prominent subcultures in every
modern society abound and especially involve
those that are built around occupations, sex,
religion, age and SES.

The term subculture has been used extensively
by sociologists and anthropologists to cast
attention on the diversity of norms found in
modern societies and the normative aspects of
deviant behavior. The concept, however, suffers
from vagueness, Milton Yinger asserts, and is
strongly influenced by both individualistic and
moralistic interpretation.

To describe the normative qualities of
an occupation, to contrast the value
system of social classes, or to emphasize
the controlling power of the code of a
delinquent gang is to underline a sociological aspect of these phenomena that
is often ignored.

Yinger proposed as far back as 1960 that the term contraculture be used to distinguish between normative systems of sub-societies and emergent norms that appear in conflict situations. He posited that contraculture be used to replace subculture in circumstances where: the normative system of a group places unusual emphasis on a theme of conflict with the values of a total society; personality variables are directly involved in developing and maintaining a group's values; and the norms of a group can be understood only by a reference to the relationships of the groups to a surrounding dominant culture.[4]

The life style of the contraculture is a total rejection of middle class values of the DGP, of status mobility, and of the traditional work ethic. Its values elevate immediate satisfaction over future concerns, feelings over reason. Subcultures probably conflict in some measure with the larger culture, in contracultures, however, the conflict element is central. Many of the values, indeed are specific contradictions of the values of the dominant culture.

If we are to believe Bugliosi, the author of Helter Skelter, Charles Manson's family was an

[4]What Walter B. Miller, has called a subculture Yinger would label a contraculture. Miller identifies five "focal concerns" of lower-class males: trouble (with social agencies, the law and with women); toughness (having strength and endurance, the so called "tough guy" who has machismo and is a skilled fighter); smartness (the ability to achieve objectives with minimal physical effort due to mental quickness); excitement (getting "kicks" out of alcohol, gambling pursuits and sex); fate (forces are beyond a person's control, "it's all a matter of luck"); and autonomy (an unusual antipathy toward being told what to do, "being your own man").

example of par excellance of a contraculture. The
family did not believe in working; members bilked
and begged when necessary. Promiscuous sexual
behavior both between and within the sexes was the
standard. Children produced from sexual liaisons
were very neglected; V.D. was endemic in the
family; murder occurred both inside and outside
its ranks. Death was extolled and drugs were a
way of life.

Barriers to Re-entering Society

Even though ex-prisoners' debts to society
are supposedly paid, that does not mean their
troubles are over. The laws in the majority of
states permanently deprive felons of the right to
vote. Other rights often denied them are holding
public office, serving as jurors, testifying in
courts of law, making contracts or suing in court.
The greatest disadvantage, however, is the psychic
cost of being unemployed.

Up to five times as many released prisoners
are unable to find work as non-offenders. If
offenders under twenty years of age are looked
at--the age category that is involved with half
the arrests for serious crimes--the rate is as
high as 36 percent. ALLEN:269 The two basic
reasons for such high rates are lack of job
skills and criminal records.

In most European countries an arrest with
no conviction cannot be used against the person in
later actions. In America, even a pardon does not
remove the incident from one's record.

When an ex-prisoner returns to society he
may be harrassed by the police and placed in line-
ups without real reasons. Socially he is stig-
matized by society even with respect to whether he
is talked to in public; no wonder that he turns to
other ex-cons like himself for companionship.
(The daily population in correction in 1975 was
1.8 million, of which about 98 percent return to
society.)

233

Consider an ex-convict's station in life while keeping the above points about socialization in mind. He can not easily re-enter the main stream of society after leaving prison. His prior identifications are never totally returned to him, i.e., his status--ex-con--is permanent. He is never completely entrusted with jobs that require "integrity" of character, cannot get bonded, is not generally allowed to handle large sums of money. He may be socially censured in not being invited to social occasions, by denial of occupational promotions. His major problem is, however, his formal criminal record, a record that will always exist regardless of where he goes or what he does the remainder of his life. The limits it may place on his life chances are hard to conceive.

Consider also the fact that a young adult male does not usually stay in prison for a long period of time if for no other reason than it is usually his first felony conviction. However, his commitment to the inmate code of ethics acquired in prison may be life long.

There is a monumental and paradoxical contrast between the small time, non-professional, law violator who gets caught and punished by society and the well-connected member of organized crime who violates an infinitely greater number of its laws but is protected and, perhaps, even lauded by the very same society.

The President's Commission on Crime calls attention to the goals of organized crime which are: (1) providing that which the public demands including gambling, loan sharking, narcotics, prostitution, bootlegging as well as other goods and services; (2) infiltrating legitimate businesses and labor unions with an eye toward take-over or/and control.

Obviously, organized crime depends on weak law enforcement and seeks to ensnarl politicians,

234

judges, prosecutors, and police in its fisherman's
net. Most of the important hoodlums in organized
crime have immunity to arrest--or prosecution, if
arrested--and this immunity is effected by the
fix. The government has failed to make a very
concerted effort to prosecute organized crime, the
usual justification being that it is too hard
to gain convictions.

Summary and Conclusions

Sociological concepts such as "we groups"
and "they groups," "socialization" and "resocialization," "subculture and contraculture" have
proved to be of great benefit in adding to an
understanding about how criminal behavior develops
and persists in society. There is no doubting
the fact that within prisons a resocialization
process called "prisonization" occurs whereby
inmate codes of behavior emerge. Such codes have
been observed in prisons throughout the world
and in every country where prisons exist. These
codes set prison inmates against their "keepers"
and against important norms and values which
help form society's codes of ethics.

It is patently clear that the American prison system does not "work" in any utilitarian
sense of the word: it does not work for the
individual whose rights are abrogated as he sub-
serves the total community of prison; it does not
work for the society since the prison contraculture creates more criminal tendencies than it contains or eliminates; it does not work from an
ethical point of view since, clearly, the
prisoner's code of ethics contravenes the society's
code of ethics and a positive and direct relationship exists between prisonization and the rate of
recidivism.

Ronald Dworkin's question, extended and paraphrased, asks, "Does imprisonment contradict the
moral principles underlying a society's compre-

hensive system of ethics?" We believe the fore-
going discussion answers that question with an
emphatic "Yes!"

BIBLIOGRAPHY

Allen, Harry E. and Clifford E. Simpson. Corrections in America: An Introduction. Beverly
Hills, Calif.: Glencoe Press, 1975.

Beccaria, Cesare. On Crimes and Punishment.
Trans. Henry Paolucci. Indianapolis: Bobbs-
Merrill, 1963, ix-xxxiii.

Bugliosi, Vincent and Curt Gentry. Helter Skelter. New York: W.W. Norton and Company, Inc.,
1974.

Clemner, Donald. The Prison Community. 1940;
reprinted . New York: Holt, Rinehart and
Winston. 1958.

Dworkin, Ronald. Taking Rights Seriously. Cambridge, Ma.: Harvard University Press, 1977.

Friedmann, W. Legal Theory. 5th edition. New
York: Columbia University Press, 1967.

Geis, Gilbert. "Jeremy Bentham." In Herman
Mannheim ed. Pioneers in Criminology. Paper
ed. Montclair, N.J.: Patterson Smith Publishing Co., 1973.

Goffman, Irving. Asylums. Garden City, N.Y.:
Doubleday, 1961.

Horton, Paul B. and Chester L. Hunt. Sociology.
New York: McGraw-Hill, 1964.

Mill, John Stuart. "On the Connection Between
Justice and Utility." In Mill: Utilitarianism
ed. by Samuel Gorovitz. New York: Bobbs-
Merrill Company, Inc., 1971.

Miller, Walter B. "Lower-class Culture as a
    Generating Milieu of Gang Delinquency."
    Journal of Sociological Issues, Vol. 14, 1958.
    President's Commission on Law Enforcement and
    the Administration of Justice, Report on Cor-
    rection, Washington, D.C.: U.S. Government
    Printing Office, 1973.

Rawls, John. A Theory of Justice. Cambridge:
    Harvard University Press, 1971.

Reid, Sue Titus. Crime and Criminology. Hinsdale,
    Ill.: Dryden Press, 1976.

Sumner, William Graham. Folkways. Boston: Ginn
    and Company, 1906.

Sykes, Gresham. The Society of Captives.
    Princeton, N.J.: Princeton University Press,
    1958.

Sykes, Gresham and Sheldon L. Messinger. "The
    Inmate Social System." In Richard A. Cloward
    et al, eds. Theoretical Studies in Social
    Organization of the Prison. New York: Social
    Science Research Council, 1960.

Vold, George B. Theoretical Criminology.
    New York: Oxford University Press, 1958.

Yinger, Milton. "Contraculture and Subculture."
    American Sociological Review, 28, October,
    1960.

Zimbardo, Philip G. "Pathology of Imprisonment."
    Society, Vol. 9, April, 1972.

David B. Miller, who is presently at Westfield State College, Westfield, Massachusetts,
obtained his Ph.D. from Mississippi State University in 1975. He has, both before and after that
time, taught in a variety of colleges and univer-
sities; examples are--Salisbury State College,
Salisbury, Maryland; Western Carolina University,
Cullowhee, North Carolina; and Tennessee Technological University, Cookeville, Tennessee.

Dr. Miller has taught a number of courses
including ones in criminology and/or criminal
justice, social psychology, the family, geron-
tology, and sex roles. He and Dr. Mostafa Noury
have just made use of a Sperry and Hutchinson
Lectureship Grant to educate the Greater Springfield Community in Massachusetts about violence
in the American family and its consequences to
society at large.

Mostafa M. Noury received his Ph.D. from
Iowa State University, Ames, Iowa, and is now an
Associate Professor and Chairman of the Sociology
and Social Science Department at Westfield State
College. He is a sociologist with special
interests, and has directed several workshops
dealing with elderly citizens; these include a
pre-retirement program and one on improving
communication and counseling skills of social
service workers.

Dr. Noury has published papers on: change in
Egyptian communities; the usefulness of reference
group theory in adoption--diffusion work; the
adjustment of selected foreign students attending
Iowa State University; the impact of the informational source on the adoption of innovations in
Egypt; the changing work ethic; and the changing
conception of marriage in America.

238

Joseph J. Tobia is presently an assistant professor in the philosophy of education at Westfield State College, Westfield, Massachusetts. Professor Tobia's interests, studies and teaching have ranged from the psychology of selling to language analysis, behaviorism, moral philosophy and higher education administration.

He holds a B.S. Ed., State University of New York, College at Fredonia and an M.S. in Communications from Syracuse University. He is a Ph.D. candidate at the University of Connecticut where his dissertation is on the Ethics of Behavior Control.

See also Tobia, Joseph J. "An Interpretation of B.F. Skinner's Beyond Freedom and Dignity." What is Man? Edited by B.J. Fleury. Dubuque, Iowa: Kendall-Hunt Publishing Co., 1974.

The Do-Gooder on the Parole Board:
Ethical Dilemmas of a Parole Decision-Maker

Ralph O. Marshall, Ph.D.

Introduction

Several years ago the writer was summoned to
the office of the Director of Correction in the
capital city where he was briefly interviewed by
the chairman of the Board of Correction, and then
invited to serve as a member of that state's
Parole Board.

The criminal population of that state,
although apparently increasing in size, was
small enough that this Parole Board was able to
maintain the structure which was traditional in
the early days of parole in the United States--the
part-time lay parole board. The writer joined
the other Board members at the state penitentiary
two days each month (later, three days) where
they reviewed inmate records, interviewed inmates
applying for parole, made decisions and then
announced the decision to each inmate in a face-
to-face confrontation.

At the time he was invited to join the
Parole Board, the writer was uncertain as to
the reason. Later he learned that it was because
a neighbor, who was politically connected, had
identified him as a "do-gooder." In other words,
he had somehow acquired a reputation in his community for thinking well of people, and believing
that if they were in trouble they should be
helped. And, although that assessment grossly
oversimplified his perspective, the direction
of that assessment was correct. The writer's
personal ethical stance is rehabilitative rather
than punitive. He holds, on ethical as well as on
theoretical grounds, that a person cannot be
helped until he is, first of all, understood and
appreciated on his own terms. When this occurs,
relevant prescriptions can be given which will
produce the strengths which will enable the

241

deviant to surmount the barriers of circumstance and temperament and construct a useful and satisfying life.

When the writer joined the Parole Board, the other members of the Board perhaps even exceeded his zeal for rehabilitation. The statutes of this particular state specified indeterminate sentences. Although there was soon to be a legislative modification specifying a minimum sentence for serious crimes, in a majority of the cases the Board could regard the inmate as eligible for parole on his first day of incarceration. Clearly it was the intent of the legislature in specifying indeterminacy that parole is desirable when there has been a significant change in the inmate's character or circumstances which increase the probability that he will avoid further criminal activity. And the Parole Board regarded it as an obligation to parole inmates--as many as possible, as soon as possible.

It was not long before the pendulum began its downward arc. Various local law enforcement personnel became very vocal in their protest of the number and quality of inmates being granted parole. Through normal attrition the composition of the Parole Board changed. The Board became sensitized to the literature supporting fixed term sentencing which began to proliferate. The more experienced Board members began to be discouraged by what appeared to be an increasing proportion of parole failures.

During this period of service the author, from time to time, experienced ethical malaise. He has, therefore, responded gratefully to the opportunity to look systematically at his own loosely-articulated ethical principles with reference to the correctional task. From his various experiences of ethical perplexity, two themes have been abstracted: the dilemma of punishment, and the dilemma of the two societies.

The Dilemma of Punishment

The current debate between advocates of the
fixed term sentence and the indeterminate sentence
appears to be based on one or another exclusive
view of the purpose of punishment. Supporters
of each position appear to construct their arguments within the context of a particular view of
"the good society." These perspectives will be
referred to as the citizen perspective and the
correctional perspective.

The citizen perspective appears to have
assumptions in common with the so-called "clas-
sical" or legal perspective. Its view of the
good society is that it will have safety, pre-
dictability, fairness, and morale. Because it is
mandatory that citizens be free from the fear
of being hurt or forcibly deprived of goods, it
is regarded as essential that dangerous persons be
removed and incapacitated. A society cannot
function without a high degree of trust. A
society would be crippled if, in every interaction
and transaction, the participants were required to
calculate whether, in view of the situation,
the relative power of the participants, and the
apparent needs of the participants, each will act
malevolently or benevolently. Therefore, norms
are developed to make behavior predictable, and
a system of threatened punishment to deter
individuals from behaving in unexpected and non-
normative ways is enacted. If a member of the
society does harm another person, or has reduced
another person's advantage to increase his own,
he has effected disharmony in the society by
creating disequilibrium. Therefore, a means for
restoring the balance through retribution is
guaranteed.

The above is a summary of three of the four
traditional purposes of punishment--incapacitation,
deterrence, and retribution--in terms of the social
necessities which each is assumed to protect. A
less traditional purpose of punishment was proposed in the last century by Durkheim. He

243

suggested that a healthy society is one in which people want to do what is right; and that this desire is developed by rewarding them with the punishment of evildoers. In other words, the society's morale is strengthened through the members' awareness that criminals are being punished. Vengeance, therefore, might be said to be a fourth purpose for punishing.[1]

A caricature of the public is created by defining the public in terms of the above views of punishment and identifying the rehabilitative perspective as the correctional professionals' exclusive property. Certainly there are many ordinary citizens who believe that the way to deal with crime is to change the lawbreaker. It is probably from such persons that correctional personnel are recruited. Their vision of the good society is that it is achieved through the improvement of its individual members. Although this perspective has a garden full of roots-- conversionist Christianity, progressive education, Freudian psychoanalysis, to mention a few--it stands in the positivist tradition that criminal behavior, as all behavior, has an external cause, and, when the cause is correctly identified, the behavior can be modified through some kind of intervention.

When viewed in the context of the ethical perspectives which are related to them, it appears that the views of punishment discussed above can be grouped into two categories: society-centered punishment, and individual-centered punishment. These correspond roughly to the legal approach to crime, which views crime in terms of the act, and the rehabilitative approach, which regards the actor as the crucial factor. If the state in which the writer served is typical, the statutes,

---

[1]Emile Durkheim, The Rules of Sociological Method (New York: Macmillan Publishing Co., 1966), pp. 65-73.

244

in most instances, focus on the actor and appear to assume that correction can commonly occur. In contrast, it is clear that a large segment of the public, which the Parole Board represented, thinks in terms of vengeance and punishment.

The emphasis of those who would abolish parole appears to be purely legalistic and society-centered. Fairness appears to them to require a system of punishment in which the assessment of something as imprecise as change will not be involved. Although persons legally oriented may confine their arguments to a retribution philosophy, the public--or so it seemed to Parole Board members--is as interested in vengeance as in fairness.

The Parole Board on which the writer served did not adhere to a consistent philosophy of punishment. Its members tended to distinguish between acts which were so incomprehensible that they must be viewed as the products of perverse minds, and acts which were regarded as the products of comprehensible forces, and which could be modified through some measure of control. Crimes such as forcible rape, incest, murder for hire, and repeated violent crimes were regarded as examples of the former. In such cases, retribution and incapacitation theories of punishment informed the parole decision. The Board regarded it as its duty to protect society from further depredations, or to see that "justice" prevailed. In contrast, the Board regarded many crimes as the product of youthful mischief, abuse of intoxicating substances, disorganized living patterns, the encountering of utterly intolerable circumstances, and so forth. These were determined to be correctable behaviors. Although there was among the members an unformulated consensus that a certain amount of time should be spent in incarceration before "enough time" had been served, the imprisonment for these crimes was viewed as deterrent ("Well, young man, have you learned your lesson?") or rehabilitative

("What kind of help have you received here which will keep you out of trouble in the future?") in purpose; and these inmates as legitimate candidates for parole.

It appears, in retrospect, that a common thread running through all assessments of parole worthiness was the extent to which the members could identify with the reported experiences of the offender. Forcible rape, incest, armed robbery, and other crimes of this magnitude were viewed as acts whose motivations were attitudes or impulses which Board members had not recognized in their own lives, or, if recognized, were so shameful that acquiescence would have been intolerably damaging to self-concept. Therefore, punishment for these offenses was understood as having the least constructive purposes: some abstract "retribution," or the neutralization of the offender's malevolence through incapacitation. In contrast, the Board members could understand asking with poor judgment while inebriated, impulsive breaking and entering while with a group of youthful peers, fighting to enhance one's image of his manliness, or the desire to supplement a marginal income. And because Board members, most of whom have punished children of their own, believed that one can learn through being punished, or that a normal person can change for the better if given a little help and a second chance, the deterrent or rehabilitative approaches were believed to be appropriate punishment rationales for these "normal" offenders.

In sum, it is the view of the writer that parole decision-makers do not operate with a single punishment orientation. Although the current debate argues in either-or terms--either retribution or rehabilitation--it appears that those who are removed from occupational involvement with the correctional system and must intercede, as it were, between the correctional system and the free world take a more utilitarian approach to punishment. The Parole Board believes that there are some inmates who are serious

enough offenders that they should be expected
to be punished in proportion to the harm they
have done; others who are dangerous to the
extent that society must be protected from them;
and others whose punishment will be of greatest
benefit to society if they are given an object
lesson in the unprofitable nature of crime; and
still others where society is benefited by their
transformation into productive citizens.

The Dilemma of the Two Societies

Nowhere is the conflict of perspectives
within the criminal justice system more apparent
than in the beliefs of the various segments of
the system about the quality of the offender.
The apprehension and adjudication tasks focus
on the act which was committed. The investigative
procedures of the police and the adversarial system of the courts inevitably lead the agencies
to define the offender in terms of the crime. In
recent years, in some courts, the sentencing
phase of the adjudication process has been somewhat separated from the adversarial phase
enabling the court to take the character and
circumstances of the offender into account when
determining the sentence. Nevertheless, the
preponderance of the criminal justice effort
prior to incarceration is devoted to the question:
What sort of person would do a thing like this?
However, when the parole board's deliberations are
brought to bear, the importance of most criminal
acts is diminished (exceptions were noted above),
and the operational question becomes: What sort
of person is this? It is then that the agony of
parole decision-making becomes acute, because two
worlds must be taken into account: the conventional world and the criminal world.

This conflict of perspectives will be
approached through two examples. The policies of
this particular Parole Board did not permit parole
to be granted without verified employment or a

247

bona fide educational or treatment plan. Employment and self-improvement tended to be regarded
by the Board as sufficient evidence that the
inmate intended to live a conventional life. A
small employment development staff moved throughout the state and effectively mobilized a corps
of employers willing to hire parolees--often for
attractive and desirable blue-collar jobs. However, frequently reports filtered back about
employers who had been "burned" by a parolee
who left the employment after several weeks and
at about the time when he had learned the job
well enough to be fully useful to the enterprise.
The prison's education staff and the admissions
dean at a local university worked diligently to
prepare educational programs and find funding for
inmates who then applied for parole to a vocational or academic educational program. It
eventually became apparent that it was a rare
parolee who lasted more than a semester in the
program; yet the Board's optimism where this
symbol of conventional resolve was offered was
undiminished.

The Parole Board was guided by a particular
vision of "the good man." The good man regards
any employment as the means by which he validates
his membership in the human community. His
dependability, his punctuality, and his produc-
tivity are taken as indicators of a basic worth
of character. He will live his life with care.
He will scale his appetites to his resources. He
will be moderate in his drinking, his accumulation
of possessions, and his recreations. He will
have a hobby or some other means of self-expres-
sion or self-improvement; and he will be early to
bed. He will have a proper degree of remorse for
his crimes, and his declaration that he is
determined to change his life will be sincere.

Parole decision-making is not a farce because
of the proportion of inmates who do approximate
this ideal. However, the Parole Board manifests
a degree of ethnocentrism by its inability to

appreciate the deviant perspective of many of the inmates. Schmalleger eventually acquired this insight:

> Most of us believe that the majority of convicts are simply people who fell on hard times and turned to crime. But over the past decade I have talked to prisoners throughout the United States--first as a student and later as a professor of criminal justice--and I have learned that most of us are wrong. Although my conclusion is bound to be controversial, I am convinced that the habitual offender lives in a world apart from what may be called conformist society.
>
> . . . the career criminal sees himself as a legitimate professional, a view reinforced by his peculiar subculture. He is indeed a member of an "underworld." Perhaps it is time we recognized that there may be validity in the claim by policemen and district attorneys that most repeat offenders are criminals out of choice and not out of necessity or unhappy circumstance.[2]

Rather than self-discipline, there is self-indulgence; rather than care, there is excitement; and, rather than prudence and planning, life consists of day-by-day responses to what the day may offer. Preferring the night to the day, the risky to the safe, and the novel to the predictable, he soon tires of the pretense of maintaining a conventional life for the benefit of his parole supervisor.

[2]Frank Schmalleger, "The World of the Career Criminal," Human Nature, March, 1979, pp. 50-51.

It appeared that many inmates were perceptive
enough to recognize this duality of perspectives.
The socially-skillful inmate could prepare a
convincing imitation of the conventional value
system; and, although his institutional reports
did not reflect that commitment, he stood a good
chance of convincing the Board that he held
most values and norms in common with them. However, if the inmate lacked thespian skills, or if
his sense of personal integrity would not permit
him to engage in deception, the parole interview
represented a conflict of culture.

It was very clear that the Board represented
a utilitarian point of view. The members appeared
to have had little doubt about the utility of
their life style and moral system. "Why aren't
you like we are?" was the unverbalized question
which intruded into nearly every interview. The
subjects were urged to admit how wasteful their
lives had been, and to recognize the superior
utility of the Board members' ways of solving
problems. A correctional counselor commented to
the writer one day: "You guys waste an awful lot
of time trying to get an inmate to admit that
your denial of his parole was the logical thing to
do." The Board members appeared to assume--
Bentham-like--that man is rational, and that
reasoned judgments will always result in the
greatest good.

There was a sense of outrage among the Board
members when a set of deviant values was
encountered head-on. This feeling became more
intense during parole revocation hearings when,
as was often the case, the Board would trace the
inmate's parole performance which was punctuated
by employment irresponsibility, family negligence,
heavy participation in the city's marginal night
community, increasing substance abuse, greater
police surveillance, and, finally, arrest for
criminal activity.

This outrage was a very human response. In

250

the first place, this breach of trust was viewed
as an attack on social order. As was mentioned
earlier in this paper, trust is regarded as a
social necessity. If the members of a society
act is unexpected ways--if we cannot base our own
behavioral decisions on the reliable behavior of
our fellows--the ability that all of us have to
coordinate our activities with each other is
weakened, and society becomes less possible.
It is interesting that some parolees, upon first
being returned to the prison with a conviction
for a new violation, would express a similar outrage. When apprehended committing a crime, they
are angry. They feel betrayed that the police
were not where they thought they would be, or
that there was a burglar alarm where one wasn't
expected, or that the crime partner proved to be
unreliable. They are outraged because their
understanding of the way things are supposed to
be ordered in the world has been proven false.
And the Board's response to the parolee's
violation of the Board's trust is like this.
There is a helplessness which is felt whenever
the social order is believed to be under attack.
There is a kind of existential anxiety which is
activated when a person who is being counted on
proves to be untrustworthy.

There is a second cause of outrage: the
Board members appeared to feel that their gener-
osity had been rebuffed. It is perhaps inevitable
that when a parole is granted--especially by a
non-professional Board--the grantors feel a sense
of noblesse oblige. The response of many inmates,
upon being returned to the hearing room and told
that they were receiving parole, reinforced that
feeling. The profuse expressions of gratitude,
the collapse of the facade of steely control, the
radical shift in body language all indicated to
the Board members that they had a performed a
gracious act which would be the beginning of a
redemptive process restoring the felon to his
fervently-sought place in the conventional society.
But alas! Too frequently when former free-world

251

patterns repeated themselves, it appears that
what had been witnessed in the hearing room was
the third and final act of the drama. Where one's
charitable intentions are repudiated or exploited
by the recipient, the giver perceives this as an
attack on his very being. He expected a warm and
satisfied feeling; instead, he was made a fool of.

Another cause of this outrage is the slowly-
emerging recognition that there is a group of
inmates in the prison who have contempt for the
total way of life--the value system, the belief
system, and the tastes--of the Board members and
everyone like them. The parole revocation hearing
is held. The Board reads the judgment of conviction for the new crime and studies the police
report and pre-sentence investigation report. It
is incomprehensible to the Board members that
this could have happened when the parolee had so
many things in his favor. The parolee is asked,
but he does not have the verbal ability to
describe his view of the world; or he recognizes
the futility of trying to make members of the
straight world understand. So he says a few
meaningless things which he hopes will lead
quickly to the termination of this pointless
encounter; one or more of the Board members will
scold him for his stupidity or his immorality;
and he will continue serving his sentence.

With the publication of Yochelson and Samenow's The Criminal Personality,[3] and with the
junior author's flurry of speech-making thereafter,
correctional professionals in the United States
responded with a variety of reactions. The
authors' contention that criminals all approach
the world with a unique antisocial way of thinking

[3]Samuel Yochelson and Stanton E. Samenow,
The Criminal Personality, Volume One: A Profile
For Change (New York: Jason Aronson, 1976).

was received as a devastating attack on traditional therapies by many correctional professionals. Others responded with joy believing that at last there is professional validation for the assessments they had already made of their own clients. The writer's view is that when the entire population of convicted felons is considered, the variations among them are more obvious than their similarity. There are very competent national data which show clearly that a majority of parolees return to law-abiding lives. (It is puzzling that these data are so seldom referred to in the current debate.) Nevertheless, when reading Yochelson and Samenow's descriptions of the thinking errors characteristic of the criminal, it is probable that most correctional personnel think of various of their clients who are being clearly described. There is a growing body of criminological literature which describes the culture of the habitual criminal which is clearly so dissimilar from the conventional culture of Americans of all social classes that it must be regarded as a counter-culture.[4]

The criminal counter-culture represents a major ethical challenge to all of the corrections profession. First of all, the presence of this counter-culture challenges the assumption of much traditional ethical enterprise that there is a universal ethic. It is proposed here that some unspecified (and unknown) proportion of felons recognize and conform to an ethical system which is so in opposition to the conventional ethical system which most of the society adheres to that

[4]Among these are Jackson, Bruce, A Thief's Primer, New York: Macmillan, 1969; Petersilia, Joan, Peter W. Greenwood, and Marvin Lavin, Criminal Careers of Habitual Felons; Schmalleger, op. cit.; Willwerth, James, Jones: Portrait of a Mugger, New York: M. Evans, 1974.

we may refer to it as a counter-ethic. It would be a major metaethical task to describe it. An attempt will not be made here because one quickly realizes that in doing so, he is restricted to using the terms of the conventional ethical system; and these are highly pejorative (e.g., "exploitative," "manipulative," "malicious," "brutalize," "egocentric," "hedonistic," etc.).

Most of our contemporary theories of criminal behavior assume a commonality of ethics between convict and corrector. If crime is viewed as mainly the product of a corrosive environment, it is further assumed that least we all want the same thing and, therefore, we hold many values in common. If a lack of the kind of social attachments which inhibit criminal behavior is regarded as the cause of crime, it is concluded that if these attachments are effected, a similarity of values will follow. The radical criminologist finds a degree of acceptance, because his disgust with exploitation and alienating life circumstances have strong conventional and ethical overtones. But an outright repudiation of every central feature of the conventional ethical system is disorienting. "How can you help someone who despises everything you stand for?" is a question which has the quality of a shock of recognition when the reality of the two worlds is acknowledged.

Conclusion

This essay began with a somewhat whimsical title. And yet, the term "do-gooder," when it is stripped of its pejorative connotation, represents an honorable ethical tradition in Western civilization. This tradition is that the society will become the setting in which all its people will be able to experience the actualization of all their potential when those who are alienated from the society are healed and welcomed within its fellowship. The ethical mission of every man and woman of good will, therefore, is for each to do

254

his or her duty toward the creation of the conditions in which alienation can no longer exist. However, this orientation apparently does not take the existence of a counter-ethic into account.

If the existence of a counter-ethic within the culture of the criminal repeaters is acknowledged, it appears that the parole board concerned for ethical consistency should adopt a proximate ethical perspective and an ultimate ethical perspective. The proximate perspective is, first of all, an acknowledging of the existence of a criminal counter-culture with its counter-ethic. The proximate perspective will also recognize that the acquisition of vocational skills, participation in the traditional therapies, the earning of the G.E.D., or the changing of the environment will do nothing to induce the transference of a committed criminal from a counter-ethic to a conventional ethic. Therefore, the parole board's appropriate conclusion appears to be that the most ethical decision is to be made regarding this type of criminal--the decision which is most utilitarian--is to do what the board can to keep him from hurting or otherwise taking advantage of those who do share the values and ethical norms of the dominant society.

The ultimate ethical perspective is that the self-actualizing society can become a reality when the resources and skills are developed for converting the criminal subculture to a truly social ethic.[5]

[5]For a proposal for conversion therapy, see Schmalleger, op. cit., pp. 55-56.

BIBLIOGRAPHY

Durkheim, Emile. The Rules of Sociological Method. New York: Macmillan Publishing Co., 1966.

Jackson, Bruce. A Thief's Primer. New York: Macmillan, 1969.

Petersilia, Joan, Peter W. Greenwood, and Marvin Lavin. Criminal Careers of Habitual Felons. Santa Monica, California: Rand Corporation, 1977.

Schmallager, Frank. "The World of the Career Criminal." Human Nature. March, 1979, pp.50-56.

Willwerth, James. Jones: Portrait of a Mugger. New York: M. Evans, 1974.

Yochelson, Samuel and Stanton E. Samenow. The Criminal Personality, Volume One: A Profile for Change. New York: Jason Aronson, 1976.

Ralph O. Marshall is an Assistant Professor of Criminal Justice at Sam Houston State University. He was a member of the Idaho Commissions for Pardons and Parole for seven years and its Executive Secretary two of those years. He taught at The College of Idaho for sixteen years. He received the BA degree from Monmouth College, the BD degree from McCormick Theological Seminary, the MA degree from the University of Iowa, and the Ph.D. degree from Washington State University.

Ethics in Research and Evaluation

Lawrence Bennett, Ph.D.

It is easy for the emerging professions of criminal justice evaluation and research to fall back on the broad scientific guiding principle that all studies should be strictly objective and therefore totally value free. Needless to say, since the advent of the atomic bomb, such a simplistic position cannot be adopted without the clash of strongly divergent views. No longer is the scientist able to deal only with the technical aspects of discovery, development and improvement, leaving the determination of the application of new technologies to political leaders, democratic processes or military strategists. Scientists must now face and accept responsibility for both short and long range implications of their contributions.

Thus, ethical considerations come into play at the onset of any research or evaluation undertaking. As soon as any idea is presented, either through the spontaneous emergence of an original idea or from the request from administrative or legislative authorities, the test of appropriateness must be applied. What will be the implications of the findings of the study being contemplated? While extreme cases make the determination to proceed an easy process, the situations containing hidden consequences present difficulties.

As we look at certain situations we see that much more subtle issues come into play. What programs are studied, the surroundings and the manner of obtaining informed consent, the data elements chosen for incorporation into a management information system --all may present ethical dilemmas.

If one grants these serious concerns, the question arises as to what is an appropriate

cause of action on the part of the researcher/
evaluator? While each kind of situation will
dictate the most appropriate kind of response,
there comes a point beyond which the social
scientist should participate. One could raise
the question as to how that action could be of
value, since often certain kinds of decisions
will be made, action will be taken even if the
researcher makes no contribution. The position
suggested here is that indeed many controversial
predicaments are likely to arise leading to
withdrawal of the researcher, leaving the administrative decision maker to reach a conclusion
without assistance from the knowledge of the social
scientist. Thus, the researcher by his non-
participation does not sanction the resulting
decision but leaves it appropriately in the
administrative/social sphere.

In the material to follow, a variety of
situations will be presented, illustrating the
kinds of dilemmas that can be engendered within
the criminal justice system. Along with the conflicts will be a suggested set of principles;
while it is doubtful that everyone will agree on
the positions taken, the material presented can
serve as a fruitful focus for discussion.

Selection of Area of Research

Let us look at some of the cases where the
conclusion concerning the involvement of social
scientists would seem clear-cut (although even
here, there will be some who argue for our
involvement). Take the case of executions.
Should the researcher or evaluator be involved
in searching for ways to improve the methods for
the taking of human lives--for assessing the
effectiveness of different methods--for attempting
to find "more humane" ways to carry out the
sentence of capital punishment? Although scientists of past times have become extensively involved (see Crime Control Digest for an inter-

258

esting, if somewhat gruesome account of the controversy between Edison and Tesla[1]) the position taken here is that the criminal justice researcher or evaluator qua social scientist should avoid involvement in such projects.

Similarly, any intervention that causes or creates irreversible organic changes in the human organism are probably also outside the area of study of the evaluator, even if the procedures themselves are carried out by professional practitioners whose training and qualifications might be deemed to be appropriate.

Soon we see that the issues become less clear cut. When Dr. White, President Eisenhower's physician suggested that preschoolers be screened for delinquent tendencies so that appropriate treatment could be made available, a great hue and cry was heard from both social scientists and the civil libertarians. From the point of view of proponents, common sense suggested that something be done. Consistently treatment experts in the field claimed that not much could be done to change a criminal because by the time he or she found their way into prison, the personality pattern and characteristic reactions have been well established. At the same time, almost everyone agreed that teachers could identify quite early those children headed for a life of strife. If identification is that easy, then it seems reasonable that the application of scientific techniques should improve the selection of those that need help. Knowing who needs the help can then lead to intervention strategies that would represent the best in preventive medicine.

The civil libertarians, on the other hand, claimed that all sorts of civil and human rights were being violated by subjecting individuals to treatment that they probably did not need, especially treatment that was of questionable value, even if they did need it. Further, the very fact of being selected for special attention

259

was liable to stigmatize those chosen, causing negative reactions to them (the "labeling theory") or leading others to believe they were somehow "bad"--the "reverse halo" effect.

Social scientists were more concerned with the problem of the "false positives"--the great number of children who might be designated as potentially delinquent and in need of treatment who, in fact, might never become involved in descriptive or illegal behavior, whether treated or not.

So we see that even where intentions are good--or, perhaps, especially where intentions are good--the potential for considerable harm is present. The parallel should be noted between this illustration and the problem presented later of predicting which inmates are likely to exhibit violent behavior--a problem of social control with which researchers continue to be involved.

The suggested principle concerning the selection of topics to be evaluated or researched is:

Social scientists should not apply their professional skills in any area of study or investigation that offers potential harm to individuals.

Objectivity and Values

Again criminal justice researchers can retreat to the stance of the scientist in general and insist that their duty is to observe and report; any action must be the total responsibility of others. But what are the realities? The field of criminal justice is value laden. Each decision made has implications for either the safety of the person or property of the citizen or the life circumstances of the offender. Thus, values inevitably become a part of research/ evaluation process.

In addition, of course, the development of the entire field of evaluation has led to the recognition that study findings are seldom applied in the decision making process if they are presented in the usual objective manner. Busy administrators, legislators and program managers often fail to see the implications of reported facts. If research and evaluation are to be maximally useful the findings must be presented in terms of recommendations for action. It should not be inferred from this statement that the research determines the most appropriate course of action. Quite the contrary. The researcher functions in the role of a consultant, providing advice and guidance but leaving final decision making to the responsible authority. Thus, recommendations are most useful if they outline the potential consequences of alternative courses of action based upon current findings. The decision maker can then choose among options. He may decide that he will reduce the number of individuals going through a program to obtain greater impact or he may feel that unless a program can affect fairly large numbers of people it should be discontinued.

Many social scientists feel uncomfortable moving beyond the results of their analysis. They may be willing to note, for example, that, "ex-inmates, in this study, who had been incarcerated for burglary who received moderate financial assistance during the first 90 days of parole, showed a significantly higher percentage in the favorable parole outcome category than those with similar characteristics who did not receive financial assistance." However, to go on to recommend, "If the desire is to reduce recidivisms, direct financial assistance is likely to affect X% of parolees at a cost of Y dollars," makes them feel as though they were assuming too much control.

A suggested principle might be:

Researchers and evaluators in criminal justice
should be prepared to present recommendations for
alternative courses of action, outlining potential
consequences based on research or evaluation
results.

Objectivity and Involvement

A variety of concerns emerge when one
attempts to assess the objectivity (truth) of
findings that are presented by a branch of the
same organization that is conducting the particular study. Thus, for example, findings presented by the research division of a police
agency that clearly substantiates the need for
increased personnel is likely to be highly suspect. Even if the quality of the work is
unquestioned, there will be those who will more
readily accept the views of almost any "outsider"
on the basis that the results are likely to be
more "objective." It seems more likely that the
level of objectivity is determined to a greater
extent by the degree of professional integrity
than by organizational placement.

It must be made clear that care must be
taken to insure that the organizational structure
does not exert undue pressure toward cooptation
of the research effort and that the political
or philosophical positions of participants are
either neutralized or clearly taken into
account in the presentation of the findings.
Thus, for example, if a strong proponent for a
moritorium on prison construction is given the
assignment of studying the impact of parole
policies, safeguards must be taken to insure that
data collection and analyses are adequately conducted. If, in interpreting the findings, the
ideological concerns tend to shape the recommendations, the researcher's biases should be
made explicit. In this manner, the reader of the
report has the opportunity to weigh the extent
to which recommendations might be discounted; the

262

facts, however, should be solid.

The argument of in-house evaluators vs. outside evaluators raises a number of serious issues. While the dangers of the potential for agency-supported researchers to be supportive of the administration is obvious, the dangers on the other side are perhaps more insidious because they are less recognized. First, outside evaluators seldom have a complete grasp of the complexity of the operation under study or the nature of organizational influences on a given program. The danger involved is misinterpretation of findings because of limited knowledge. To protect the evaluation from this danger may involve the expensive proposition of training the outside evaluators in the culture of the organization. Second, outside evaluators are not free of bias simply because they are external to the organization. For example, the group or individual is likely to wish to obtain further financing of projects. Thus, it is conceivable that the evaluators may wish to please the key decision makers, tending to slant their findings in a positive direction, for negative findings are usually not well received. Third, and this is particularly true of university-oriented evaluators, it may be that the evaluators have a basically different set of objectives than the administration. The decision maker may want information that will assist in improving the operation. The researcher, on the other hand, may be more interested in building knowledge, discovering the "truth" or in developing a reputation. Iconoclastic reports are often readily accepted for publication, leading the academically oriented evaluator toward exploring how the program fails to work when the need of the administrator is to learn how it can be made to work better. Support for such a view is provided by Binder[2].

Out of these concerns the following principle is presented:

Evaluations, whether conducted by in-house staff or outside firms, should provide objective evidence for findings. Where personal bias may have a potential influence in the interpretation of findings, the concerns should be made explicit.

Scientific Distance or Program Involvement?

Most researchers entering the field of criminal justice were trained in one of the more scientifically oriented disciplines. As such, the experimental model is almost sacred and the ideal is a situation in which all human elements have been removed. As the practice of program evaluation has developed as an area of study over the last ten to fifteen years, it has become apparent that to be useful, the evaluation process must be closely involved with program implementation. There are those that would argue that the evaluator/researcher must be a non-involved observer; others, however (see Patton, for example[3]) would say that a major value of evaluation is the providing of feedback to program managers so that corrective action can be taken when a program innovation is obviously not achieving the desired objectives for which it was designed. It would appear that the researcher/evaluator makes little contribution if, in the interest of science, the stance is taken that one stands by passively but objectively while a program flounders and fails. It seems clear, on the other hand, that the evaluation should not assume program responsibility and rescue the operation but there must be an acceptable middle ground. It would appear that the role of the consultant might be appropriate to the situation. The evaluator, in fulfilling his responsibilities to the program should report at the earliest time possible and at frequent intervals thereafter, the extent to which the program is progressing toward stated objectives as well as the implications of these findings for the program functioning upon full implementation. In addition, unexpected

264

side effects of the program should be brought to the attention of the program manager.

As noted earlier, the findings need to be presented in terms of anticipated consequences. Thus, rather than confronting the program manager with what he should do, information is provided in terms of future consequences. Suggestions might be presented somewhat as follows, "If program A is fully implemented along present lines it is anticipated that less than 50% of objective 1 will be achieved and severe side-effects in terms of program drop-outs may be expected. Present evidence suggests that if program intensity can be increased by 50% by the addition of two staff counselors the target set in objective 1 will be achieved. To avoid the undersirable side effects that seem to be emerging a special public relations effort might serve to reduce tensions." It is then the responsibility of the program manager to decide what should be done. The additional resources may not be available, requiring the program to be discontinued or severely reduced. Thus, it is the program administrator or manager who has the authority to act and who must assume responsibility for the situation.

Thus, in terms of a suggested principle, in this case it is more a matter of extending latitude rather than erecting rigid barriers. The principle might be stated as follows:

Those criminal justice researchers involved in program evaluation should provide timely feedback of progress to allow correction or modification of objectives, objectivity being maintained by the careful observation and recording of changes and the basis of modification.

Prediction of the Rare Event[4]

In discussing the kinds of tasks to be under-

265

taken by criminal justice researchers/evaluators, the concern about false positives was noted. In this section that particular concern will be strongly highlighted for there is a trap into which the unwary can easily fall.

Let us take the prediction of violent behavior as an example. It does not matter whether the behavior of concern is violence within the institution or after release while on parole, the central issue is the same. The offending behavior, when limited to observed, officially recorded events, is relatively rare in either setting. Usually less than five percent of any inmate population of a correctional system will be guilty of assaultive offenses during their prison stay; less than one percent of murderers released to parole are again convicted of murder. The fact of the matter is, that the tools are simply not available to predict the rare event. Meehl and Rosen[5] noted that in order to develop a reasonably accurate predictive device, the incidence of a given behavior should occur in about 50 percent of the population. Rosen[6] subsequently illustrated the inappropriateness of attempting such predictions by examining suicidal patterns. Despite these warnings numerous attempts have been made, usually with serious, but relatively unrecognized, results.[7]

To illustrate let us say that a scale could be developed that could detect 80 percent of the violent individuals in a group of 100 inmates made up of both aggressive and nonaggressive men. Further, let us assume a very high rate of violent behavior of 10 percent. The device then would select 8 violent men and 20 nonviolent men, while losing two who could represent dangerousness. It is the imposition of restrictions on the false positives--those who have been misclassified as potentially assaultive but who are, in reality, not--that is of major concern. This concern applies to the prediction of violence in prison, violent assaults on parole, escapes from custody and almost all classification processes associated with the correctional process.

Well, what's so bad about false positives if we manage to control a fair percentage of those likely to cause trouble? One might make the argument that on a cost benefit basis the gains outweigh the unnecessary controls placed on a few more inmates. Andrew von Hirsch takes strong exception to this point of view:

> . . . cost-benefit thinking is wholly inappropriate here. If a system of preventive incarceration is known systematically to generate mistaken confinements, then it is unacceptable in absolute terms because it violates the obligation of society to individual justice.[8]

As can be seen, it seems extremely difficult if not impossible to predict dangerous, violent behavior. Given the high ratio of false positive generated--the number of individuals incorrectly identified as dangerous when they are not, compared to those correctly identified as violent prone--it would also seem to be apparent that the application of prediction devices at this time would be quite dangerous for individual justice.

There may be a way out of this dilemma. It is suggested that in each situation where the demand is made for the prediction of future violence a reverse prediction formula be developed. Thus, if the desire is to predict which individuals are too dangerous to be placed on probation the suggestion is made that a prediction be made as to which candidates are likely to handle probation in a safe manner. Such a procedure can actually be placed in operation.[9] Similarly, readiness for release from parole supervision can serve as an example.[10]

But isn't this technique just the reciprocal of predicting dangerousness and won't it lead to the same results? At first glance it would appear so but further review will reveal it to be quite different. First, the accuracy of prediction is consistently quite high. As long as emphasis can be maintained on how well the system is working, support will be maintained, for most such efforts are around 90 percent accurate in their predictions.

Second, when we look at the consequences of false prediction we see that no individual is penalized. Upon present approaches those incorrectly classified have to undergo restrictions on their freedom, are subject to treatment they neither need or want and are generally treated like second class persons. In the process of applying the proposed system, those not correctly categorized gain greater freedom, are placed in less restrictive settings and are considered to be free of the need for treatment intervention.

Third, as previously noted, there is a constant pressure for conservative decisions at all stages of the criminal justice system. Large numbers of individuals will be locked in controlled settings no matter what kinds of predictive techniques are employed. The proposed procedure would insure that at least some of these people would be afforded the opportunity to demonstrate their lack of threat to the prison population or to society. The application throughout the correctional continuum does not seem beyond consideration.[11]

Out of these concerns the principle that is suggested might be something like the following:

Criminal justice researchers/evaluators should avoid involvement in predicting the rare event but rather should urge the prediction of the individual's tolerance for lowered controls. The adoption of this proposition is to insure

that the consequences attendant upon errors of
classification will result in an increase in
individual freedom and an improvement of the
person's life situation rather than increasing
the risk of unwarranted deprivation of liberty.[12]

Values and Data Systems

With the increasing use of information systems
to assist in the evaluation programs and projects
and in a variety of decision making tasks within
the criminal justice system a new series of
ethical issues have been identified by Zimmerman
and Dunn.[13]

According to these investigators there are
a number of potential dangers, many of which have,
at this point, gone unrecognized. Included
among these concerns are: 1) the nature of the
decision model selected; 2) the clarity of communication of values from the decision maker to
the programmers, data collectors, etc; 3) the
retention of authority and responsibility by
the decision maker; and 4) the nature of data
provided. While these highlights tend to greatly
oversimplify the complexity of the issues involved,
they can serve to illustrate some of the more
important concerns.

In the case of model selection, care must
be taken that the process is seen as an assist to
decision makers and not a substitute for the
actions of those in authority. Further, the
selection must be flexible for while decision
models are not necessarily synonymous with
computerization we find the two closely linked in
application which means they function on a very
literal-minded basis. Some would argue that such
models should therefore be ideal for "routine"
decisions where a high degree of consistency or
uniformity is desired. However, even here caution
is required for "routine" decisions may dictate
"policy" decisions by limiting the alternatives
available. At the policy level the values

269

implicit in the model must be brought to the surface and closely examined. In corrections, for example, a model that shifts all default decisions toward lesser custody or toward community based options might not be appropriate to an administrator who is committed to a punishment or just deserts view of corrections. But a reasonable choice cannot be made unless these underlying assumptions are made known.

Similarly, there needs to be constant interaction between the decision maker and those instituting the technical application for at almost every juncture the manner in which data is entered, the nature of the processing and analysis, etc., may limit the kinds of decisions that can be made. For example, an administrator exploring the issue of time served in prison may view things quite differently if information is provided on the basis of mean time served, median time served, or the middle 50 percent range.

As an extension of the first point having to do with automated data systems as support for decisions, further safeguards are perhaps required. Zimmerman and Dunn,[14] drawing on the laboratory work of Milgram,[15] suggest that it is all too easy for administrators to shift from a "autonomous" position wherein he perceives himself as having control over events and therefore accepts responsibility for decisions made, to an "agential" stance that leads to a voluntarily shift to the view that the function is to carry out policy. In this case policy is reflected in the computerized model and thus, somewhat unconsciously, the level of commitment and sense of personal responsibility is reduced. When this shift occurs and is coupled with the tendency to accept what computers produce as verified truth, it can be seen that large errors of both fact and value creep into the system unless carefully checked.

270

As noted earlier, the manner in which data is summarized or analyzed can often make a major difference of policy. Even what data is collected will contribute. Let us examine the simple matter of age. If, for ease of categorization, age is recorded in terms of ten year intervals, a prison population might be depicted as having a few individuals under 20, the bulk of the population between 21 and 30, with few over 30 and almost no one over 40. However, if the same information were collected in terms of percentage of the population at each age level we might find that the bulk of these in that particular prison were either 22 or 23 - quite different than if the majority were 28 or 29. Yet the earlier approach would not differentiate.

It is obviously difficult to bring these diverse and complicated issues into a single principle. The following might represent at least the focus for further discussion:

In developing computerized management information systems or decision making models every effort must be made to make underlying assumptions explicit and insure administrative understanding of the data collection system, the method of summarization, the system of analysis and the limitations of the system logic.

Volunteerism and Informed Consent

While informed consent has long been a central principle in social science research where human subject volunteers are involved, it has only been in recent years that the process has come to be codified in various regulations. The need for formalized procedures grew out of identified abuses as well as the recognition that past approaches did not fully take into consideration some of the subtle and not so subtle influences surrounding the recruitment of volun-

271

teers.

With the increase in the recognition of
human, civil and legal rights those involved in
criminal justice research have had to reevaluate
procedures earlier taken for granted. The use
of prison inmates, for example, has become
extremely complicated. If the participants are
paid or rewarded by better food or living
accomodations or by early release for cooperation,
the researcher may be charged with exploitation.
The argument is made that coercion is implied in
that often the inmate has no opportunity to gain
the rewards offered in any other manner and
is thus punished if he does not "volunteer."
Even when fully informed consent is assured, the
criticism continues on the basis that limited
opportunities deprive the individual of full
freedom of choice.16

Along similar lines, access to records has
been seen to be violations of civil rights unless
consent is obtained. If all these principles were
pursued to their ultimate logical conclusion,
no research could be conducted in a correctional
setting--an extreme position advocated by some.
The work of Greguras, Broder and Zimmerman17
suggests that reactive regulations provide a
tone to both legal restrictions and administrative
regulations that tend to prejudice decision-makers
against making records available, making social
research even more difficult.

Psychological testing has come under fire
with the view that such procedures may be harmful
to an individual's adjustment. Greguras, et al.18
feel there is no violation of the right to
privacy if persons give general consent to submit
to such tests.

Another element to be considered is the
value of the study. Often researchers rely
heavily on the guideline presented by the Public
Policy Commission which places studies in the
acceptable category when the ". . . societal

imperative outweighs the individual's claim to protection."[19]

Another aspect of the problem has to do with confidentiality surrounding the information collected. Pelfrey[20] pointed out that there were adequate legal precedents assuring protection in that the whole matter takes the form of an implied contractural arrangement among the researcher, society and the individual.

(The researcher's) privilege, if it exists, exists because of an important interest in the continued flow of information to scholars about public problems which would stop if scholars could be forced to disclose the sources of such information. . . . As is true of other behavioral scientists, his research technique rests heavily on the inquiry of others as to their attitudes, knowledge or experience. Often such inquiry is predicated on a relationship of confidence.[21]

Let us assume that we have designed a study dealing with attitudes of inmates in the hopes of relating these attitudes to institutional adjustment and to post-institutional integration back into society. Let us further assume that the suggested procedures have been reviewed by the human rights committee of the university conducting the study and the institution in which the study is to be carried out. Further, representatives of the inmate body have endorsed the general nature of the study and have agreed that the level of compensation is appropriate for the task and commensurate with other pay scales in the institution.

Providing all these conditions have been met, we must set up an informed consent form. The existence of such a form immediately involves us in the process of voluntarism. Here new

273

problems emerge. In order to "fully inform," so much information can be provided that potential participants can be frightened away. As noted by Greguras, et al[22] in their experience, "even in the simplest versions, the consent forms remained complex documents for the average individual." When the desire is to sample on some random basis, or administer different types of tests to two different groups the assignment to which was made on a random basis, there will be individuals who will fail to volunteer.

Faced with this initial destruction, in which direction can we turn? Well, after facing the devastation of the loss of randomness (although some would argue that conditions are still random in that no systematic distortion has been introduced) the matter of the representativeness of the sample can be estimated. Or at least we can examine this issue.

But how can a comparison between respondents and non-volunteers be achieved if the non-volunteers, by their decision not to play the game, shut the door on the use of any data about themselves? Can we even legitimately identify those who failed to participate, in light of their failure to provide a signed statement of informed consent? But perhaps all is not lost. Working from a roster of those selected for possible involvement, either on the basis of random assignment or in line with specified criteria, a determination of non-volunteers can be made along with their individual identifications when participants are checked off.

Given this identification, what kinds of data can be accessed without violation of the individual's human and civil rights? It seems that a reasonable approach to use as a guideline is that developed for the restriction of criminal history data, in general. In addition, of course, the supplemental safeguard must be assured that any publication of the material must be limited to grouped, statistical presentations with no person individually identified. This means that only the data associated with convictions of high misdemeanors or felonies should be readily available. Such information, should, however, provide much of value, for included would be age, nature of offense and ethnic identification. In most jurisdictions the probation officer's report represents a public document. Thus, such concerns as claimed level of educational attainment and employment history could be available in those jurisdictions where a presentence probation report is required in most cases.

With these two pieces of information--identification of volunteers and non-volunteers and the basic demograph data--a fairly clear determination can be made as to whether the sample limited to volunteers is representative of the sample originally identified. Whether either sample is representative of the population from which it is drawn must be determined on the basis of certain assumptions as in any case of sampling. Inasmuch as there is a strong suspicion that there is some possibly marked difference between those who volunteer and those who do not, even if the two groups were found to be without significant differences on available measures, generalizations must be made with caution. If differences are found, serious doubt almost certainly enters the picture, suggesting that the resulting volunteer sample is not representative of any larger entity.

An additional problem emerges, however, if circumstances prevent a clear identification of non-volunteers. One possibility, rather than contrasting volunteers and non-volunteers, would be to move directly to the question of the representativeness of the sample drawn of the population it is alleged to portray. Again using those demographic indicators readily available

and, in a sense, non-restricted, the sample can
be compared to the entire group of which it is a
part. While part/whole comparisons tend to
overestimate the similarities because of the
overlap of subjects, the effect only becomes of
concern when the sample is large compared with
the population from which it is drawn. In most
situations, however, the sample is relatively
small compared to the total population and double
counting of subjects is of little consequence.
Thus, this kind of a procedure offers some
assurance as to the similarity of the sample and
the population, at least in terms of the
characteristics for which measurement date are
available.

Out of this array of concerns, safeguards
must be developed that do not do violence to the
legal, civil and human rights of the individual
and yet allows for the researcher to have
reasonable access to information. To this end
the following principle is suggested:

To the extent possible individual consent
should be obtained for access to data; where for
comparison purposes information about non-volunteers is required, only that data that can be
reasonably classified as "public" may be used.
In any case data must be presented in summary
form with individualized information reported
only in those cases where specific fully informed
consent has been obtained.

Confidentiality of Records

A variety of reviews, discussion and public
hearings culminated in a set of regulations
published December 15, 1976 in the Federal
Register. While the nature and extent of these
regulations which apply to all LEAA funded projects that involve the collection of information
identifiable to an individual for research/
statistical purposes, it seems like a sound
approach to reiterate these restrictions and to

276

discuss related concerns.

It should be noted that this set of
regulations is designed to permit maximum access
to data on the part of researchers while protecting both the researcher and the individually
identifiable records from being subpoenaed or
otherwise legally compelled to be produced in a
judicial or administrative proceeding. Similarly,
safeguards are provided to ensure that information
collected for research, evaluation or statistical
purposes do not inadvertently fall into the
hands of unauthorized persons.

It should be noted that the regulations do
not apply to information obtained from records
designated under State of Federal statute as
"public" under open-record policies.

Once gathered by legitimate means data may
be used or revealed on a "need-to-know" basis for
other research or statistical purposes without
the individual being advised. There are a number
of safeguards built into this transfer of data
including return of data or other appropriate
disposal following conclusion of the purpose of
study.

Safeguards are provided to require consent
for use of the information for nonresearch/
statistical purposes, with the recommendation
that the consent be recorded in written form.

In addition to these regulations most states
have special legislation on availability of data,
much of it more restrictive than LEAA. Often the
requirement is that criminal justice information
be made available only to law enforcement
agencies. There, private research groups, either
nonprofit or for profit, and university-based
institutes have a difficult task. In cases like
this, a close working relationship must be
developed between the research organization and a
law enforcement agency which has access to the

data. With guidance, the agency with direct access can process the data involving individually identified information, after which the research group can quite properly and legally deal with the summarized data.

Also to be considered are the various human subjects review bodies. Under Health, Education and Welfare regulations, most research organizations are required to establish a review board to assess the adequacy of safeguards to protect human subjects that might participate in any experiment, study or survey. Many of these boards view the collection of information, even from secondary sources, as subject to their overview. While sometimes irksome to the researcher planning a project, such safeguards play an essential role in sensitizing all concerned to the potential dangers involved in almost all research and experimentation. Where the dangers are minimal, the review clearance is usually not unduly burdensome.

In view of the clarity and extent of regulations available no statement of principle is required beyond the admonition similar to that extended to most parolees upon release from prison, "Obey the Law." In this case the principle is stated in terms of the need for a positive search to insure clearance of all relevant regulations:

In the planning of research and evaluation projects, care should be taken to identify all pertinent laws, regulations and rules dealing with control of information and data and to develop procedures in compliance with these safeguards.

Politics, Research and Action

One of the major frustrations faced by the criminal justice research, perhaps more pronounced than that of researcher in most other

278

areas, is the failure of administrators to make use of the findings of research and evaluation in the decision making process. It appears to the researcher that the direction of action is obvious and deviation from that course wrongheaded. Further, bureaucratic entanglements often prevent research findings from making their way to the most important areas for consideration--for example, the legislature.

There should be no suggestion that research utilization is rare or nonexistent for there are numerous examples where research findings have had a major impact on policy[23] but there still remains a wide array of research findings that have never been incorporated into action in the criminal justice field.

Faced with frustrations, the researcher working within an organization may sometimes feel the need to take the issue to the public, to smuggle research findings to those that may be opposing policies or positions advocated by the employing organization. However, these temptations must be avoided, for ethically the allegiance must be to the entity paying one's salary. Such a position is not to imply that one should forgo objectivity to provide false support for any administrative policy but rather once clearly established findings have been presented, the responsibility for action rests with others.

To make this position more tolerable, it might be helpful to adopt the view that the researcher/evaluator functions in the role of a consultant or advisor. The administrator accepts the advice or guidance in the form of recommendations, weighs this evidence along with other factors and comes to a conclusion as to the appropriate, for that individual, course of action. It should be noted that this forces the administrator to assume the proper leadership role of both exercising authority and assuming responsibility for the performance of the organization. The researcher has fulfilled the designated role by supplying the findings and recommendations; since he can take no responsibility for subsequent actions there should be no authority to act. It is often helpful to clarify some of these issues prior to undertaking of the research effort. Anderson and Ball,[24] in discussing the ethics of evaluation, advocate that the rights of release of findings be explicitly agreed to, especially in those cases involving an outside contracting firm.

A more troublesome problem develops when administrators or other decision makers distort research findings to support preconceived ideas about how the world should function. Here the course of action is clear. The distortion should be first brought to the attention of the individual with the distorted view on the chance that there has been a misinterpretation of data, a matter about which reasonable people might differ. Should this procedure fail then more direct action is required even to the point of bridging bureaucratic controls and making known to the public the more accurate depiction of the findings. This latter course of action should be undertaken only in the most extreme cases and after careful consideration of all factors, for the researcher may be exposed to severe reprisals including unemployment.

The principle that emerges might be expressed as follows:

The researcher/evaluator should view his duty as fulfilled when he delivers carefully supported findings and appropriate recommendations; the responsibility for action rests with others. Only in the case of gross distortions of research findings should the researcher seek ways to clarify the issues outside normal organizational channels.

Summary

A number of issues have been raised involving ethical concerns that must be faced by criminal justice researchers and evaluators. Taking into consideration humanistic value, human rights, civil rights and legal restriction plus the scientific need to build knowledge, suggested principles have been outlined. It seems likely that not all workers in the field will agree with all of the positions presented, but the tentative principles should provide a framework for subsequent discussion. A thorough review may lead to the forging of a set of guidelines that appears to be necessary at this stage of the development of the fields of criminal justice researcher and evaluator.

FOOTNOTES

[1]"Electric Chair, Its Origins, History and Use as Explained by Professor," _Crime Control Digest_, November 1, 1976, p.4, col. 1.

[2]Arnold Binder, "Diversion and the Justice System: Evaluating the Results," in Alvin W. Cohn ed., _Criminal Justice Planning and Development_, Beverly Hills, California: Sage, 1977.

[3]Michael Q. Patton, _Utilization-Focused Evaluation_, Beverly Hills, California: Sage, 1978.

[4]The material presented in this section is an exerpt from a chapter, "Challenge or Trap? Predicting Dangerousness in Corrections," in Iacovetta and Chang eds., _Critical Issue in Criminal Justice_: Durham, N.C.: Carolina Academic Press, 1979. The chapter should be consulted for a more adequate exploration of the topic, outlining a number of examples wherein prediction attempts lead to questionable administrative decisions.

[5]Paul E. Meehl and Robert Rosen, "Antecedent Probability and the Efficiency of Psychometric Signs, and Patterns of Cutting Scores," Psychological Bulletin, 52 (1953), 194-216.

[6]Albert Rosen, "Detection of Suicidal Patients: An Example of Some Limitations in the Prediction of Infrequent Events," Journal of Consulting Psychology, 18 (1954), 397-403.

[7]Recently the Department of Corrections of Michigan developed a scale or series of characteristics that seems to offer hope of identifying those likely to commit violent acts while confined. By creating subcategories, the scale was able to identify 80 percent of the aggressive inmates in one group. Closer examination, however, revealed that this high level of accuracy could only be applied to a very small percentage of violent inmates, while at the same time allowing the build up of a large numbers of false positives. Similar attempts have been made via the psychiatric approach to dangerousness. See, for example, the work of Harry L. Kozol, Richard J. Boucher, and Ralph F. Garufalo, "The Diagnosis and Treatment of Dangerousness," Crime and Delinquency, 18 (1972), 390-408.

[8]Andrew Von Hirsh, "Prediction of Criminal Conduct and Prevention Confinement of Convicted Persons," Buffalo Law Review, 21 (1972), 740.

[9]Lawrence A. Bennett, "Evaluation Feedback and Policy," Journal of American Criminal Justice Association, 41 (1979), 7-18.

[10]Lawrence A. Bennett and Max A. Zigler, "Early Discharge: A Suggested Approach to Increased Efficiency in Parole," Federal Probation, 37 (September 1975) 27-30; and Dorothy R. Jaman, Lawrence A. Bennett and John E. Berecochea, Early Discharge from Parole: Policy Practice and Outcome, Research Report No. 51 (Sacramento, California: Research Division, California Department of Corrections, 1974).

11Lawrence A. Bennett, "Should We Change the Offender or the System?", _Crime and Delinquency_, 19 (1973), 332-342.

12Lawrence A. Bennett, "Risk and Supervision," paper presented at National Institute of Corrections Symposium on Classification, Denver, Colorado, August, 1976.

13Sherwood E. Zimmerman and Charles S. Dunn, "Responsibility and Control in Computer Assisted Criminal Justice Decision Making"; paper presented at the annual meeting of the Academy of Criminal Justice Sciences, New Orleans, March 1978.

14Zimmerman and Dunn, _op. cit._

15Stanley Milgram, _Obedience to Authority: An Experimental View_ (New York: Harper Row, 1974).

16Nathan Hershey and Robert D. Miller, _Human Experimentation and the Law_ (Germantown, Maryland: Aspen Systems, 1976).

17Fred M. Greguras, Paul K. Brodie and Joel Zimmerman, "Record Access and Subject Participation in Criminal Justice Research: A Preliminary Case Study"; paper presented at the annual Conference of the American Society of Criminology, Atlanta, Georgia, November 1977.

18Greguras, et al, _op. cit._

19Privacy Protection Commission, _Personal Privacy in an Information Society_ (Washington, D.C.: U. S. Government Printing Office, 1977).

20William V. Pelfrey, "Privileged Communication in Criminological Research"; paper presented at the Annual Conference of the American Society of Criminology, Atlanta, Georgia, November 1977.

[21]U. S. vs. Doe, 460 F. 2nd 328, 333 (1972).

[22]Greguras, et al, op. cit.

[23]Lawrence A. Bennett, Evaluation Feedback, and Policy," Journal of American Criminal Justice Association, 41 (1979), 7-18.

[24]Scarvia B. Anderson and Samuel Ball, The Professional Practice of Program Evaluation (Washington, D.C.: Josey-Bass, 1978).

BIBLIOGRAPHY

Anderson, Scarvia B. and Samuel Ball. The Profession and Practice of Program Evaluation. Washington, D.C.: Josey-Bass, 1978.

Bennett, Lawrence A. "Should We Change the Offender or the System?" Crime and Delinquency, 19, 1973.

Bennett, Lawrence A. "Risk and Supervision." Paper presented at National Institute of Corrections Symposium on Classification, Denver, Colorado, August, 1976.

Bennett, Lawrence A. "The Problem of Informed Consent, Anonymity and Nonrespondents - Ethical Issues." Paper presented at the annual meeting of the Academy of Criminal Justice Sciences, New Orleans, March, 1978.

Bennett, Lawrence A. "Evaluation, Feedback, and Policy." Journal of American Criminal Justice Association, 41, 1979.

Bennett, Lawrence A. and Max A. Zigler. "Early Discharge: A Suggested Approach to Increased Efficiency in Parole." Federal Probation, 37, September, 1975.

Greguras, Fred M., Paul K. Brodie and Joel
    Zimmerman. "Record Access and Subject Parti-
    cipation in Criminal Justice Research: A
    Preliminary Case Study." Paper presented at
    the annual conference of the American Society
    of Criminology, Atlanta, Georgia, November,
    1977.

Hershey, Nathan and Robert D. Miller. Human
    Experimentation and the Law. Germantown,
    Maryland: Aspen Systems, 1976.

Jaman, Dorothy R., Lawrence A. Bennett and John
    E. Berecochea. Early Discharge from Parole:
    Policy, Practice and Outcome. Research Report
    No. 51. Sacramento, California: Research
    Division, California Department of Corrections,
    1974.

Kozol, Harry L., Richard J. Boucher and Ralph F.
    Garufalo. "The Diagnosis and Treatment of
    Dangerousness." Crime and Delinquency, 18
    1972.

Meehl, Paul E. and Robert Rosen. "Antecedent
    Probability and the Efficiency of Psychometric
    Signs, and Patterns of Cutting Scores."
    Psychological Bulletin, 52, 1953.

Milgram, Stanley. Obedience to Authority: An
    Experimental View. New York: Harper & Row,
    1974.

Patton, Michael Q. Utilization-Focused Evaluation.
    Beverly Hills, California: Sage, 1978.

Pelfrey, William V. "Privileged Communication in
    Criminological Research." Paper presented at
    the annual conference of the American Society
    of Criminology, Atlanta, Georgia, November,
    1977.

Privacy Protection Commission. Personal Privacy
    in an Information Society. Washington, D.C.,

U.S. Government Printing Office, 1977.

Rosen, Albert. "Detection of Suicidal Patients: An Example of Some Limitations in the Prediction of Infrequent Events." Journal of Consulting Psychology, 18, 1954.

U.S. Government Printing Offices. Federal Register. December 15, 1976.

Von Hirsh, Andrew. "Prediction of Criminal Conduct and Preventive Confinement of Convicted Persons." Buffalo Law Review, 21, 1972.

Zimmerman, Sherwood E. and Charles S. Dunn. "Responsibility and Control in Computer-Assisted Criminal Justice Decision Making." Paper presented at the annual meeting of the Academy of Criminal Justice Sciences, New Orleans, March, 1978.

Dr. Bennett, currently Director of the Office of Program Evaluation of the National Institute of Justice, Washington, D.C., came to that position from Southern Illinois University where he was Director of the Center for the Study of Crime, Delinquency, and Corrections. In that capacity he filled both a research and academic role, functioning as head of the Administration of Justice program. Earlier experiences span over twenty years in correctional work during which he served in a number of positions including Chief of Research and Departmental Supervisor of Clinical Psychology with the California Department of Corrections. He has worked in several prisons as a clinical psychologist and began his career in corrections as a parole agent. He has published extensively in the areas of corrections, counseling, criminology and psychology.

Towards an Ethic for The Systems
In Criminal Justice

Robert Gustafson, Th.D.

The criminal justice system in the United
States is in deep trouble! Disagreement,
suspicion and confusion within and between the
various agencies of the criminal justice system
have prompted the American Bar Association to
call it a "non-system," an indictment very
similar to that of The Starr Report to the
National Commission on the Causes and Prevention
of Violence which stated that "There is no
system of criminal justice operating. There is
only a non-system of discontent and rivalry
between the segments of the system who often
feel that their own special mission is being
undercut by the cross purpose or malfunctioning
of the others."[1]

Charges of unjust laws, unjust procedures,
unjust police action, inequality and inequity in
the courtrooms, waste in correctional systems,
confusion and conflicts of purposes are so
prevalent in criminal justice publications as
well as those not concerned directly with the
system, that restating them at this time is
not necessary for the informed or concerned
citizen or practitioner. The fact remains,
there is a lessening of confidence in the
criminal justice system. Part of this decrease
in confidence may be attributed to the
scepticism of the general public about the low
state of ethics within the system and its
practitioners.

The system of criminal justice is not
satisfactorily limiting or reducing crime. It
is not alone in the blame for the sad state of
affairs. Urbanization, mobility, racial discrimination and strife, economic deprivation, and
other social conditions contribute to the
increasing rate of crime. It is ironic that in

287

view of our national idealistic professions
the United States has the highest rate of violent
crime of any economically developed Western
country. The National Advisory Commission on
Criminal Justice Standards and Goals reporting
in 1973, declared, "State and Federal correctional
and penal codes are a hodgepodge enacted over
the generations and follow no consistent pattern
or philosophy."[2]

The criminal justice system does have a
measure of responsibility to avoid aggravating
some causes of crime while leading the way
toward making changes that are needed in the
system. Authorities are almost one in affirming
that a positive public attitude toward the
system is vital if it is to work. Respect for
law throughout all levels of society is more
effective in maintaining order than any amount
of enforcement can possibly be. Citizens
believe that the personnel and practices in the
system at all levels should be above reproach,
and yet there is documented evidence that
there is a widespread lack of public cooperation
with the police. Much of the indifference can
be attributed the lack of confidence people
have in the whole system of criminal justice
which the policeman represents on the street.
Charges of corruption and ineptness are levelled
at all components of the criminal justice
system including the police, legal professions,
court systems, correctional systems.

There is little doubt in the mind of those
men and women in and out of criminal justice
agencies that something is wrong and that something must be done to restore confidence at all
levels--and more importantly to provide the
foundation for a stronger system. It is essential
for us to increase our emphasis upon the ethical
aspects of life and this emphasis must carry over
into the public sphere! I believe John Sawhill
is right when he says ". . . it is finally, the
character and quality of our standards of conduct--

288

our ethics--that will determine the character
and quality of our lives. Unless we are
willing to abandon the goal of a more humane
future, it is essential for us to increase our
emphasis upon the ethical aspect of life, to
combine an ethical inquiry with the other sciences
in which we will surely continue to excel."[3]
While he was making a plea for an increased
ethical awareness in higher education, his
comments are pertinent to the criminal justice
system.

     The attitude toward any code of ethics
varies from eager hopefulness by unconcerned
citizens and practitioners to measured cynicism
by professionals who express scepticism with
respect to codes of ethics. Idealists still
affirm that criminal justice depends upon
public confidence and acceptance for its
effective operation. Is this the same as saying
that the ethics demanded of those in the
criminal justice system must be the same as the
prevailing ethics found in society, no better
or worse? The ethic of the people is the ethic
of the criminal justice system? Is this what is
being affirmed today? In the past, Americans
could say yes without much hesitation, for
what was implied in placing such emphasis on the
standards of society was the ingrained belief
shared by Americans that citizens and public
servants were motivated by ideals of the good,
true, and beautiful. Are not all endued by the
creator with certain rights such as life, liberty
and the pursuit of happiness? The Civil Religion
and the ethic of this American belief system
were infused with affirmations that the nation
was called, that citizens were to be responsible,
law abiding, sober people bent on accomplishing
the American dream of a government of the people,
by the people and for the people. Public
servants were assumed to be honest, but just in
case there was any doubt, the architects of our
Constitution enshrined a system of checks and
balances between the executive, legislative, and

judicial branches of government. After all, Americans are smart enough, bright enough to govern themselves--hence the democratic form of government is possible. But, the self-same fathers also recognized that checks and balances were necessary to save us from any rascal or coalition of rascals who would mount any power drives to usurp power! Moral philosophers have noted somewhat humorously that checks and balances were necessary to recognize that old bugaboo of sin!

Churched and unchurched alike shared the Calvinist-Puritan ethic of responsible citizenship, industry, and integrity. At least we are supposed to believe this to be the case. No hedonism was held up as an example of good behavior, nor was anyone seriously supporting any form of ethical relativism which was funded by the absence of any objective norm and the presence of opinions that one person's ethic was as good as the other person's. Time nor space permits any detailed analysis of the changing face of ethics, or lack of same, in public (to say nothing of private) quarters. Suffice it to say that Watergate did not reveal anything new; it only reminded us of the grim news that for a long time the standard operating procedures for many in public service, at many levels, seemed to be one that looked askance at any codes of ethic, or if there were any, to consider them as nice antiquarian holdovers from some innocent bygone period of American history. Archibald Cox, victim of the Saturday Night Massacre, put it bluntly when he decried the low state of ethics in government and in his call for greater ethical awareness and sensitivity in government--at all levels.

What should be done? Write a new set of ethical codes for all criminal justice agencies? This would be impractical and unnecessary. Codes already exist in these agencies. We may need to stand back to consider the place and importance of ideals--norms which should presuppose or influence the codes. A close look at the central importance of human beings as moral agents is also vital at this time when society and not human beings is considered to be the locus of all value and meaning.

There are a number of ideals or norms, depending on how one wants to consider them, which exert a moral influence on citizens in the public and private domain. These have the force of shaping character. They make demands on us because they evoke not merely the best in us; they represent the prized ideals and principles enshrined in religious and secular quarters in this country.

There are no quick solutions, sure panaceas, ten easy steps that will right the wrongs, move us from indifference to concern, or restore confidence. A vigilante law and order recipe is questionable. We do not need a "police state." Authoritarianism may be appealing--for a brief period of time. There are nobler possibilities, more humane and in keeping with the best of our country's past. The criminal justice system and the ethical-professional perspectives must cohere and express the deeper moral convictions of the people. The "deeper moral convictions" do not necessarily reflect the latest polls, since these may or may not reflect "deeper moral convictions." At one time in the past slavery and segregation were accepted by the people. This acceptance did not make the practices right, nor did they conform to the deeper moral convictions. Ideals and norms are not necessarily arrived at through polls, nor are they the automatic possession of any of us by being born. William Bennett, Director of the National Humanities Center, is certainly correct when he claimed that "Children are not born with an instinct for democracy or citizenship. Civility, a probity, a disinterested concern for the well-being of others are not part of the natural order.

Efforts must be made by each generation of
adults, for each generation of children, to
bring them to an understanding of a spiritual
inheritance that is their birthright but that
doesn't come with birth. Free, responsible,
thoughtful people do not emerge naturally or by
accident. Rather, such people are the result
of the intentions and efforts of parents,
teachers, communities and society at large.
This requires that at all times we consciously
nurture and support those institutions, practices
and traditions that move civilization along and
provide new participants in it."[4]

In keeping with the thrust of Bennett's
thought and of the thrust of this paper, the claim
is made that there are traditions--at least
three--of serious consequence which have provided serious contributions for ethical guidance.
These are the traditions of Judaism, Christianity
and philosophy. While there are meaningful
differences and disagreements among scholars of
each tradition on a wide variety of topics,
there is, however, significant consensus between
these traditions relating to issues affecting
justice and criminal justice. Fundamental to
this article is the belief that ethical norms
(moral standards) need to be available to be used
as criteria for determining if a law, sentence,
policy or practice is just, or whether a proposed
philosophy of criminal justice is ethically
acceptable. These norms noted below, moreover,
are instructive for the criminal justice
practitioner at any level. It is ludicrous to
claim these norms are important for a "system"
but not for the practitioners in the system.

There is general agreement from the three
traditions mentioned that the following norms
reflect valid moral standards inherent in the
traditions. A more analytical treatise would
provide detailed documentation for claims made in
each norm. Those wishing to engage in this
research may wish to refer to the works cited in

the noted reference.[5]

Fundamental to any consideration of norms is the recognition of the tension between the necessity of a stable community and the freedom of individuals in that community. A totalitarian state may provide security for certain favored citizens. A state without any legal restraints may encourage anarchy, an anarchy in which there is empty freedom. It is not within the province of this article to consider the arguments for and against law and order on one hand and individual freedom on the other since these have been debated extensively already. Both must be accorded favored status in the American criminal justice system.

1. Citizens are responsible for their community. It has become too commonplace for citizens to relegate to the criminal justice professionals responsibility for criminal justice. This tendency must be repudiated. The grizzly details surrounding the murder of Kitty Genovese a few years ago and the even more astounding lack of response by those who watched it still should haunt us. No one rushed to help her; no one phoned the police to report the assault. No one wanted to get involved! Attitudes like this, if elevated to the status of acceptable behavior, will build walls between criminal justice practitioners and citizens. The truth is simple; citizens must assume a measure of responsibility for their communities, and they must be encouraged in this endeavor.

2. When disrupted the community must be restored. This consideration may be so obvious as to warrant no discussion. But is it? When a community is held in low esteem it is too easy to ignore efforts to restore it. Pictures of communities that have suffered because of vandalism, property violence, or neglect are abundant. More tragic is the persistence of a point of view that is not committed to the restoration of

community. The more significant ethical traditions, both religious and philosophical, attest to the importance of a caring community. If the community is disrupted by crime, the values of individuals as well as those of society are undercut if not destroyed. Crime is encouraged even more. The increasing rates of homicides and suicides can be charted. Hostility between criminal justice practitioners and citizens quite logically increases to the breaking point. What can be said about property crimes and family crises in such a situation except that these too increase.

3. The Criminal Justice System must be sensitive to the need for its procedures to be consistent with the facts in a given situation. The ideal of government by law and not by persons requires consistency in both the substance and procedures in law. This ought to be clearly recognized and adhered to, but it isn't. A casual reading of the papers or a few days spent observing court proceedings unhappily substantiates the need.

4. Respect for all persons and equal treatment of all persons must prevail. All ethical traditions of consequence agree as to the importance of goodwill and respect. Steadfast love and/or lovingkindess toward every person in human relations are distinctly religious ethical statements. The moral obligation of universal benevolent goodwill and respect for human dignity are found in non-religious moral philosophical works. A consistent, dependable, respectful benevolent goodwill toward all persons is not only a fundamental requirement of ethically sensitive criminal justice practitioners, it is also tied in with the absolute requirement that all people should be treated equally. The Constitution and the 14th Amendment affirm the obligation that all share equal rights before the law. Is it always the case? Should it be?

5. The presumption of innocence must be safeguarded in the system. Closely allied with the need for respect for all persons and equal treatment for all persons is the obvious affirmation that there should be the presumption of innocence in any criminal justice process, however difficult this might be to sustain. The predominant religious ethical traditions within Judaism and Christianity include strict rules for safeguarding the rights of the accused against their accusers and placing the burden of proof on the accusers while providing injunctions against judgmental attitudes and allowing for the importance of concern and respect inherent in the principle of mutuality. This expression of mutuality is explicit in the Golden Rule and in the ethical thought of Immanuel Kant who will be discussed later. In addition, the Supreme Courts has in its many decisions affirmed the presumption of innocence until guilt can be proved.

6. Protection of the poor, weak and unpopular must be recognized. Perhaps comments in this section could have been subsumed under other headings immediately preceding, but special emphasis is necessary. Too few are willing to be concerned for the poor, weak and unpopular when it comes to fair treatment. There has been a growing wave of intolerance with respect to the disadvantaged in American society and it may become more prevalent. The reasons are many and beyond the scope of this consideration. One fact is evident. There are too many people who through no fault of their own are poor, weak and who find themselves unpopular or out of step with the momentary majority. There are ample examples from religious and philosophical writings advocating fairness and special care. There are warnings against being vengeful or of holding grudges. Rulers are to be concerned for all and not just a few who are favorites. One Old Testament law forbids taking a widow's garment in pledge and another forbids keeping a poor man's cloak in pledge after sundown if he owes money.

He may need it to protect himself from the cold.
The history of Christianity reveals an active
concern for the poor and weak, even though there
were instances when some of Christendom's
followers were less than humane. The age old
problem of practitioners not living up to the
lofty teachings of a religion are conspicuous
in Christianity   (and in any human institution!).
The expression of social concern is no more
clearly revealed than in the Social Creed
adopted by the National Council of Churches--a
concern that extends to workers placed in
hazardous work situations, to child labor, and
other forms of injustice. The ethical principle
of equity generally supported by non-religious
ethicists implies the need for provisions to
help the poor, weak and ill-equipped to cope
with modern technological society. Indeed the
western liberal democratic tradition of justice
differs from other traditions on both the formal
and substantive components of justice. It holds
that they must be consonant with the dignity of
human personality.

7. The Community must recognize the rights
of victims. Though the responsibility of society
to reform and/or rehabilitate criminals has
received much attention, it is evident that more
attention needs to be paid to the needs and
rights of victims! The preoccupation with
apprehending, trying, incarcerating and rehabil-
itating the criminal has fostered the belief
that the system works when the crime has been
solved and the criminal has been introduced to
the criminal justice process leading to trial.
But what are our attitudes with respect to the
victims? What are their rights? their needs?
Indeed victims often experience icy indifference
from the "system" and from society. In some
instances victims have been accused (rightly or
wrongly) of being the provokers of crimes against
themselves or others. Women have been reluctant
to press charges of assault or rape for fear of
being accused of inciting the crime! The claim

being made here in calling attention to the
needs and rights of victims is based on more
than being sorry for the victims. The physical,
psychological and financial aspects of a victim's
life have been assaulted. The community has
a responsibility to preserve the victim's sense
of integrity and worth.

The ethical norms stated above cannot be
confined to any analysis of systems, for systems
involve people and the norms relate to people in
the systems. The norms discussed not only
represent several significant traditions, they
also are undergirded by several assumptions.
One is that the need for and possibility of
having harmony and order is fundamental to society.
Another is that human beings are moral agents and
as such they are responsible for their actions.
They have freedom and dignity as moral agents.
One final assumption is that morality is a
theory of a system of laws, precepts, binding upon
rational people, the content of which is ascer-
tainable by human reason.

Why is it important in a treatment of ethics
in the criminal justice system to mention
such an array of assumptions? It is necessary to
present a philosophy of personhood which
unabashedly claims that there is such a thing as
personhood and that there is a philosophy of it.
Humanity continues to be in danger of being
renamed society! Environment is replacing
individual autonomy. Belief in individual
responsibility, accountability and freedom are
considered outmoded and to be relics of the past.
Human dignity, freedom and responsibility count
for little in a mass culture given over to
maximizing emotions, feelings, and pools, to say
nothing of public opinion. B.F. Skinner
expresses a popular attitude thusly: "As a
science of behavior adopts the strategy of physics
and biology, the autonomous agent to which
behavior has traditionally been attributed is
replaced by the environment--the environment in

297

which the species evolved and in which the behavior of the individual is shaped and maintained."[6] Where is individual responsibility, dignity and freedom? It is not bestowed by society now.

The claim of this paper is that individual life has meaning and purpose and that the deeper moral convictions of our country are supported by the need for harmony and order. We must take seriously not only the claim that people are more than their environment but that indeed they can rise above environment or in spite of it! Responsibility implies accountability and accountability implies the capacity to make rational decisions. Growing out of this assumption is another one which temporarily will be posed as a question. Can moral principles be rationally justified? On the answer to this question depends the possibility of constructing the differences between moral right and wrong as objective and universal and therefore as knowable by moral judgments on which all persons who use rational methods must agree. (There are affirmative answers to this question from Plato's idea of the good and Aristotle's rational mean (Golden Mean) to various views of Natural Law, Kant's Categorical Imperative (more about this later) and Mill's principle of utility. Dissenting voices range from Sophists and skeptics through Hume, Marx, and Nietzsche to contemporary emotivists and noncognitivists.)

Again, the important consideration for ethics in the criminal justice system and particularly for the individual in any of the systems is that rationality is internal to morality, not external to it and that individual people have a stake in ethical decisions uniquely. Moral judgments appeal to reason and lay claims to justification or correctness. To evaluate moral judgments by consideration of the ultimate criteria of rational justification is to use and respect their own internal rational structures.

298

Several philosophers-ethicists including Imanuel Kant, Alan Gewirth, Alan Donagen, and Marcus Singer have argued that morality can be rationally grounded. They would generally agree with the assertion that moral conduct is the practical exercise of the noble capacity to be rational and self governing, a capacity which sets us apart from the lower animals and gives us dignity.

The influence of Kant's Categorial Imperative, "Act only on that maxim whereby thou canst at the same time will that it ohould become a universal law," is powerful and persistent as evidenced by Alan Gewirth's Principle of Generic Consistency (called PGC). The PGC requires one to act in accord with the generic rights of your recipents as well as yourself. The words "generic rights" refer to the claim that every person must hold that he has rights to the necessary conditions of agency, freedom and well being. The principle of generic consistency is necessary for a person. To deny or violate it is to contradict himself. Why? He would be in the position of holding that the rights he claims for himself are not possessed by other persons who have these qualities. Gewirth like Kant universalizes his principle: "To act in accord with the generic rights of our recipients as well as of yourself means that when the agent engages in transaction by acting toward other persons, he should respect their generic rights as well as his own."[7]

Marcus Singer has revealed the influence of Kant in his own version of rationally justifying morality by means of what he calls the "generalization argument." The generalization argument asks, "What would happen if everyone did that? If everyone did that, the consequences would be terrible, therefore you ought not to do that."[8] By use of this approach in a variety of ways Singer has demonstrated how moral judgments can be rationally supported, although he has done this by what appears to be a negative approach to the

Kantian imperative.

Alan Donegan, the last of contemporary
philosophers whose views will be considered,
claims that "the ground on which the principle of
morality is structured involves an end for the
sake of which action is done (and not merely something to be produced by doing it), something
already in existence to be respected in doing it.
Again, the ground of the fundamental principle of
morality is that rational nature exists as an end
in itself! This means that no rational being
should be used as merely as a means. . . he must
at the same time be treated as an end."9

It is logical to claim that human beings
conceive their existence as an end in itself. It
is contrary to reason to conceive it in any other
way. To do so is to court the state of mind
expressed by Macbeth:

> Life's but a walking Shadow, a poor Player,
> That struts and frets his hour upon the Stage,
> And then is heard no more. It is a Tale
> Told by an Idiot, full of sound and fury
> Signifying nothing.

What distinguishes human beings from the brute
animals is a two-fold capacity: for rational
deliberation, which enables us to call in question
not only whether a necessary means to a contemplated end should be chosen, but also whether
the contemplated end shall be pursued; and for
making the choices rational deliberation presents.

The claim made in this paper is that there
are a number of norms from the important philoso-
phical-moral traditions in the Western world that
can be considered to be positive contributions
toward developing an ethic for the systems of
criminal justice. Among the assumptions operating
in these traditions is the belief that human
beings affirm harmony and order and that they will
work toward achieving harmony and order. The

300

several variations of Kant's Categorical Imperative illustrate the centrality of human beings in grounding morality in rationality and in extending moral claims beyond self. Shakespeare reminds us of this point tersely:

> This above all----to thine own self be true,
> And it must follow, as the night the day,
> Thou canst' not then be false to any man.
> (Hamlet)

FOOTNOTES

[1] James S. Campbell, et al., *Law and Order Reconsidered* (New York: Praeger, 1971) p. 268.

[2] The National Advisory Commission on Criminal Justice-Standards and Goals: Corrections (Washington: Government Printing Office, 1973) p. 601.

[3] John Sawhill, "A Question of Ethics" *Newsweek*, October 29, 1979, p. 27.

[4] William Bennett, "Simple Truth" *Newsweek*, January 1980, p. 7.

[5] Arthur A. Cohen, *The Myth of the Judeo-Christian Tradition* (New York: Harper and Row, 1970). H. LA. Hart, *Law, Liberty and Morality* (Stanford, California: Stanford University Press, 1963). Milton R. Konvitz, *Judaism and Human Rights* (New York: W. W. Norton, 1972). Emil Brunner, *Justice and the Social Order* (New York: Harper, 1945). Paul Ramsey, *Deeds and Rules in Christian Ethics* (New York: Charles Scribner's 1967). James Gustafson, *Theology and Christian Ethics* (Philadelphia: United Church Press, 1974). Richard B. Brandt, *Social Justice* (Englewood Cliffs: Prentice Hall, 1962), Harold DeWolfe, *Crime and Justice in America* (New York: Harper, 1975).

[6]B. F. Skinner, <u>Beyond</u> <u>Freedom</u> <u>and</u> <u>Dignity</u> (New York: Bantam, 1971) p. 9.

[7]Alan Gewirth, <u>Reason</u> <u>and</u> <u>Morality</u> (Chicago: University of Chicago Press, 1978) p. 163.

[8]Marcus Singer, <u>Generalization</u> <u>in</u> Ethics (New York: Alfred Knopg, 1961) p. 4.

[9]Alan Donegan, <u>The</u> <u>Theory</u> <u>of</u> <u>Morality</u> (Chicago: University of Chicago Press, 1977) p.31.

ANALYSES OF ARTICLES

Robert Gustafson, Th.D.

In the pages that follow I will briefly
summarize each article and then discuss several
pertinent ethical motifs that have been stated
or that are implied in the articles.

Some Constraints on Ethical Behavior in Criminal
    Justice Organizations

John P.Matthews and Ralph O. Marshall

The influence of any given criminal justice
organization on the type of ethical behavior by
one of its practitioners is immense and often
ignored. Organizations have two categories of
needs, those that relate to the internal needs for
preserving and maintaining the organization
itself, and those that relate to the service
provided by the organization. The argument of the
authors is that criminal justice organizations
reward participants whose behavior focuses on
organizational rather than on client needs.
Behavior is influenced by conformity to the belief,
not always articulated, that the organization
must prevail and that any actions by participants
which draws away resources to meet client and
service oriented needs will not be rewarded.
Those participants who ignore problems as well as
those who either don't create problems or solve
problems seem to remain within the system in
either changed or otherwise secure positions.
The problem-solver participant as typified by
the policeman who endeavored to use police
resources to stimulate the initiation of a health
inspection as well as to identify appropriate
social service agencies for the victim, on the
other hand, may not be rewarded and may be the
recipient of negative comments, lowered efficiency ratings and charges of being a "do gooder."

The situation where the organization defines
a no-risk kind of behavior is intolerable to
Matthews and Marshall who do not hesitate to
state their own views which are summarized as
follows: 1. Ethical action requires risk. The
policeman who is a problem solver is the ideal.
2. Some sort of service ideal is necessary.
There has been too much stress on meeting the
needs of the organization. 3. A situational
ethic which stresses the greatest good for the
greatest number is preferred over any "absolutist"
ethic which holds that the participant must do
the "right" thing regardless of the consequences
for himself or others. 4. The organizational
climate must be conducive to ethical behavior
characterized by the willingness to take risks.
5. The primary ethical dimension which modifies
all considerations of effectiveness is justice.

A closer look at the ethical terms and
definitions used by the authors will indicate
the sense in which there are conflicts and problems raised for ethical analysis. Utilitarianism
affirms the greatest good for the greatest
number. There are variations but the focus
is on the greatest good for the population
considered. Nothing is stated regarding what
this "good" is to be. Situational ethics affirms
that the situation determines not only the issue
or problem but that one must, at least in a
religious or moral theological perspective,
do the loving or benevolent action in the situation.
What that action is cannot be determined in advance,
nor can one develop any type of catalogue of
possible actions--in advance. Missing from the
situation approach is any suggestion that there
are norms or sanctions or principles that will
help individuals decide with any degree of
intelligent discretion.

Lurking beneath the surface there may be
hidden factors which influence how one responds in
a given situation, but these are not put on the
table. I call this the hidden agenda in any

ethical situation. This agenda is often overlooked or ignored. In a discretionary police
situation, how does the participant determine
the "good" where there are conflicting claims?
Consequentialism, a rather formidable term in
ethics, affirms that one must be concerned for
the consequences of any act of behavior more
than for any sense of obligation or sense of
oughtness one might feel in a situation. If the
emphasis is on the consequences of an action,
we run the risk of dissolving any idea of
obligation or sense of imperative that claims
that certain acts are right or wrong in themselves. If the emphasis is only on obligation
(absolutist), the charge is made that human
needs or problems will be ignored.

What is needed is a focus that for our
purposes can be called "inprincipled concern."
Simply stated there are principles--norms, if
you will--that represent society's understanding
of what it considers to be acceptable and
unacceptable behavior. Practitioners are aware
of this. Also recognized is the fact that
there will be situations which by their very
nature require a mitigation or adjustment of
any absolutist application of the sanctions of
the law. Discretionary decisions are made
against the backdrop of established norms or
principles more than against the backdrop of
having situations determine everything. Inprincipled concern allows for exceptions and adjust-
ments to be made from a stance.

What will make organizations change? Not
merely the realization that criminal justice
organizations serve organization rather than
client needs. This information is known. The
time is ripe for recognition that organizations
need to be aware that social legitimacy will be
granted to criminal justice organizations that
reward their problem solving participants, and
that these participants will be supported in
their endeavors. This may very well be a

political decision. Needed is a reaffirmation
of the accepted place of "risk" by criminal
justice participants.

Police Ethics and International Police Cooperation

André Bossard

The scope of this article is broader than
the other articles that have focused on the
national scene. He is appropriately interested
in the topic of ethics on an international scale.

The code of ethics (he uses the term
potential code) for international police forces
contains a number of principles that should be
included in all international code. These are
respect for national laws, compliance with the
terms of the Universal Declaration of Human
Rights, non-intervention in cases of political,
military, religious or racial nature, justification of requests for cooperation by reference
to a violation of ordinary criminal law, and
finally indirect sanctions in the form of a
refusal to cooperate.

These principles provide the foundation for
a number of rules which are applicable to the
conduct of police officers in any country. They
involve: 1. respect for the law; 2. the
intention to serve the law and nothing but the
law; 3. the necessity to be objective and
impartial; 4. the belief that the police officer's
duties must be socially acceptable.

Repeated throughout the paper is his claim
that police ethics cannot be dissociated from the
ethics of justice or of government, or for that
matter from the ethics of society as a whole.
Police and crime investigation departments
reflect the society in which they exist and the
moral standards which they have to defend. "The
police did not spring fully armed from the

306

legislator's brain; they were born of necessity
and experience and have to adapt to the conditions
of life within society and to the civilization
of which they are but one component part." Elsewhere he states that "the search for a code of
ethics for the police is in fact a search for a
balance between the law and man, between society
and the individual, between order and freedom."

Bossard's positions has been articulated
from a set of principles which are relevant for
police systems throughout the world. From
these principles several rules were deduced which
influence the conduct of police. Respect for
the place and importance of professional ethics,
in turn, is strengthened by a number of factors
including staff recruitment, training, discipline
and training of commanding officers, career
planning, and technical resources.

There is a utilitarian procedure present
in Bossard's understanding of ethics in the
international sphere. If the basic principles
or norms are agreed upon by each police system
and if these can be generally agreed upon by the
systems, it is then incumbent on police in the
systems to try to achieve the utmost good within
each system. In a sense he is working to achieve
international acceptance of a code that will
enable police professionals throughout the
world to work within agreed upon limits.

Law Enforcement Ethics: A Theoretical Analysis

Charles L. Johnson and Gary B. Copus

The Code of Ethics is in trouble! So state
Johnson and Copus in their examination of ethics
in law enforcement through the perspectives of
anomie and cognitive dissonance. There is a
"disjunction of reality and idealism." The
idealism of the code clashes with the reality of
the environment within which police must function.

Idealism crumbles at the onslaught of pressure
from the "real" world.

Does the police code contribute or detract
from the ethical practices of the police? The
authors believe it detracts. What to do? Several
questions are to be considered. Can a code of
ethics exist? Yes! It must be modified with
input coming from the line officers so that it
reflects reality to a more reasonable degree.
The input should take into consideration the
current occupational culture and the related
attitudes and assumptions held by the culture.
Failure to do so will invite the continued exclusion of a workable code of ethics from police
practice. The present code, therefore, as now
written is unsatisfactory. The ostentatious
words, so considered, must be examined in the
light of what is known from the world in which
police must function.

Johnson and Copus have raised serious
questions relative to the code of ethics. But is
the problem with the code or with society? Is the
idealism so demanding that the code needs changing
or elimination? Yes, and the authors suggest
modifications in keeping with the attitudes and
behavior of the time.

There are several questions to be raised,
some of a hypothetical nature. Are we moving to
some form of ethical relativism in the prescrip-
tion to modify the code in keeping with relevant
pressures? With pressure being applied to modify
the recognized idealism in the code considered
to be out of touch with reality, there is room
made available for some form of ethical reductionism to become operative. Reductionism affirms
that a shift has taken place from a focus on the
importance and relevance of norms to a consideration of what will be permitted by a given
constituency. Idealism yields to what will be
granted! In the absence of a norm or set of
principles, the situation dictates what will be

accepted, and the situation is defined not merely by the particular problem but by the prevailing attitudes and behavior of the public at any given time.

There are problems in any consideration of a code when the tension between ought and is persists. How can the demands of ethical idealism centering as they do on norms and principles and the demands of society for change be satisfactorily settled. I believe that a way can be found that keeps ideals and realities in a realistic tension so that the pressure is kept on maximizing the ideals while recognizing the force of society. The word used to describe this process is casuistry. Casuistry is not the science of compromise. It is the reasonable service of the conscience which calls people to express concern for their fellow man within the limits of social possibility. Casuistry, in order to be genuine, must be concerned with principles and relationships between the ultimate and proximate levels of ethical decision. The focus on casuistry being advanced will be to let principles guide conduct in circumstances.

Casuistry must not, as some legalistic ethics do, fail to take account of the ambiguities and uncertainties that attend all human efforts to do what is considered to be obligatory. Neither must it, as ethical relativism does, fail to take account of the decisive quality of the importance of norms or principles. There is a helpful concept for holding to both sides of this tension called the "middle axion" (I am borrowing insights from John Bennett and from J.H. Oldham). Middle axioms are attempts to define the directions in which, in a particular state of society one's ethical commitments must be expressed. They are not binding for all time, but are provisional definitions of the type of behavior required of people at a given time and in given circumstances. A middle axiom is more concrete than a universal ethical principle and

309

less specific than a program that includes
legislation and political strategy. Here is an
approach that sets definite goals that draw
society beyond itself without setting goals
that are irrelevant to society. Middle axioms
ought to enunciate goals higher than the practices
of present culture, but somewhat less demanding
than the demands of any pure form of an ethical
norm or obligation.

Continuing Cycle of Systemic Police Corruption:
A Prognosis for New York City

Paul E. Murphy and T. Kenneth Moran

Moran and Murphy are worried about the
continuing cycle of systemic police corruption
not only in New York City but in all police
systems. What is wrong in New York is wrong elsewhere! Cynicism and anomie have negative and
counterproductive effects on police performance,
and according to the authors, "they must be
eradicated when found to exist and safeguarded
against even when not actually identified."

Corruption exists; police are held in low
esteem; a blue wall of secrecy exists between
police and public when charges of police
corruption emerge. Nevertheless, Moran and
Murphy believe that attitudinal changes can occur
and that these changes can be brought about by a
return to the idealism and professionalism
inherent in the existing standards.

The key to the problem of and cure for
corruption rests with the police's willingness to
accept the responsibility for change. "The emergence of a cadre of police officers who are
willing to stand up and fight for ethical police
practices is an encouraging recent phenomenon."
Moreover, professional organizations can contribute to this movement. The Code of Ethics
adopted by the American Academy for Professional
Law Enforcement represents a clear linkage between

the concept of police professionalism and a
commitment to take all necessary steps against
unethical or corrupt practices no matter how
painful. Professional organizations and the
professional codes representing these organizations are vital and necessary factors in
effecting change.

Their approach is different from that of
Johnson and Copus in that Moran and Murphy
believe that the performance of police professionals must improve to meet the standards of
the code. Ethical relativism or reductionism
give way to a serious consideration of ethical
idealism which stipulates that practice must
conform to norms, ideals. A climate of professionalism must be established, maintained, and
undergirded by a desire to adhere to the
standards.

In the absence of any stated mechanism to
adjudicate difficult issues when police and
public have conflicting perceptions or behaviors,
it is evident that the authors wish to adhere to
the standards adopted and to the positions of
professional organizations. One's behavior, one's
conduct is to be evaluated by the extent to which
the norms and ideals are supported more than by
what is expected to occur in terms of anticipated
results.

Prosecutorial Ethics

John Jay Douglass

Douglass acknowledges that guidelines are in
many cases quite specific and in other instances
vague and of little assistance. The Code of Professional Responsibility developed by the American
Bar Association in 1969 and amended in 1975 is
"almost devoid of direct and explicit behavioral
advice to a large group of lawyers." The same can
be said regarding the American Bar Association's

311

Project in Standards of Criminal Justice and the
National Prosecution Standards of the National
District Attorneys Association. The A.B.A.
standards define professional conduct as "conduct
which it is recommended be made subject to
disciplinary sanctions. The NDAA Standards treat
professional ethics thusly:

> To ensure the highest ethical conduct
> and maintain the integrity of prose-
> cution and the legal system, the prose-
> cutor shall be thoroughly acquainted with
> and shall adhere at all times to the
> Code of Professional Responsibility as
> promulgated by the American Bar Associ-
> ation and as adopted by the various
> state bar associations."

Experienced prosecutors, however know the
"rules" and when delicate situations arise they
are capable of adjusting and of remaining within
the Code. Douglass admits that the written
codes and canons, philosophical discussions,
statutory admonitions, court rulings, and standards for the various practitioners often do not
capture the particular nuances and problems
of a particular situation to provide explicit
guidance. Because of this vagueness in codes
and standards, prosecutors must rely upon a
personal code of ethics as a guide to official
public actions. Since prosecutors are often
forced to make ethical decisions rapidly, the
importance of a personal code of ethics is
magnified. He concurs with the notion that the
prosecutor's personal instincts must arise from
an in-dept intuitive understanding of the ethical
responsibilities demanded of a lawyer-prosecutor-
public official.

Prosecutorial conduct is influenced by a
variety of sources including case law, the Code
of Professional Responsibility in the A.B.A.
Standards, and by specific court pronouncements
on instances of misconduct, such as recommendations
of reprimands, retrials or dismissal of an errant

attorney. Of paramount importance, again, is
the lawyer's own personal code.

Douglass has not advocated the need for a
rigid code to be legalistically applied. Such
a code would be unable to deal with the myriad
of issues which arise in the courts and are not
covered by a specifie "rule." The citizen's
safety lies in the prosecutor who tempers zeal
with human kindness, who seeks truth and not
victims, who serves the law and not factional
purposes, and who approaches his task with
humility.

The qualities he describes are as illusive
and impossible to define as those which mark a
gentleman, but Douglass has not indicated just
how the prosecutor will come to possess them! We
are considering the qualities and characteristics
of a humane person whose education and life are
tempered by humanistic values, but how these
values came to be held is not considered directly.

Douglass' contention that a prosecutor's personal instincts must arise from an in-depth
intuitive understanding of the ethical responsibilities demanded of a prosecutor suggests what
is called in moral philosophy an ethic of
intuitionism. The claim in this perspective is
that one can intuit from the nature of the
situation the desired course of action, and that
one somehow is able to know or to discern what
course of action is required. The question of
content to a specific decision is not considered
by ethical intuitionism, since the specific
decision is determined by one's own disposition or
inclination at the time. Ethical intuitionism
ultimately depends on a particular disposition of
the person as to how one will react in any given
situation or how specific content in a situation
once understood through intuition will be decided.

Douglass' position combines the dimensions of

principled-humanism wherein the human qualities of a prosecutor interact with the standards of the profession in a specific situation with ethical intuitionism. He has avoided the pitfalls of ethical legalism while retaining the flexibility of a situational response.

Correctional Ethics: The Janus View

Carolynne H. Stevens

"Correctional Ethics: The Janus View" is an impassioned criticism of the militaristic-adversarial model prevalent in correctional systems and a plea for a different approach, a new model. Correctional systems are plagued by problems ranging from a lack of sensitivity by practitioners in the system, the absence of professional status, and a flawed ethical sensitivity.

Stevens claims that corrections as a profession which entails, among other things, a general ethical humanitarian orientation which gives rise to a sense of duty expressed in the content of a special body of knowledge and applied skills. In short the characteristics of a discipline are lacking.

Stevens does more than criticize; she proposes a way out of the "conceptual mindfield and philosophical wilderness." Rather than search for a solution to the varied problems, she proposes an ethical search process, a process that is guided by several premises. Inherent in her approach is what she calls correctional pathfinders who must be responsible for choosing, among unlimited possibilities, the courses they will follow to educate the public, to stimulate concern, to cause moral reexamination to bring the public into corrections. These pathfinders will have to choose the time, the rhythms of change. They must decide how to select the most difficult

tasks and how to incorporate people whose contributions may be more mundane but nonetheless
valuable to the overall process.

At issue is the development of an ethical
search process which is guided by certain
logically derived beliefs and premises and not by
any sense of a final destination or envisaged
solution or result! While no fixed destination
or specific type of solution guides the activities
of the pathfinder in the process, it is evident
that each premise in the process is intended to
increase ethical sensitivity by a number of
considerations, some of which involve having
more alternatives from which to choose, improving
the amount and diversity of viewpoints available
to examine correctional systems decision making
procedures, eliminating public alienation by
encouraging new approaches to policy formation
through more public participation, and changing
the present political processes as they apply to
the correctional system. These "premises" as
she calls them are developed to some extent in
her paper and they reflect while they create
ethical sensitivity.

In reading the article, one question comes
to mind. Will the ethically sensitive person be
likely to consider more alternatives, or will the
consideration of more alternatives make one
ethically sensitive? The willingness to consider
more alternatives is itself a manifestation of
ethical sensitivity. Without the willingness,
there is no consideration of any alternatives.
Something more than process is involved in
seeking new possibilities for heightened ethical
sensitivity! Stevens is appropriately concerned
that change will occur through a process that is
recognized as being an important component in
affecting new directions! Her understanding of
premises (guidelines, beliefs and assumptions in
my terminology) can be viewed in terms of
obligation or imperatives which are intrinsic to
the process. There is less concern for a fixed

315

destination or envisioned solution. There is
an emphasis on a process which begins with a
number of stated premises.

Ethics and the American Prison System

    David B. Miller, Mostafa M. Noury, and
    Joseph J. Tobia

    Imprisonment does not correct criminal
behavior. The institutional structure of the
prison system does not lead to correcting criminal
behavior. Inmates' code of behavior which have
emerged over the years are more powerful than
the norms and values of the non-prison community,
and they will and do prevail. Such are the views
of the authors--pessimistic to say the least.

    The authors have examined the ethical foun-
dations supporting current competing theories
of justice and have concluded that the criminal
justice correction system does not work in any
utilitarian sense. It does not work for the
individual whose rights have been abrogated,
nor does it work for society. The prison contraculture creates more criminal tendencies than
it is able to contain or eliminate. Ethically it
is a disaster, since the code of the prisoners
contravenes society's code of ethics.

    What can be done? What courses of action
are open? The authors are pessimistic about
the level of ethical sensitivity in society;
there seems to be precious little to support
any meaningful societal system of ethics.
Organized crime, they state, depends on weak law
enforcement and seeks to ensnarl politicians,
judges, prosecutors, and police in its "fisherman's net." Immunity is granted to important
hoodlums, and where they are arrested the fix
gets them off with often nothing more than a slap
on the wrist. "The government has failed to make
a very concerted effort to prosecute organized
crime. . . ." The President's Commission on Crime

enunciated the goals of organized crime and
in doing it reiterates the sentiments of professionals in criminal justice as well as those
concerned citizens who are alarmed. The goals
are to provide that which the public demands
including gambling, loan sharking, narcotics,
prostitution, bootlegging. In addition organized
crime infiltrates legitimate businesses and labor
unions with an eye toward take over or control.

If the correction system is a reflection
of the moral principles of prisoners and if
crime exists because it is meeting the demands of
large numbers of citizens, then there is little
of an optimistic conclusion to any approach that
would reverse the status quo. The authors have
opted for community corrections as the best
answer we have to curbing or containing crime in
America. A decentralized approach might be worth
trying if communities are not now too disinte-
grated to be of help.

The concept of an ideal community exerting
powerful changes in the lives of people has
support from religion to the idealistic communes
which have dotted the American landscape for
years. These "ideal communities," however, were
founded on some ideal or set of ideals usually
prompted by a perceived deficiency in the prevailing society. One wonders what ideas and/or
ideals more than the questionable ones that now
prevail in society will be presented in a community corrections program.

The Do-Gooder on the Parole Board: Ethical
    Dilemmas of a Parole Decision Maker

    Ralph Marshall

    Ralph Marshall's experience on a parole
board has caused him to be less idealistic and
more realistic about the value of efforts in the
parole system to change criminal behavior. The

counter-ethic which exists within the culture
of crime and criminal repeaters contradicts
the values of parole boards and the society
they represent.

Faced with the pessimistic assessment,
parole boards are obligated to adopt two perspectives. A proximate ethical perspective must be
developed that acknowledges the existence of the
criminal counter-culture with its counter-ethic.
We must recognize that little that is done to
change the environment through education or
other socializing processes will induce the
transferrence of a committed criminal from a
counter-ethic to a conventional ethic. The
second and ultimate perspective is that the
"self actualizing society can become a reality
when the resources and skills are developed for
converting the criminal sub-culture to a truly
social ethics."

The parole board must operate between the
realities of the counter-culture and the idealism
that the self actualizing society will become a
reality to change the criminal sub-culture. The
board must be guided by a utilitarian purpose
"to do what the board can to keep him (the
criminal) from hurting or otherwise taking
advantage of those who do share the values and
norms of the dominant society."

Utilitarianism has many shades of difference.
Generally utilitarianism asserts that one ought
to produce the greatest good for the greatest
number. Or one ought to produce the greatest
possible good over evil. The greatest good for
the greatest number is one reading of this
perspective. Act utilitarianism focuses the
question as to which act or acts will produce
the greatest balance of good over evil. Rule
utilitarianism poses the question as to which
rule will produce the greatest balance of good
over evil. It is logical to assume that the
board would have to make its decision on

utilitarian grounds in terms of two possibilities:
1. Which prisoner when paroled will be most
likely to do the greatest good for society. Which
prisoner has the greatest potential for doing the
greatest good. 2. Which prisoner will do the
least harm given the understanding that little
can be done to effect significant changes in
behavior.

The utilitarian approach advocated by
Marshall is tempered by the reality that little
can be done to change the environment of the
counter-ethic to a conventional ethic. Marshall
has not so stated that there is a problem in
human nature that does not yield to environmental
manipulation, but the suggestion is there. The
"do-gooder" perspective when facing the harsh
realities of a counter-ethic has severe
difficulties.

The ultimate perspective points to some end,
some good, that is, the self actualizing society
where resources and skills are developed--the
good society. This ultimate ethical perspective
has a utopian tone to it; it has not been realized,
and indeed it may not be, but the vision is
present to evoke the desire for something better.

Marshall's casuistry expressed in utilitarianism permits the parole board to make decisions
between two poles--realism and idealism. He has
not used the term "middle axion" which was
referred to earlier, but the principles are
evident.

Ethics in Research and Evaluation

Lawrence Bennett

Bennett raises a number of issue involving
ethical procedures that must be considered by
criminal justice researchers and evaluators. The
issues he raises and the conclusions he comes to

are informed by humanistic values, human rights, civil rights and legal restrictions, and scientific needs to build knowledge.

The principles focused on desired stress consequences from research or from anticipated results. There are principles which must be considered. These principles lead to some consequence or results in contrast to an ethic of obligation or oughtness which stresses the doing or not doing of an act as being good in and of itself.

A few examples will illustrate the direction of his perspective. Evaluation should provide objective evidence for findings. Where personal bias may have a potential influence on the interpretation of findings, the concerns should be made explicit. Researchers and evaluators in criminal justice should be prepared to present recommendations for alternative courses of action, outlining potential consequences based on research or evaluation results.

One delightful conclusion that can be drawn from this paper is that he has advocated the rights of individuals over the need to know or the demands that "science" or "the organization," however conceived, might make. Nowhere does he suggest that the nation's needs or the interests of science must prevail in shaping the principles of ethics in research and evaluation. This is refreshing!